Praise for *Rocket*

"Whether you work with an apostle brand or are falling victim to 'schismogenesis,' *Rocket* will help guide you toward the critical factors that cause apostle brands to stand out and thrive. The authors illustrate the necessary traits to build, maintain, and grow successful brands. Very interesting and practical stories covering some of the best brands in the world. A great read for anyone building a brand."
— Bob Carter, Senior Vice President–Automotive Operations, Toyota

"*Rocket* is an extraordinary book. The book tells the stories and secrets of so many successful companies. The 'secrets' are fascinating and extremely thought-provoking. *Rocket* emphasizes the values of integrity and human dignity; values which we consider to be the keystones of our operations."
— Brunello Cucinelli, Founder and CEO, Brunello Cucinelli

"A powerful book that offers the keys to growth—deep insight into consumer behavior, stories that energize and excite. A primer for marketers, innovators, and change agents. *Rocket* can help you open doors and drive growth."
— John Mackey, Co-CEO and Cofounder, Whole Foods

"Much has been written about Four Seasons' legendary service model and the 40,000-plus people that bring it to life every day, but *Rocket: Eight Lessons to Secure Infinite Growth* takes a unique approach. By exploring our deep commitment to employees within the context of growth, *Rocket* shows exactly how a passionate team of employees can transform any brand and position it for success. *Rocket* is an essential read for any business leader focused on long-term growth."
— Isadore Sharp, Founder and Chairman, Four Seasons Hotels and Resorts

"Engaging and clever lessons that can be applied in any business."
— Tony Hsieh, CEO, Zappos.com, Inc.,
and *New York Times* bestselling author of *Delivering Happiness*

"Powerful stories from real people who are delivering extraordinary results. Practical ideas that can be implemented immediately. If you have one business book to read this year, this is the one!"
— Irene Rosenfeld, Chairman and CEO, Mondelez International

"A compelling blueprint for realizing your full potential. A superb guide for reimagining your approach to driving growth."
— Douglas R. Conant, Founder, ConantLeadership; Chairman,
Avon Products; and former President and CEO, Campbell Soup Company

ROCKET

EIGHT LESSONS TO SECURE INFINITE GROWTH

MICHAEL J. SILVERSTEIN
DYLAN BOLDEN
RUNE JACOBSEN
ROHAN SAJDEH

The Boston Consulting Group

New York   Chicago   San Francisco   Athens   London
Madrid   Mexico City   Milan   New Delhi
Singapore   Sydney   Toronto

1 2 3 4 5 6 7 8 9 0   DOC/DOC   1 2 1 0 9 8 7 6 5

ISBN 978-1-259-58542-5
MHID 1-259-58542-5

e-ISBN 978-1-259-58543-2
e-MHID 1-259-58543-3

McGraw-Hill Education books are available at special quantity discounts to use as premiums and sales promotions or for use in corporate training programs. To contact a representative, please visit the Contact Us pages at www.mhprofessional.com.

* * *

*To our spouses and children, in gratitude
for their support and inspiration
To Silvia, Heather, Charlie, John, and Kyle (Michael)
To Carla, Jack, Anna, and Claire (Dylan)
To Mette, Nicolai, and Julia (Rune)
To Masha, Sohail, and Taara (Rohan)*

* * *

CONTENTS

Rocket is dedicated to the proposition that mere mortals can create immortality. You can build a brand that lasts forever. You can grow faster than your rivals. To do this, however, you need to understand the theory that a very few people—the very few focused consumers—create most of the value in any business. If you have loyal consumers and you turn them into your apostles, they will spread the word about you, and they will propel you to growth. *Rocket* is your guide to understanding the physics of growth.

We tell 16 stories about entrepreneurs in the retail, consumer packaged goods, and travel sectors who have done precisely this. They are stories of love and emotional connections. These entrepreneurs focused on their core consumers. They vowed to understand those consumers' hopes, dreams, and wishes. By doing this, they created businesses that have grown to be worth billions of dollars.

In the book, we talk about an *eight-to-one ratio*. One loyal consumer—an apostle—can generate eight times his or her own consumption through word-of-mouth advocacy to friends and family. Also, we talk about a rule called *2/20/80*: 2 percent of your consumers directly contribute 20 percent of your sales and drive 80 percent of the total volume by their recommendations. They deliver more than 150 percent of your profitability, buying products and services without discounts and they do it year round.

Rocket is a storybook about how to create a great brand. Yet it is not about genius. It is not about accident or luck. It is about the apostles, the cravers, the brand ambassadors—and what you need to do to nurture them.

Most companies don't get this. They still do research with the general population. They still launch products that end up largely cannibalizing their own business. They still launch products that consumers dismiss as "me too" products.

If you run one of these companies, you need to change your strategy. Conduct research with the consumers who count, the consumers who really matter. Focus on the 2 percent who drive the 20 percent who drive the 80 percent. Learn how to rocket toward stellar growth with your best consumers.

None of the master branders in this book started with a master plan. None of them laid out a strategy on a sheet of paper on their first day and said, "This is what we're going to be." Each of them found his own way to success. Nevertheless, their stories do share many truths.

To be successful, you must demonstrate a presence at multiple levels—emotional presence, intellectual presence, and presence in the moment. It's about curiosity. It's about humility. It's about a secret sauce. It's about invention. It's about learning every day. It's about not spending a huge amount of money on R (research), but spending a lot of money on D (development). It's about not believing that the first time you launch a product is the end of the story. It's about leaders who care about their followers, who consider them full partners. It's about managers who treat the consumer as the boss. It's about being both fearless and fearful: fearless in the sense of being willing to take risks; fearful in the sense of worrying constructively every day.

Your starting point should be what we call *consumer "demand spaces,"* as we will explain in the book. Create an understanding of demand by occasion and you will understand what really drives consumer choice. We dedicate this book to your success and to the businesses you invent—or reinvent—as a result of reading the stories and fully integrating the lessons.

INTRODUCTION

Cultivate the Apostles to Become a Beloved, Iconic Brand

Human beings are curious. They love to explore. And they love to shop.

Many consumers—up to 25 million Americans—go to malls on any given Saturday or Sunday. Sometimes they arrive with a list of priority items that they're ready to purchase. Sometimes they just wander and browse. Sometimes they are looking to touch items that they will later buy online.

If you have a brand, this is your chance to stand out from the crowd. Retailers tell us that the strong brands sell without promotion. Consumers come into the store and ask for signature products. They say no to substitutions. Weak brands sit on shelves, waiting to be scooped up at a steep markdown by bargain hunters.

Great brands are forever if you work on them. Customers want them to be available forever. Brands make their lives easier and more predictable. They take the anxiety out of decisions. If a customer buys a gift, choosing a great brand reduces the risk that the receiver will show disdain for it. Great brands celebrate consistency and deliver smiles.

Consumers love to love brands. They love to talk about them. If you get consumers talking about a brand that they care about, there is no detail that's too obscure. They love bending your ear with little facts. They want to show everyone that they *really* know. But what they know is never enough. They will ask: Where is the product made? What are the ingredients? How is it tested? Will it stand the test of time? Will my friends express envy that I own it and they don't? They always want to know more.

They want access to more. They want to have a totally transparent relationship with you. They want to know who you really are. They seek the truth. They search out not only all your brand's technical and functional features, but also all its emotional elements. They care about your social policies: How do you treat and pay your employees? How do you treat your suppliers? Do you have a clean environmental footprint?

For successful brands, the payoff from having the first position in consumers' minds is very high. Its owner will have a valuation that is a multiple of sales. Often it will deliver a cash margin in excess of 25 percent. When consumers love you, it's a memorial. They will provide you with loyalty, a stream of purchases, a price premium, and advocacy with friends and strangers.

But if you ever fail them, it's an abomination. They will damn you. They will scold you. They will scowl at your name. Worse, they will tell everyone they know what they think of you. And, in this digital age, word spreads quickly. They can tell the world with the click of a button on their keyboard. Reputations can be tarnished unfairly and fast.

To stay on top, your job is to deliver magic—every day, in every way. Your customers expect you to provide them with a flawless, complete experience. They expect you to provide value for money. Not a low price, but value, which includes their experience. They expect you to deliver with energy and passion.

Brands are fragile. Most companies waste them. Too often, once brands are big, the executives get sloppy. In a big company, they count the number of big brands in their roster. You need to go down four levels in the organization to find the individual who is responsible for a particular brand. That person's job is to deliver predictable sales, sales growth, margin, and margin growth. Top management often does not see all the data—brand rank, brand advocacy, and share of category requirements among the most important consumers. They see a P&L, and they promote those who deliver "good numbers." They get greedy. They prioritize short-term profits. They let competitors steal their market. They lose their first position in consumers' minds. They add overhead that does not add value. They cut primary research. They cut materials research. They eat their seed corn. That's one reason why in industry after industry, it is the new entrants that are growing fastest and taking share. These nimble companies live and die on the basis of a single position.

For the big brands that are lost in big companies, recovery once losses have started is very challenging. Generally this comes at a time of management change and shareholder activist pressures. Our prescription for success is best carried out before the activists turn their attention to your brand. You have more time when you're not under the gun. We preach preemptive action. You have to move before you lose your core consumers. In *Rocket*, we talk about schismogenesis. This is an anthropology term that means that relationships are not stable. They are always moving either up or down. Conditions are always fluid. Once brands become sick, it is rare to see a full recovery. Generally we have seen long, slow declines. Sick brands become like inner-city homes in Detroit—abandoned, unloved, and unsalvageable. Teardowns of the future.

Preventing this requires a stream of innovation. It requires a constant, formal, qualitative appraisal by your best customers. It requires you to have all your senses switched to "on."

Ask yourself this: When your customers use your products or services, what do they see? What do they experience? Is that experience pleasing to them? Does it touch them in an emotional way? Does it contribute something above the everyday? Is it elevating?

Answer these questions with energy, excitement, and pizzazz, and you will take a magic carpet ride. Answer the questions with negatives, and you face death by a thousand cuts.

It's all about creating a bubble for your consumers, about surrounding them with happiness, joy, inner peace, and validation for their purchases.

Why do 75 million people per week go to Starbucks for coffee when they could crawl out of bed and brew their own coffee or grab a free cup at the office coffeepot?

Howard Schultz says that the answer is the brand and everything that has been built into that cup of Joe—the highest-quality beans, perfect roasting, fresh brewing, personalized combinations, ambiance, cachet, attachment, a real break, a familiar barista, and more. Starbucks has found a way to forge an emotional connection with its customers and its employees. Schultz and his team call each worker a *partner*. In 1991, Starbucks introduced Bean Stock to enable eligible part- and full-time employees to own shares. He says it was aimed at connecting their contributions to growth and the value of the company. Starbucks has configured its network of 22,000 stores to provide you with not only your morning coffee, but also late-morning lounging with friends on weekends, working with free Wi-Fi and power in the afternoon, using the local Starbucks as an office for a meeting, or rushing in for a quick pick-me-up drink. It knows how to romance you with a broad variety of coffee-based beverages and sell you a bagel, a lemon cake, or a croissant.

Before Starbucks, American consumers just drank coffee, purchased at a coffee or doughnut shop. Now many proudly carry a handcrafted beverage made exactly to their specifications. For these customers, the Starbucks latte, cappuccino, flat white, caramel macchiato, or espresso is *their* drink.

THE INTERVIEW: HOW HOWARD SCHULTZ APPLIES THE EIGHT BRANDING RULES AT STARBUCKS

You don't need to apply all the rules all the time. But one company that has applied all the rules is Starbucks. It is a company with a $68 billion valuation[1] that shows that the rules, when applied together, have a powerful impact.

Howard Schultz did not invent Starbucks. He was first an employee. Then he left. Then he engineered a buyout. His original plan was to have 150 stores, not 22,000. He did not have a full vision of a global footprint. He worked his way into becoming a powerhouse brander. He started with entrepreneurial spirit and courage.

In his own way, Schultz pursued the eight branding rules. He understood naturally that the engagement of employees—*partners*, as they are called—was the key to success. His intent was to become the employer of choice—to pay decent wages, provide healthcare benefits to even part-time workers, and create mechanisms for broad employee ownership. He worked every job in the store. He listened critically to suggestions. He invested in beautiful architectural designs. He created open access to his phone and e-mail for a broad cross section of employees, from baristas to office workers. And he listened with vigor, interest, and genuine appreciation. Starbucks mobile and loyalty platforms—with their payment options, status levels, store location capability, and gifting access—make it a leader in the digital space. Starbucks has proved the value of incremental stores and density in a range of geographies from Manhattan to Shanghai. It is the American Dream realized for a boy who started life in the housing projects of Brooklyn.

Schultz believes that credit for the success of Starbucks goes to its culture and its partners, the employees.

"We created a business based on connecting humanity. We want all our partners to benefit," he told us on a rainy day in Seattle early in 2015. He explained that the invention of Starbucks was a result of bringing people together behind a common vision. It was about creating a responsible and caring place of employment and treating everyone with dignity.

Early in our conversation, Schultz mentioned the story of his father, a World War II veteran. His father was a blue-collar worker who, when Schultz was seven years old, was injured and laid off from work. The family had no savings, it had no health insurance, and there was no safety net. Schultz has created a company where employees share in the wealth, including healthcare, Bean Stock (equity in the form of stock options), access to college tuition reimbursement, and many other benefits, even if the employees are part-time.[2]

"I was trying to create the kind of company that my father never got a chance to work for—trying to balance profitability with conscience [for everyone] regardless of your station in life," he said.

Schultz is a man who is willing to tackle tricky social issues: government gridlock, the challenges facing returning veterans, marriage inequality, and race relations. He has recently held a series of town hall meetings with store managers and baristas to talk about diversity and equality.

"We have had good fortune. We remember where we came from," he said. "Success becomes more full and complete when it is shared. Our company has been able to grow fast for a long time because we share a tribal knowledge. Our culture has defined us."

Starbucks has more than 22,000 stores and 300,000 employees.[3] Sales per store are still under $1 million. Market value is now just 30 percent less than that of titan McDonald's and three times that of industry darling Chipotle.

Schultz is very articulate about the Starbucks DNA. "More often than not, profit as a goal and primary purpose gets people in trouble. Performance is the price of admission. We have to perform, but we are a performance-driven organization through the lens of humanity," he states. "The culture has defined the company. The equity of the brand has always been built from within. We always recognize that the brand was defined by the people wearing the green apron. We are a people-driven, culture-based organization."

The Starbucks headquarters is located at the former site of Sears, Roebuck & Co. Placards call out for "coffee passion," "engaged partners," and "connecting humanity." Schultz's words are written on the walls: "Grow with discipline. Balance intuition with rigor. Innovate around the core. Don't embrace the status quo. Never expect a silver bullet. Get your hands dirty. Listen with empathy and overcommunicate with transparency. Tell your story, refusing to let others define you. Use authentic experiences to inspire. Stick to your values—they are your foundation. Hold people accountable but give them tools to succeed. Be decisive in times of crisis. Be nimble. Find truth in trials and lessons in mistakes. Be responsible for what you see, hear, and do. Believe."

Schultz is altruistic and impassioned, and says that he aims to use the company's scale and success for good.

Inside Starbucks, there is a belief that store presence drives sales—that looks do count. At investors' meetings, a clear relationship is shown between store density in a city and sales per capita. The company is also intent on creating new occasions—for example, full breakfasts, lunches, cold refreshment beverages in the afternoon, and tasting menus for the evening.

The seven-point strategy[4] for Starbucks is simple:

1. Be the employer of choice.
2. Lead in coffee.
3. Grow the store portfolio.
4. Create new occasions.
5. Grow the brand in consumer packaged goods.

6. Build Teavana.
7. Extend digital engagement

Schultz is able to connect with employees who are many levels lower in the Starbucks hierarchy. He says that this allows him to stay in touch with what's going on. "I have deep-rooted relationships all over the world with our people, and I've encouraged it. I think people feel they have a license to communicate directly with me. With that comes a level of understanding and insight that you would not get through a survey or by walking around."

Headline: Willing to Tackle Many Issues— Business, Social, and Political

It is no wonder that Schultz's first book about Starbucks was titled *Pour Your Heart into It*. It is about "imagination, dreams, and humble origins." It is the story of the company's early days: how he used values, culture, pride, and ambition to grow from a few stores to 1,600 at the time of the book's publication in 1999, and developed a culture that stretches across lands. He has a core belief that big companies can act like small companies and that doing the right thing pays off every day.

Schultz believes that retailers need to rigorously control quality and the customer experience. "Success is fragile, and you've got to earn it every day, and we can't be a company that is sitting here celebrating and embracing the status quo, because the customer is not celebrating what happened yesterday. We've got to perform today. We've got to be hungrier, smarter, and push for reinvention and self-renewal more than any other time because of the seismic change in consumer behavior as a result of technology and mobile phones."

He states, "We're now processing almost 7 million mobile transactions a week. That's about 16 percent of tender. The loyalty program has been a major source of success. We're now piloting mobile order and pay. We'll bring it to the rest of the country in calendar 2015. We're experimenting with delivery soon. All these things are designed to make Starbucks relevant. We have to be hyperrelevant, and we've got to surprise our customers and in doing so galvanize our organization about working for a company that's innovative and in-the-know."

Schultz's advice to young entrepreneurs is to follow your dream— but to do it with rigor and study, and to get experience. "I say to young entrepreneurs, 'If it's not personal, if you don't love it, if you're not willing to sacrifice almost anything for it, then don't do it. You've got to dream big and have a little bit of luck.'" Schultz continues, "I don't think any of us had the audacity to believe we'd have 22,000 stores. . . . But now that we're here, we realize the opportunity is much, much greater. I think it's okay not to know how big something could be. Just keep dreaming about it and keep pushing."

Tribal knowledge has been imprinted into the company in its heritage and tradition. Schultz engages his leadership team in town hall meetings about key business, social, and political issues. He uses the discussions as a platform to demonstrate that Starbucks is more than just a coffee retailer.

Within a short drive of its headquarters, at 1124 Pike Street in Seattle, Starbucks has opened its first Starbucks Reserve Roasting and Tasting Room. This is a 15,000-square-foot former Packard car showroom that has been meticulously turned into a flagship for everything Starbucks. As the Starbucks partner at the counter explained to us, "This space truly has heart. You can tell the minute you walk in here. I am excited to come to work here every day."

The store is a stage on which to tell the story of Starbucks. It is as much about theater as it is about retail. For $15, you get to taste three types of espresso, from bold Kona with notes of chocolate to a lighter blend with citrus and vanilla. The baristas educate you on the choices. You are in the center of a live coffee-roasting facility where all of Starbucks's global specialty coffees—called Starbucks Reserve—are processed for distribution around the world. Starbucks says that food is an essential part of the Roastery experience. The food menu was created to complement the flavors of the coffees offered—like wine pairings in fine restaurants. Tom Douglas and his team provide fresh seasonal pizzas from the Serious Pie restaurant inside the building, as well as the pastries, sandwiches, salads, and sweets offered in the Roastery café.

Schultz says the company is prepared to invest in other Roastery locations around the world—like the one on Pike Street—to celebrate and authenticate the brand.

He is not blindly confident: "We have a lot of challenges. We have a lot of issues. Change requires great thoughtfulness and sensitivity well beyond strategy and execution. It requires a deep level of understanding of how to move the organization forward, how to share success, how to build trust, how to bring people along. This is built around leadership, and leadership comes in many forms and many shapes. The hardest part of leadership is leading when it's inconvenient and not when the wind is at your back, being decisive, and making decisions when you don't have perfect information. And it's lonely."

He continues, "Challenges are the soft side of the business: maintaining and enhancing and improving the culture, taking responsibility for 300,000 people and their families, making the kind of decisions that make our people proud, betting on the right things, maintaining the entrepreneurial DNA of the company while it gets bigger, having courage and conviction, celebrating success, not punishing failure, encouraging risk taking in the company."

He understands that the partners entering Starbucks today are different from the first generation of employees. "It's a more idealistic workforce. I think they expect more from the company they're working for. I think most people have worked for other companies before they come to Starbucks, and they've been disappointed, so there's a level of cynicism, and the burden of proof is on us to perform early on—show them we're different."

When asked about the ability of hot coffee beverages to travel and, as an extension, about the real prospects for delivery, he smiles. "You will see," he says securely. "We have mastered that challenge. It is all about incremental volume on top of a good business."

He continuously pushes the boundaries to avoid becoming "predictable, inaccessible, or irrelevant."

Starbucks has generated an 18 percent operating margin, a 10 percent target global growth rate, and successive 30 percent total shareholder returns, adding 1,500 stores a year—more than half its locations are now outside the United States. In China, there are 1,500 stores with 20,000 partners.[5] The company has completed the rollout in the United States and Canada of baked goods from its acquired bakery company, La Boulange. Starbucks Evenings stores serve coffee, wine, beer, and small plates. Starbucks furthered its commitment to innovation and transforming the tea industry by acquiring Teavana mall stores and opening new Teavana Tea Bars.[6] The company launched Oprah Chai tea. It now has more than 9 million My Starbucks Rewards loyalty members.

At the company's headquarters, Schultz is quoted in big bold letters on the wall:

We inspire and nurture the human spirit—one person, one cup, and one neighborhood at a time.

We live these values:

▶ Creating a culture of warmth and belonging, where everyone is welcome
▶ Acting with courage, challenging the status quo, and finding new ways to grow our company and each other
▶ Being present, and connecting with transparency, dignity, and respect
▶ Delivering our very best in all we do, holding ourselves accountable for results
▶ We are performance driven through the lens of humanity
▶ We are on a journey

Schultz concludes, "I'm more inspired today than I ever have been. We have a chance to be the kind of company that makes history in the world. It's about redefining the role and responsibility of a public company and doing what's right for our people and the communities we serve."

There is a *science* to building a brand. It involves extensive quantitative and qualitative research. You get deep inside the consumer's head. You understand how and why she buys. You understand her hopes, her dreams, and her aspirations. You understand the context of her life and the trade-offs she has to make. But this is not sufficient to create a brand.

There is an *art* to brand building, too. Great brands anchor themselves in the customer's emotional space. A great brand is about loyalty. It's about love. It's about providing the customer with enough truth and enough myth to carry her through her day.

It's about stories.

It will be the backstory about your brand—the one your customers repeat to their friends with energy and force—that will allow your company to earn extraordinary returns and create annuities that last forever.

In *Rocket*, we tell the stories of companies that have done this. Some of the stories you'll know or have heard about—for example, those of Apple, Amazon, and Toyota. We offer you the chance to understand their evolution and the thought processes of their founders. Other stories may be new to you. But we find that the stories of mortals—the hard-working business executives who built brands that stand the test of time—are just as insightful and perhaps more inspirational given their ordinariness. You don't have to be a genius like Steve Jobs to create a great brand like Apple.

There are many secrets to success. In the course of our work for more than 80 percent of the world's largest brands over the past five decades, we have encountered many similar patterns of winning. In this book, we have synthesized our findings to create a set of eight branding rules. You need to follow them if you are to be truly successful, if you are to build an enduring brand.

Rule No. 1: Don't Ask Your Customers What They Want (Because They Don't Know Until You Show Them)

The most famous story concerning this rule is about a global communications giant that was exploring the development of the cell phone. In focus groups, the company asked salespeople to look at the box phone and then asked, "When will you use it?" The salespeople said that they would sooner put a quarter into a phone booth rather than pay $500 or $1,000 for an unwieldy box. As a result, the company put cell technology on a back burner. This was an expensive error. It cost the company billions of dollars to buy its way back into the business after it had taken off. The consumer could not imagine a better way to make a phone call and certainly could not imagine paying for it. The big leap forward requires curiosity and courage, instinct, and a taste for the jugular. It requires you to look beyond simple answers and impulsive consumer rejection.

Rule No. 2: Woo Your Biggest Fans (Because They're Absolutely Worth It)

Few companies count the value of their best customers' purchases and the value of the purchases that those customers promote through word-of-mouth advocacy. Our research supports the rule of "4+." Generally, the best customers—we call them *apostle consumers*—are personally responsible for a full 20 percent of the sales and 40 percent of the profits of their favorite brands.[7] They are also responsible for between four and eight times their own sales through advocacy with their "followers"—family, friends, and colleagues. Their hearty recommendations and trial by friends can deliver more than the balance of your total profits.

One apostle begets many others. The math of multiplication of $1,000-per-year consumers is amazing. In 12 generations, you can achieve more than $1 billion. This cycle of 12 generations can happen within three years. The law of propagation is this: *innovation times trial times uniqueness and power equals uptake.*

Rule No. 3: Always Welcome Your Customer's Scorn (Because You'll Come Back Stronger)

Toyota says that a complaint is a gift. The company uses process control and redesign to track and process any customer complaints. This operates as a system to stamp out design errors and repeated customer complaints. Complain once, let me fix it. Complain twice, shame on me. Complain three times, and I should be replaced.

Toyota's approach—reliability, durability, and "complaint as a gift"—translates into higher resale value, a higher repurchase rate, and deeper loyalty. When the complaints are vehement, listen and get ready to change. As CEO, open your e-mail to get direct feedback. Always give a polite and thankful response. Capture and respond to scorn. Change as a result.

Rule No. 4: Looks Do Count (Because People Really Do Judge a Book by Its Cover)

Humans use their eyes in every purchase. They look for beauty. They look for vision. They dream about a better world for themselves and their loved ones. You can create a storybook.

The best dreamscape company in the world continues to be Disney. Little girls visiting Disney World go to the Magic

Kingdom. They see Cinderella and Snow White. They carry the image in their subconscious. For many, it draws them back when they decide to marry. Disney has created a rich business by fulfilling fantasy. Customers can be princesses marrying their prince—and they do it in droves. You can count thousands of bricks with the names of couples who took their vows in the fantasy world of the Magic Kingdom (at Disney World), now celebrating its sixtieth birthday. They paid up to $250 to have their names immortalized. Visual brilliance costs a lot, but its value is priceless. It allows you to put a framed picture in the minds of your most important consumers.

Rule No. 5: Transform Your Employees into Passionate Disciples (Because Love Is Truly Infectious)

Walk into a Container Store with a vague idea about a storage problem and ask for help. Within moments, a counselor will have you spellbound as you describe your problem or problems, and soon he will be offering solutions. The employees know how to charm you into better organization so that you can manage your closet, kitchen, bath, and office more productively. It is a perpetual favorite company to work for. Container Store associates are treated with respect, are paid twice the wage of competitors' employees, and turn over at a fraction of the average rate.

Passion equals knowledge. Knowledge equals solutions. Solutions translate into sales. It's so simple but so infrequently exercised.

Rule No. 6: Better Ramp Up Your Virtual Relationships (Because That's What Your Customers Are Doing)

The world has moved to 24/7. The consumers with the greatest disposable income have the least time. They have the greatest education. They have high-speed Internet lines at home and at work. And they want to buy what they want to buy when they want it.

Amazon is an emotionally cold company. You search and get a random list. It has telephone support, but the company never flaunts it or makes it easy to access. But millions of people are now in Prime, a membership program where customers pay $99 to get free two-day shipping and other perks. Amazon gets to process all your purchases. The company calls this *collaborative filtering*. It is the ultimate in suggested sales. There is no "person" choosing for you—it is a computer algorithm. But in 21 years, with relentlessness and a passion for growth and share gain, this company has garnered a market value of $137 billion and sales of $90 billion. The value of Amazon is now greater than the combined value of Macy's, Nordstrom, Kohl's, JCPenney, Best Buy, and, of course, Barnes & Noble. This is not an accident. It is the future. Digital is not just a channel.

Rule No. 7: Take Giant Leaps (Because You're Not Going to Win with Timid Steps)

If you want to win big, you are highly unlikely to succeed if your plan is built on tweaking your current competitors' products. Big wins require big dreams. They require innovations in product, packaging, source materials, distribution, sales system, customer engagement, after-sale service, and meeting the needs of the apostle consumers. Timidity and incremental improvements to existing products is the road to World War I trench warfare. Giant leaps permit rapid growth and share gain. All of the top 10 brands in BCG's consumer index got there with easy-to-describe, graphically dynamic, simple value propositions. Each has a major consumer catch point and a symmetric set of consumer support points. They were not extensions. They did not reflect value engineering. They grabbed the consumer by the shorts.

Rule No. 8: Find Out What Schismogenesis Means (Because It Will Save Your Relationships)

We have always believed that brands are not stable. Our research for this book proves it. Consumers say that brands are either getting better faster or sinking fast. The world of retail is the best case in point for rapid growth, fast shrink. Once the dark winds are in your sails, it is almost impossible to break their hold. Think Sears, Kmart, or JCPenney. How do you know where your brand advocacy is headed—up or down? Learn how to use quantitative metrics, such as BCG's Brand Advocacy Index. Track them like the third leg of your P&L—revenues and profits, share of the properly defined universe, and advocacy. If you are not improving, you are in decline. If you are not top dog, you are likely to be surpassed.

The Apostle Brands

You may think you know why you love Apple, Starbucks, or McDonald's. Who hasn't bought an iPhone, gotten a *grande latte*, or picked up a Happy Meal for a ravenous child?

But our eight rules provide you with a game plan for converting your customers into loyal shoppers—customers who advocate your brand and urge their family, friends, and colleagues to try your products. We have formulated the rules on the basis of BCG's 52 years of client experience, a unique quantitative study of U.S. consumers, and a series of in-depth interviews with top executives.

In the course of our work, we have discovered that there are ordinary brands and what can be called *apostle brands.* Apostle brands are rare. Few companies have brands whose signature products and services are widely revered everywhere. There are 10,000 multimillion-dollar consumer companies around the world, but only 100 of them can properly claim to have apostle brands. They offer magic and light. They provide entertainment, nourishment, imagination, and utter joy. They inspire enduring trust, loyalty, love, and almost evangelical endorsements and advocacy. To their fans, followers, and believers, they are like religions. They capture a disproportionate share of discretionary dollars.

The list of apostle brands is based on the BCG Consumer Sentiment Survey, which offers deep quantitative research from some 15,000 adult consumers of all ages and incomes. This survey is founded on a database that we have developed over more than 10 years that covers 20 major countries and contains more than 400,000 consumers.

The top 10 U.S. apostle brands are Apple, Amazon, Walmart, Netflix, Costco, Samsung, Coca-Cola, Target, JetBlue, and Chick-fil-A.[8]

It should be no surprise that Apple tops the list. If you ask most consumers in the United States or Europe to name one favorite brand, they usually say, "Apple." But the company has not always enjoyed global success. For much of its history, it was actually struggling. For many years, it was a microcomputer firm in a secondary position. It created beautiful, technically differentiated, elegant products that were broadly rejected by the largest potential market: business organizations. Eventually, the company's founder was fired by the board and replaced by a marketer. But this didn't work. The organization floundered. In desperate straits, it asked its founder to come back. It was the return of the prodigal son.

The young Steve Jobs was driven and impatient, but he had an instinctive understanding of what customers really wanted. He appreciated the importance of the emotional connection between the brand and the customer. When Apple finally reached into the soul of millions of music lovers, its fortunes skyrocketed.

In our survey, we asked customers how Apple made them feel. The top five answers were, "Smart, like I made a good decision," "Excited," "Worry-free," "Comfortable," and, "Like I did something good for myself."[9] Another emotion that respondents expressed was that Apple made them feel "successful and accomplished."[10] The company offers a classic story of innovation, apostles, and legacy. Steve Jobs was the innovator. Music fans became his apostles. And the legacy is a company boasting $500 billion in market value some five years after his death.

Apple delivered record figures for the last quarter of 2014: $74.6 billion in revenue. Its net income for the quarter was $18 billion, up 37 percent year-over-year. *Business Insider*, a news website, waxed enthusiastic: "Apple just delivered an earnings report for the ages. It simply demolished expectations thanks to fantastic iPhone sales. Apple sold 74.5 million iPhones, up 46 percent compared to the year prior, its biggest ever quarter by 23.4 million units. Analysts were only expecting 65 million units sold. This growth is truly phenomenal."[11]

The other companies in the top 10 can tell a similar story of brand growth. They have found a way to connect emotionally with their customers—and then deliver the technical and functional features that satisfy those emotions. For Amazon, it's about the variety of the products, the prices, and the shipping. For Walmart, it's all about prices. Walmart demonstrates the simplicity of a formula for consumers. It has a unique, powerful appeal for lower-income consumers. For Netflix, convenience, accessibility, and entertainment factors are dominant. For Costco and Target, it's a combination of price, selection, quality, and range. For Samsung, Apple's great rival, it's about the quality of the products and the value. For Coca-Cola, the overriding theme is taste, refreshment, and accessibility. For JetBlue, it's all about the service. For Chick-fil-A, it is about uncommon value, the quality of the product, and customer service.

At the end of this Introduction we have provided an exhibit. It is a Wordle—a visual depiction of the most common words consumers use to describe the top brands. For the most valued companies, this is often one to five words that every fan utters. It is a simple test of your brand to ask, "What is the Wordle we are trying to evoke?" If you, as the founder, can't create it, your consumer is unlikely to be able to do so.

Apostle Customers: Looking for the Elusive "Demand" Space

What apostle brands do better than their rivals is convert customers into ultraloyal followers. We call these people *apostle customers*. They are the reason why the apostle brands are so successful. They are worth a multiple of the value of their own purchases. They recommend the brand that they love passionately and unequivocally. They take friends and family members who might be tempted to go to another retailer or buy another product, and they prod them to embrace the apostle brand instead. They bring them to the store. They carefully explain the backstory behind their beloved brand: the quality differences, the value, the authenticity, and the reasons to believe in it. They do this using the language of their peers. This is the power of word-of-mouth advocacy. It's so much better than a slick advertising campaign. Apostle brands win on the words of their users.

An apostle customer can be an eight-year-old elementary school student, an eighty-year-old retiree, or someone anywhere in between. Likewise, apostle purchases can come in many different sizes. They can take the form of a $4 espresso at Starbucks, an $8 burrito at Chipotle, a $16 ticket to a Pixar movie, a $660 Rimowa suitcase, a $7,500 Hermès Birkin bag, a $74,000 Audi A7, or a rare $250,000 Patek Philippe watch.

How do you convert customers? Apostle brands provide a complete expression of trust, loyalty, and knowledge; a commitment to standards of quality and purpose; and a promise of uniform delivery, pleasure, and personal fulfillment.

They can do this because they understand what really determines customer choice. It is generally thought that demographic factors hold the key: a customer's age, gender, or economic group. These all do play a part, of course. But during our client work and extensive research, we have established that the biggest determinant of customer choice is the *occasion of use*, which is typically *grounded in an emotion*: when customers consume the product, whom they are with at the time, and, most important, how they want to feel. In other words, they prioritize different products with different features on different emotionally based occasions.

So you need to focus on your customers' needs and wants or demands. Ask the right questions, and you can create a map of different kinds of demands. In the jargon, these are "demand spaces."[12] A "space" is an occasion or an emotional moment, and each unique space has a unique set of demands. These spaces are usually expressed in everyday language—the kind of language used by apostle customers when they advocate brands to their friends and family.

When Frito-Lay, PepsiCo's snack-producing subsidiary, reviewed its business as a series of demand spaces, it found that it should be competing not just in the salty snack market, but in the much larger macro snack market. As we show in Chapter 3, it mapped out the different spaces in a market where Lay's and Tostitos compete with crackers, nuts, candy, and chocolate, but also fast food and frozen snacks. The largest space was called "Fun Times Together."

The secret to discovering the right demand spaces is to do the right kind of research. Ask the right questions. Don't base your conclusions on syndicated data (the historical purchases by category reported by Nielsen and IRI). Once you've created a map of the demand spaces, and can see your business and your market in a very different way, you can very easily establish whether you have a "right to win" in one or more of the specific demand spaces. You can do so only if your brand owns the relevant emotional attributes of the space.

For instance, Hilton Worldwide found that the "cool and hip" demand space, while attractive from a marketing perspective, was not aligned with its flagship Hilton brand. It was too small, and Hilton really didn't have a right to win against some of its boutique rivals. Instead, it opted for the "recharge and refresh" space, which was large, encompassing both business and leisure travelers.

Finally, you can close the loop by establishing the commercial opportunity of the demand space and the share of the market where your brand has a right to win. Once you know this, your challenge is to create "bull's-eye" products to match all the demands in the space precisely. You can fully align all the activity of your organization—from marketing and finance to R&D and operations—around the idea of winning your target demand space.

We call this process *demand-centric growth*.

Schismogenesis: Why Brands Fail

Brands are fragile. They are subject to the laws of schismogenesis. They always were. But now, in the digital age, they can be wiped out in an instant. To be successful, they need constant nurturing. You can't afford to switch off—not for a second. If you do, you won't endure. You won't create an apostle brand.

Even the greatest brands need to be on their guard. Apple, as we've seen, is the world's favorite brand. But it is also among the world's least favorite brands. "I think they are overpriced, overhyped, and more flash than function," one consumer told us. Others said that Apple was "arrogant," was "secret and elitist," and "rips people off." In other words, if things ever turned against Apple, there are consumers who would happily denigrate it further.

Right now, Apple is standing tall. Few companies have done what it has done and created an apostle brand. However, often the next generation of executives loses focus. They don't understand the demand space they are playing in. They "forget" the rules—assuming that they knew them in the first place. They become insular, arrogant, and complacent. They become the person who "speaks to investors" and caters to the needs of the board. They lose the passion that got them to the top. They become blind to the market and to competitive intruders.

Many companies allow their great ideas to be squandered by obscure, poorly executed strategies, by doubting or delaying colleagues, or by other misguided organizational prerogatives. They value-engineer their product—saving on short-term costs while sacrificing integrity—and end up devastating their customer base. They skimp on ingredients. They compromise by revising beloved recipes. They stop listening, and they stop learning. They retreat to what they know, doing more of the same even when new and vital consumer values become obvious, when distribution channels shift in radical new ways, and when vibrant start-ups and global challengers are growing around them.

You don't need to be one of the failures.

These companies urgently need to learn the lessons of the apostle brands. In the chapters that follow, we tell the stories of how consumers find out about and follow their favorite brands, and why they love the brands they love—and how brands and businesses can build enduring trust, advocacy, and love.

During the course of the book, we identify the critical elements for success as an apostle brand. These are brand principles, and they complement our brand rules:

> **Inspire.** Behind each of these brands is a singular inspiration. Apostle brands begin with a bold, unique vision aimed at a big market and a broad arena of consumers, a vision that is conceived and articulated by a highly committed, creative, often obsessed leader. The vision is authentic, purposeful, and motivating.

Empathize. Apostle brands are built on unique consumer insights. These brands offer first-time solutions and answers to consumers' profound fears, dissatisfactions, and unmet needs. The creators of apostle brands are listening to and empathizing with consumers. They fully understand their consumers—who they are, and when, why, and to what degree they experience these needs, longings, and wants. They are surveying the landscape to look for and identify critical new demand spaces. They communicate that they care deeply and longingly.

Dazzle through design. Apostle brands design products, services, and retail spaces that provide functional, technical, and emotional benefits that are almost magical. They develop the "no compromises" ideal and build it at virtually any cost. Their products, services, and retail systems include features that respond directly to consumers' most ardent needs, wants, and dreams. They deliver highly interactive design that anticipates and responds to fundamental human desires.

Innovate and refine. Apostle brands continuously innovate and respond to consumers and what they're asking for, refining and improving their offerings with boldness, specificity, simplicity, and conviction. These brands make their fundamental value proposition clear, real, and widely known. They learn from and adapt to consumers.

Engage and evangelize. Apostle brands engage early users in a shared experience. They help those first consumers understand the company's value proposition, and then rapidly work to build a full portfolio of offerings catering to these consumers' needs. They then recruit these apostle consumers to spread the word worldwide. Apostle brands make their money not just from the net present value of their early adopters' purchases, but also from the value of all the referral customers whom the early adopters, in turn, recruit, attract, or both. They stoke new users to offer other consumers their personal endorsements, positive reviews, and gushing enthusiasm and encouragement.

Treat people well. An increasing number of apostle brands also boast a positive, holistic "good business" philosophy that reflects consumers' values, personalities, and ethics. They aren't just paying lip service to corporate social responsibility. They are not engaged in superficial "good cause" marketing. Instead, they're doing well by all the people they touch—their customers, their employees, and the communities where they make and distribute their goods. Treating people well and helping others is at the core of their strategic vision and everything they do. They do this because they deeply believe in it and because they believe they can recruit better people with that bedrock belief.

The Structure of the Book

Rocket is our bible on apostle brands—and how to become one. The eight chapters are devoted to the eight rules. In general, there are two featured companies in each chapter, with insights drawn from exclusive interviews, deep research, and decades of client work. Each chapter tells the story of the entrepreneurs behind the companies—and does so in a detailed way, with the backstory of their success. We could have presented a narrow story that is concerned solely with the rule in the chapter heading. But we knew that you would want to hear the whole story. As with their brands, you can't begin to understand these people's success without understanding the backstory—how they got to the top, what drove them, and what inspired their thinking about business and brands.

Throughout the book, many themes recur, uniting the different rules. They include the following:

▶ Put your apostle customers at the center of everything you do. Listen to them, collect feedback from them, pay attention to them, and regard them with admiration and appreciation. Every apostle brand has a way of articulating this point. Juan Roig refers to the customer as *el jefe*: the boss. Isadore Sharp talks of his "golden rule": "Do unto others as you would have them do unto you." Focus on the advocates of your brand. Identify the "cravers"—consumers who love your products and will tell everyone they know to buy them. Don't worry about the general population.

▶ Discover what really determines what your customers want and need. Create a map of the demand spaces and the "bull's-eye" products that will satisfy them and turn you into a winner.

▶ Always be switched on. Don't rest on your laurels. Renew or die. Innovate with urgency and authenticity. Create a powerful, believable story that inspires customers.

▶ Establish an emotional connection with your customers. Technical and functional features are important, but they need to meet the customer's underlying emotional needs. These are the things that endure. These are the ties that bind.

▶ Above all, use the demand-centric growth process to chart your course. It can unlock enormous opportunities.

Follow the Eight Branding Rules, Create Your Own Stories, and Achieve Immortality

Apostle brands represent a new class of brand winners. These companies behave differently and better. They source ethically, pay fairly, establish an advantage based on design, boast keen insight into consumer dissatisfactions, and have relentless experimentation in their veins. They do not exploit their followers, but seamlessly and completely respond to their hopes, dreams, and wishes. They follow what we call the *yellow brick road*—creating a path to home and providing safety, a sense of being cared for, and emotional satiation. They lay the seed for the telling and retelling of highly positive, inspiring stories.

Follow our eight branding rules and you'll have the power to create your own apostles—consumers who will carry your message, teach and convert, listen and tell you more, and help you deliver to your full potential.

Throughout the book, we show you how the rules have been applied across a range of companies. We hope they make the concepts and principles of success come alive for you. We also provide you with a set of tools, including demand spaces and the Brand Advocacy Index, that you can use to renovate your own brands.

We recognize that you can't simply replicate the Apple or Amazon story. Your company will have its own constraints, market conditions, challenges, and opportunities. But we think that you can imagine a better future. You can take your brand to a stronger and more powerful position.

We hope that you will be able to weave your own story with the help of the rules and the tools in *Rocket*.

This book is, therefore, a manual for mortals who want to build a brand that lasts forever.

Top 15 Brand Wordles

THE BOSTON CONSULTING GROUP

TOP 15 BRAND WORDLES

Source: BCG 2014 consumer survey.[13]

Don't Ask Your Customers What They Want (Because They Don't Know Until You Show Them)

THE CHAPTER IN A BOX

The Main Point

Consumers cannot think in abstractions. They cannot envision a new concept. They cannot predict their behavior. They can only compare an idea against their current frame of reference. So you need to make the big leap for them. You need to provide them with a reason to buy, a reason to exclaim to their friends. Expect new-to-the-world ideas to fall on deaf ears. People will, however, change their tune when they can see, touch, and explore something new. That's why, when you deliver a truly breakthrough idea, it has so much traction. There is a lot to talk about. There is a lot to praise. It is so different, so pleasing, so unique.

Why This Story for This Chapter

Les Wexner is one of the few inventors who has done this time and time again. He has invented and redefined the rules of specialty retail. His original invention was Limited. Women's sportswear as a category was ripped out of the sleepy department stores, where it wasn't well defined. He put it front and center in a small-footprint store. It guided women to comfort, security, fashion, and color. On a concept board, it would have fallen on deaf ears. On a busy street or in a mall, it became a "must shop." He did it again with Express, aimed at younger women. He did it again with Limited Too for girls. He bought Abercrombie & Fitch when it was near bankruptcy and focused it on clean-cut, preppy clothing at premium prices. And then he found a way to take "sexy" mainstream with Victoria's Secret. He knew that women have "every side of sexy" in their heads, and he delivered "playful, impulsive, fresh, optimistic, sparkling" products under one roof. He took lingerie, then laddered up into fragrance and body care with higher margins, higher velocity per square foot, and immediate international appeal.

In sequence, Limited, Express, Abercrombie, and Victoria's Secret broke the markets they attacked. Limited brought sportswear with conviction—it piled large quantities of merchandise in big displays. The merchant dictated fashion for middle- and upper-middle-class women. It delivered wow in its day. Express brought that vision to younger women. Abercrombie made preppie and proper available to all. It marked up the goods to give people a sense of higher quality and value. Victoria's Secret answered the call for sexy, glamorous, and comfortable by selling lingerie, not underwear. These brands revolutionized their categories with a unique reason to buy. As each trend became common, Wexner, the shrewd investor, either sold the brand at a high valuation or reinvented it to develop the next idea.

Chapter Overview

Les Wexner, the grand master of specialty retail who has built Victoria's Secret into the largest lingerie retailer in the world, doesn't believe that consumers can tell you what they really want. He does not believe in traditional market research. He has more than 50 years of glorious retail success and billions of dollars in product sales to support his views.

In his view, consumers react. They know what they love, but they can't explain why. They know what they hate, but they can't explain why. And they shift on a dime. To Wexner, success in business is about anticipation, instinct, insights—and, ultimately, curiosity and experience. He will, however, listen to tight summary findings of in-depth consumer profiles and is always trying to understand what we call the *wheel of consumer emotions.* Consumers don't fit neatly into any one segment. Their behavior and the way they purchase vary depending on context. Where are they going? What are they doing? Who are they doing it with? What conversations have they had? What media have they most recently seen or heard?

What will drive their behavior at the moment when they are finalizing a purchase?

Headline: Curiosity and Experience Provide the Basis for Investment and Brand Power

On any given Saturday, Wexner is likely to be shopping. He'll most often be wearing a casual jacket, a baseball cap, and a pair of sunglasses. He is often accompanied by one of his four children or his wife. He'll be looking in the most unlikely places—the side streets of Shanghai, the shopping extravaganza of the Rue du Faubourg Saint-Honoré in Paris, supermarkets, Costco, and the Easton Town Center, which he developed in Columbus, Ohio. He'll talk to consumers—personally. He'll ask them about what they like, and why. He will study the operations of a store, looking to see whether the manager is visible and engaged or caught up in mundane tasks and missing the action. He will notice what is out of stock, study merchandising, and watch consumers look at windows and decide whether to enter a store. He has little time for conventional research reports. He'd rather use his curiosity and his experience as his guide. He will try to see patterns and find reasons for consumer choices.

Wexner is insatiably curious. When you walk into the library of his home in New Albany, near Columbus, you enter a room that is more than 1,000 square feet. It's a perfectly organized maze of books, with shelves rising 16 feet high. Pull out any title, and he's read it. Ask him about American history, and he'll give you an answer about the life and times of each president. Ask him about Picasso, and he can give you an encyclopedic account of the artist's life from his childhood to his last work of art. Talk about automobiles, history, or architecture, and Wexner is an expert. Wexner wears his curiosity on his sleeve.

His curiosity and his experience have allowed him to give customers what they really, really want. He talks about "seeing around the corner" in anticipation of changes in shopping behavior and trends.

At 77 years old, Les Wexner still comes to work every day with a bounce in his step and big dreams. He still finds energy and excitement in the sale of bras, panties, fragrances, and candles. He believes that the best apostle for a brand is its creator, and he is the ringleader and impresario of his brands. Victoria's Secret, PINK, and Bath & Body Works are his primary sales engines. He also invented and profitably sold off Abercrombie & Fitch, Limited, Limited Too, and Express.

"Creators know how difficult it is to create a brand. They understand how fragile their brand's equity is," he says. "We know that the force of gravity is likely to bring you down. We know that success breeds competition. And the most loyal consumer is loyal for about 32 seconds. You can't and shouldn't count on them for their loyalty. You need to win them back with reinvention. Everything changes. So if you don't exercise the change muscle, then you just lose the ability to change. You either go out of business or you evolve into a different position."

Wexner believes in the power of big brands to capture consumers' imagination and to influence the way they spend their money. He knows from experience that leadership requires continuous evolution and continuous investment. What's hot today is cold tomorrow. He has studied and lived the history of consumer shopping and consumption. He knows that where there is success, imitators follow. He believes that where there are retailers earning price premiums, there are discounters coming. He says that to earn above-average returns, you need to bring innovation, news, and depth to a category.

Wexner started in 1963 with nothing but his dreams. He was one man with one store, working from 7 a.m. to midnight running Leslie's Limited, a start-up women's sportswear store operating out of a small storefront near Ohio State University's Columbus campus. He had borrowed capital from his aunt and gotten a $5,000 loan from a local bank.

Today, his retail empire has $12.1 billion in sales and a market cap of $27.5 billion.[1] Five years ago, at the bottom of the Great Recession, its shares sold for $8 each. As we write now, they are $94 each. He operates nearly 3,000 stores in the United States, Canada, and the United Kingdom and has 1,000 franchised stores in other markets. More than half of his company's profits are made in November, December, and January. Foreign stores are among the highest grossing in the company. Typically, they have a very small footprint but extraordinary velocity. The Victoria's Secret store on London's Bond Street has sales of $80 million per year. Dubai's is the third-largest store in the world. A small store in Chengdu, China, has sales of $14 million per year. His international expansion has been patient and careful. He generally finds a trusted local company and partners with it, tightly controlling the brand, the merchandising, and operational training.

Wexner made sexy lingerie mainstream without offending anyone. He gave customers what they really want. They want a sexy self-image and confidence.

Headline: Let Your Curiosity Rule—And Then Reinvent

Wexner says that his greatest advantage in life is his natural curiosity. His story is a profile in curiosity—how a constant search to find patterns and understand them through the eye of a merchant can be a path to riches, notoriety, and joy. It is also a story about reinvention—moving from one category to another, transporting business skills and insights, and investing for advantage.

We have known Wexner for 20 years. He is a naturally modest, soft-spoken man. He listens a lot and reads even more. When you talk to him one-on-one, he is engaged, entertaining, and vibrant. He loves retail businesses—he loves to watch other brands, and he spends weeks in the market, looking for patterns in fashion and winning concepts, and talking on the sly with consumers in his stores and in other people's stores.

In this digital age, he has no fear of e-commerce. "Humans are social creatures. They like to go out. They like to touch the goods," he says. "People have come to the marketplace to buy goods for 4,000 years. People like to be with other people, and the shopping experience is the greatest form of free entertainment. They buy online for convenience, but this is not the end of the store. The stores that remain have to deliver energy, excitement, freshness. The ones that do will prosper."

We also believe that curiosity is the greatest source of ideas, retail revolutions, and insights. A curious mind armed with skill, experience, knowledge, and patterns can give birth to a big brand revolution. A curious mind does not ask consumers, "What do you want?" A curious mind understands context, understands behavior, and understands spending and spending patterns—the accumulation of a day's purchases, or spending over a week or a year. A curious mind asks the questions that open up the consumer to talk about her latent dissatisfactions, hopes, wishes, and dreams. A curious mind knows that functional goods sold en masse earn a good return, but breakthrough profits come from satisfying consumers' emotional needs. A curious mind does not jump to conclusions but tests carefully and thoroughly. A curious mind will draw on all of life's experiences to get to the big "aha." The curious cut the data by quintile, by segment, and by user.

"Brands naturally drift away. Whether the brand is Disney or Starbucks or any of the great brands, it requires constant constructive curiosity," Wexner says. "Just being curious can be destructive if it takes you to the wrong place, so you have to test. You have to make sure your curiosity is continuously relevant, and you can test it in the marketplace. You can train yourself in pattern recognition. I have to see things to have ideas. If you just give me a blank piece of paper, I'll give you a blank piece of paper."

In Wexner's case, he decided that apparel was a "cold space" where consumers wanted to buy either low-cost products or the highest luxury. However, he was unwilling to either make a speculative bid for one of the luxury fashion houses or attempt to configure his business to become cost-competitive with Zara and H&M. So, in the 1980s, he looked at the women's "underwear" market and imagined a new market with a lead competitor that called it "lingerie" and made it a product that was about seduction, romance, and love.

He used his curiosity to reinvent the women's underwear market. He is the leading proponent of "reinvent or die." He taught us that when a brand is on top, it has the most to lose and needs to be investing fiercely. Together we defined who is the "best at" in a category—first for Wexner's businesses, and then for many other consumer products and retail concepts. The "best at" is the dominant supplier—the one that provides great depth, assortment, and variety, and that also leads the category with news.

"The people that ran the stagecoaches didn't invent the railroads and the guys that ran the railroads didn't invent the steamship lines and the steamship lines and the railroad guys didn't invent the airlines. Businesses have to be reinvented or they become obsolete by their successor," he spouts, like poetry. "So, in retail, the department stores didn't invent the discount stores and they didn't invent the specialty store. They are being obsoleted by both of them."

Retail is a particularly harsh environment. The barriers to entry for that first store are low. Wexner needed only $10,000 in cash in 1963. Today, you can do it with $100,000 or less. Success is easy to read: new assortments either work or don't work. If they work, it is relatively easy to grow from one store to 100 and from 100 to 500. But Wexner warns that launching new stores is like skiing in a mountain resort known for avalanches. "If you are skiing and you believe there could be an avalanche, waiting until you hear it is too late," he jokes. "Are you scanning broad enough so that you see the avalanche before you hear it?"

In his view, fashion businesses require fast response, continuous patterning, and investment in new technical, functional, and emotional benefits. He can point to many retailers that had it and lost it. He can also point out many retailers that are teetering precariously today.

Curiosity and the readiness to reinvent are necessary for survival.

Headline: Be a Serial Inventor, Develop Patterning Skills, and Explore New Territory

"My wife calls me the ultimate disrupter," Wexner says. "We disrupted the shopping centers. We disrupted the lingerie category. We disrupted with fashion specialty. But *disruption* is just a contemporary word to describe a fundamental phenomenon that happens in the world. The question is, are you the disrupter or the disruptee? If you have a position and you get lazy, you get disrupted."

Wexner should know. He disrupted women's sportswear, then clothing for college women, then bath and home fragrance products, then preppy college clothing, and then lingerie.

Wexner says he does not believe in market research. That's not quite true. As with many things he says, there is a bit of Plato's dialogues in this: he is teaching with rhetoric in his commentary. What he is really saying is that he doesn't believe in delegated market research. He puckers his face at the thought of the type of market research in which a brand assistant hires the principal of a market research firm, who then turns to a young associate and says, "Tell me about usage in the client company's category." Wexner wants to know himself. He doesn't want a thick, dense, circular market research report.

He has a hunger to know and to understand. He will devour topics and become expert in art, architecture, history, historical figures, and the history of the world. He is an expert in leadership patterns, from the Roman emperors to George Washington to George W. Bush. We call him the *long gun*, a nickname we have had for him for 15 years. It is a reference to the knowledge advantage that he has developed during his long life. In sixteenth-century Europe, armies with long rifles could shoot farther—and decimate their enemies.

One Saturday, we were meeting him in his home in Aspen, Colorado. We were working on the brand strategy for his company. We had concluded beyond a shadow of a doubt that his two best businesses were Victoria's Secret and Bath & Body Works. They both had great profit, a strong market share, loyal core consumers, and strong prospects for growth. For this man who scoffs at market research, we had just completed 100 in-home interviews with 26-year-old single professional women in urban markets. We had gone into their homes; counted, measured, and appraised their lingerie; and asked "why" a hundred different ways. We had boiled it down to one slide with one fraction: "2/7ths." This was Victoria's Secret's share of lingerie with its top consumer targets. These young, sophisticated women told us that they wore Victoria's Secret on Friday and Saturday nights. They said that the lingerie was sexy, glamorous, and worth sacrificing a little comfort for.

Wexner liked this new fact. He could do something about it. He could figure out underwear for Monday—and for the rest of the week, too.

"How do we change it?" he asked out loud, without directing the question to any of us specifically. At that moment, we were staring out the window at the magnificent view—lines of groomed aspens and the distant mountains with a bright sun in a blue sky. It was indeed a magnificent day, and all we had to do was deliver a single insight to justify our turkey burger lunch.

We had told him that young women love Victoria's Secret bra-and-panty sets for Friday and Saturday nights—date nights. They say they are willing to dress up for a date or a possible social encounter. They want to feel feminine and sexy. They know there is some chance that a new beau will see what they are wearing underneath their jeans, skirt, or dress. But on weekdays, it's different. They want to be comfortable. Hence the slide that said "2/7ths." Our findings showed that from Sunday through Thursday, they mostly wore cotton underwear—comfortable, cheap, and functional. Victoria's Secret was perceived to be "special occasion" apparel.

Wexner knew the answer to his own question. He usually does. He said: "Pattern—find me product anywhere in the world that will break the compromises of sexy, glamorous, *and* comfortable." Our all-female team immediately got on planes to Brazil, Japan, France, Italy, Holland, and other lingerie hotbeds. They came home with samples that solved the problem: products that used microfiber instead of satin, plus a wide variety of "engineered" solutions. We found a way to use fabric instead of metal to provide support.

Headline: Use Your Experience; Don't Delegate; Change the Rules

So began a journey for Victoria's Secret from a specialist that was stuck at $2 billion to an $8 billion-plus brand that is aiming at a global $20 billion sales target. It was a journey that defined focus, careful experimentation, bold multimillion-dollar marketing investments, and careful, methodical expansion—first to Dubai, then to Kuwait, Brazil, Singapore, and eventually China.

Wexner was present at each early-stage investment and all the major negotiations. A savvy serial retail entrepreneur, he is a retail genius with the instincts, curiosity, and experience that allow him to see things that others miss.

Wexner grew up in Columbus, Ohio. He is the small-town boy who made good, and he has not forgotten his roots. In his hometown, where he came of age in retail, he is considered the second coming of the Wizard of Oz, with a difference: the output of his genius has led to thousands of local jobs and a major quilt of philanthropy across education and health care. Many Columbus investors are millionaires thanks to his success.

His Russian immigrant father and American-born mother had a modest women's clothing store. They worked hard and eked out a living. They sent their son to Ohio State to become a lawyer so that he could escape the punishing life of single-store retail. Of course, he never became a practicing lawyer. For Wexner, law was not a creative business.

Once, when he was left alone in the store while his parents went on their first vacation in decades, he did some line-of-business accounting and saw that they made all their money in women's sportswear. Formal clothing, outerwear, and dresses were losers. When he told his father the news, his father dismissed the finding and then dismissed his son. In response, the 26-year-old bachelor borrowed $5,000 from his aunt and $5,000 from a bank and opened Leslie's Limited—a sportswear-only store for women in suburban Columbus.

Wexner was merchant, cashier, cleaning man, and chief procurement officer. The store sold its first load of sweaters in a week. In Wexner's first year, he grossed $165,000 in revenues at the store and made roughly $20,000 in profit—more than he could imagine. Today, that would be the equivalent of just over $1 million in revenues and $100,000 in profit. After this, he rapidly expanded throughout the Midwest. The chain was an innovator, with big displays of single items and a focus on fast selection and purchase. He took share from tired old regional department stores. He offered depth of selection, fashion merchandise, and fast service.

The modern specialty apparel store was born.

After about six years, Wexner did his IPO—an intrastate IPO, available only to Ohio residents. It cost less money and was less regulated than a regular SEC IPO. He gave founder shares to his parents. His father and mother sold a small part of their holdings. L Brands' investor relations department estimates that $1,000 in IPO shares—with all dividends reinvested—would be worth more than $43.3 million today.

Until his late thirties, Wexner says, he had only work as his passion. He finally got married at age 55 and is the loving father of four children. In his office, there are life-size pictures of his beautiful wife and kids. As Wexner's wealth grew, he discovered art, travel, architecture, and charity. He is famous at Ohio State for his devoted time as a board member, for his funding of the Wexner Arts Center and the Wexner Medical Center, and for the single largest gift in the history of Ohio State. He has also been a major donor to the Kennedy School at Harvard, the United Way, and his own Wexner Foundation.

Wexner remains keenly competitive. He has always compared his enterprise to all the big names of U.S. specialty retail. Now, he is comparing it to the biggest global specialty-store operators in Spain, Japan, and Scandinavia. Wexner says he is "on top" on measures of growth, profitability, and return to shareholders. He operates a retail invention factory. He has never had a losing quarter. He has always been smart enough to invent, bring the business to scale, and then either spin it off or sell it.

Headline: How He Did It—The Secret of Victoria's Secret

Working with Wexner, we helped develop a framework for brand development that we call the 9 Ps of a successful retail brand. It all starts with Positioning—determining the essence of the brand, the personality, the story of the founder, the point of view, the attitude, the motivations, the uniqueness, and the aspiration. In the case of Victoria's Secret, the founder is the mythical Victoria, the daughter of an English lawyer or businessman and a beautiful, sensuous French model.[2] The attitude is English with French sensibility. Sexy, glamorous, and sensuous without being cheap—these attributes are the brand's calling card. Looking beautiful, fit, and desirable are wholesome and worthy goals for Victoria and her customers. The brand is lingerie—not underwear.

That fundamental set of decisions defines the brand core, with which all other elements need to be consistent and coherent. Positioning is surrounded by Price (and value), Product (occasion of use, best-at category, and innovation), Promotion (cadence, calendar, events, and communication), Place (the store environment, navigation, and visual "wow"), People (the employee, the interaction, the relationship, the selling script, the brand culture, and the execution detail), Projection (from point of sale to visual merchandising to broadcast and online), Patterning (competition, customer, and fashion trends), and Profit performance (financial, customer metrics, share, and operational controls).[3]

Victoria's Secret was the racehorse in Wexner's portfolio. It evolved dramatically in aspiration, positioning, and performance. He directed a set of initiatives to take the business on offense—to launch new products at unheard-of levels of intensity backed by the principles from a movie premiere. He drove sustained unit-volume growth and transaction value increases. He delivered higher levels of productivity and margins.

Wexner, the merchant king, orchestrated design, marketing, stores, display, planning for speed, depth of assortment, certainty of merchandising, and innovation according to a defined cadence. He removed a lot of time from the manufacturing cycle, reducing 18 months for a launch to a matter of weeks. The Victoria's Secret stores are colorful, with big-screen video and dramatic presentations of bras and panties in abundance. They stretch back, with lingerie as far as the eye can see. In the back, where there is a set of cash registers, there are fragrances, hair care products, and accessories. The products are not cheap: a bra is $58, and panties are $20. Yet most product lines are sold at full retail, with store gross margins of 60 percent or more.[4]

Victoria's Secret has enjoyed tremendous category growth, proving Wexner's hypothesis that businesses with emotional benefits are not defined by the level of current consumption. The company's secret is to compete on what we call *benefit layers*. It offers customers uniqueness in a series of technical and functional features at different price points. This allows the company to keep moving up, build the brand's credibility, and reinforce its emotional position.

By our count, you can now buy a Victoria's Secret bra in 167 distinct types whose differences include coverage, padding, lining, closure, closure location, material structure, material style application, and materials used. The company became "best at bras," and this allowed it to sell matching panties.

Wexner always aims to take first position in his target consumers' minds and in their share of wallet. With Victoria's Secret, he has powered scale in lingerie and now has more than a 40 percent share of the dollars in the category. That's at least 12 times his nearest competitor's. As a retailer and a producer, he gets double markups—the margin for retail and the margin for wholesale. His global business has an almost infinite return on capital. Outside the United States, his footprint is that of a franchise—other people invest in the stores, the inventory, and the start-up expense. Wexner earns a profit on the sale of goods and controls all elements of the retail operations.

Wexner's success with lingerie has enabled him to extend into adjacent categories—sleepwear, swimwear, yoga and exercise clothes—and, with PINK, into the younger generation of consumers. It opened the door for the large prestige fragrance business.

Scale is something that Wexner understands intuitively. He gets it that being "best-at" in a category delivers traffic and, ultimately, sales. If you can maintain this, you get the benefits of depth, breadth, and cost. He sees major promotional investments as his weapon for driving awareness, trial, and traffic. In 2014, the Victoria's Secret Fashion Show was held in London. Begun in 1995, the show is the brainchild of Wexner's long-term colleague, Ed Razek. Razek has, he says, organized a show that profiles "the world's most beautiful women wearing Victoria's Secret lingerie." The show is about romance, dreams, passion, and art. It is conveniently aired before Christmas each year. "All the lace, all the beauty, all the joy," the announcer says, as people enjoy the show. "Give the gifts the angels want. Say you love me. I want to fall in love. Take the show home with a tote with purchase."

Scale advantage allows Wexner to spend as much as $20 million on the show every December, to invest millions of dollars in media promotion, and to create more styles, more patterns, and more new products than anyone else.

Headline: The Apostle Interview—A Victoria's Secret Fanatic

We met a Victoria's Secret customer in her home in the Crown Heights neighborhood of Brooklyn, New York. Jenny is 27 years old and educated at the University of Chicago and the Kennedy School of Government at Harvard. She makes $70,000 a year working for a not-for-profit organization. She is 5 feet 7 inches tall and wears her dark hair medium-length. She was born in Korea but moved to the United States as a child and speaks without an accent. She wears wire-rim glasses and is proud that she is athletic—she runs, bikes, and hikes. Jenny is a Victoria's Secret apostle. She swears by the brand: "I like the style. I want my underwear colorful and fun. I like to go to VS because it's new and exciting. I like the displays."[5]

She says that the occasion is a key deciding factor when she is choosing what to wear. "Some underwear I would classify as 'fun and cute,' and that I'd just wear around the house," she says. "Then there's some that I wear when I go on a date. For date nights, I like the lacier stuff. I can always feel confident with what I'm wearing. I could always show somebody my underwear."

"When girls talk about underwear or bras, I mention that VS is the only thing I purchase, and it's really great," says Jenny. She visits Victoria's Secret once a month and spends about $500 a year. Some 75 percent of her bras and panties are from Victoria's Secret. She rotates her underwear and tries to maintain an inventory of 30 sets for work, for going out on weekdays, for exercise, and for weekends. She loves having a rainbow of color in her underwear drawer.

She blurts out: "It just adds another element of fun when you pick something out on purpose with the intention of showing it to someone else." She adds, "That's heightened when the other person appreciates it."

Jenny says she is currently seeing a man, but just casually. She is not looking to get married. She has too many places to go and too many things to do to settle down now. Victoria's Secret makes her feel sexy, glamorous, and comfortable. The way she connects with the brand is distinctly different from the way women connected with the brand when we conducted interviews a decade ago. Her fraction is six-sevenths, not two-sevenths. The one-seventh in her lingerie drawer that does not come from Victoria's Secret is normal consumer promiscuity. She will try other brands as a way to validate her loyalty.

Headline: A Long Way from 2/7ths to a 12-Times Advantage over the Next Best Competitor

Wexner has recreated Victoria's Secret for consumers like Jenny. In a decade, he has moved from having 2/7ths of women's purchases to having the vast majority. He has figured out how to get these consumers to visit the stores almost every month, and to go from just lingerie to sports bras, fragrance, skin care, swimwear, and other accessories. He sells to the Jennies of the world through the Omni channel—they can buy 24/7 and learn about the fashion models, the new products, and the "technology" of bras. He has Jenny's loyalty now, and his superior depth of assortment locks her in.

The fashion shows and extensive PR have made the brand an international property. Store openings in international markets are mob scenes. It is clear that there is a lot of bottled-up demand for underwear that is sexy, glamorous, and comfortable. In the Middle East, South America, and Asia, young female consumers believe that Victoria's Secret will make them more desirable and more datable. Around the world, more liberated sexual mores make underwear choice a source of confidence and enticement.

Headline: Forever Young, Forever Current, Forever Shoppable

In our closing moments with Wexner, he walks us to his outer office. On the wall is a long quote from Samuel Ullman, a somewhat obscure southern businessman who retired to write poetry. He tells us that it was originally on Douglas MacArthur's office wall during the occupation of Japan following World War II.

> Youth is not a time of life; it is a state of mind; it is not a matter of rosy cheeks, red lips and supple knees; it is a matter of the will, a quality of the imagination, a vigor of the emotions; it is the freshness of the deep springs of life.
>
> Youth means a temperamental predominance of courage over timidity of the appetite, for adventure over the love of ease. This often exists in a man of sixty more than a boy of twenty. Nobody grows old merely by a number of years. We grow old by deserting our ideals. . . .
>
> Whether sixty or sixteen, there is in every human being's heart the lure of wonder, the unfailing child-like appetite of what's next, and the joy of the game of living. In the center of your heart and my heart there is a wireless station; so long as it receives messages

of beauty, hope, cheer, courage and power from men and from the infinite, so long are you young.

When the aerials are down, and your spirit is covered with snows of cynicism and the ice of pessimism, then you are grown old, even at twenty, but as long as your aerials are up, to catch the waves of optimism, there is hope you may die young at eighty.[6]

Ullman's words frame Wexner's view on the world. He sees himself as being youthful in spirit, as being adventurous and seeking the next round of improvement in both his businesses and his philanthropic activities. He has never written a book on retail, but he nevertheless wants to leave a legacy. At his company there are video recordings of him leading sessions on merchandising, store navigation, retail economics, and big-idea creation.

He is very free with advice. He has made it beyond his wildest youthful imagination—global retailer, philanthropist, devoted husband and father of four successful children, a multibillionaire. "Leaders must have discipline," he says. "They must demonstrate strength. Leaders are curious. They need to have references in history and learn from those references so that they can see into the future. They need to be reflective and see the patterns. You don't need to be first. You need to be best."

Wexner still has a profound youthfulness of spirit and his original curiosity. He is, of course, emboldened to take risks and to raise the ante in his retail businesses. He is shrewd and careful. His mind is vibrant, and he takes a very active hand in running the businesses. He can be directive and specific, he can go deep into the details of retail execution, and he is tough. By continuously refreshing his brands, he has given them the fountain of youth—they are forever young, forever current, and forever shoppable. Curiosity and courage are, of course, the prerequisites.

*****

Lessons from Victoria's Secret

Curiosity and experience provide the basis for investment and brand power. You need to test and explore. You need to be patient and learn as you go. You can use others' experience as a proxy for the future, but do not expect a different outcome unless you have different inputs. Experts—those with a knowledge advantage—have much less risk when they boldly strike out.

Serial invention requires patterning skills, vision, and the courage to explore new territory. Remember, brands sink without newness and invention. If you have sufficient category leadership, you can create massive advantages of scale. When you go global, be cautious. You don't need to be first—just best.

Another lesson is this: retail scale, properly defined, gives fuel for advantage. Bigger and better means higher sales per square foot. It translates into better lease terms. It gives you prominence in the consumer's mind and allows you to achieve first position. If you get ahead, competitors have to try to take what is yours. If you are vigilant, responsive, and decisive, you can cut them off immediately. You can lay claim to a category for multiple generations and deliver extraordinary profit for years.

Above all, remember that although there is much to be learned from consumers, successful dialogue involves more than simply listening. It requires the "ears" of experience, confidence in your interpretation, and a bold goal to invent beyond today's reality.

Three Takeaways

1. **Be inventive.** Seeing what the world cannot imagine is critical to success. Wexner introduced lingerie while the rest of America was still talking about underwear. He helped female consumers—ages 12 to 80—move up emotionally. Like Wexner, invent a new reality. Help your consumers discover a new world.

2. **The economics have to support the business model.** Wexner's lingerie business is expensive. It requires beautiful stores, extensive inventory, significant investment in design and fabrication, and a global supply chain. Promotional events such as the Victoria's Secret Fashion Show are a multimillion-dollar fixed cost. Wexner's genius is that he imagined a business five times the size of his nearest competitor's. He knew that with five times the scale or more, he could deliver cost advantages in design, sourcing, store sales, advertising, and promotion. As the inventor, he set

the price and established the margin structure that delivers the highest profits in specialty retail. Like him, create a business that gives you an economic advantage. Don't settle for anything less than extraordinary returns and a high multiple. It's not about being greedy, it's about being smart.

3. **Know when to get out.** When you invent a business, there comes a point when you should sell. Wexner took the cash returns from Limited, Limited Too, and Abercrombie & Fitch for years. He used the funds to create enormous wealth. Just $1,000 invested in Limited's original IPO is worth more than $43 million today. Wexner, the merchant king, is also a trader. He knows which horse to ride, when and where to race, and for how long. He knows when to retire a horse, too. Remember: you invent a business—and a brand—with the idea that you will eventually sell it.

SOME KEY ACTION POINTS

1. Invent according to an economic anomaly—for example, almost all the profits from an umbrella store come from a small number of departments.
2. Relentlessly fill space.
3. Create waves of demand, with invention delivered every quarter.
4. Build out a demand chain that sources at the best price, delivers seamlessly, and permits you to chase trends with reorders.
5. Invest in fixed-cost promotions that can be amortized against your superior scale.
6. Create adjacent businesses that target consumers of the same gender at different ages (very young, young, contemporary, and mature with young eyes).
7. Use your cash to invent the next big wave.

Exercise your creativity. Ask yourself these questions: Where is the profit core? How can I build a business based on this core idea? How do I fill it out completely so that I own every segment? How do I take my core users and satisfy their every demand? How do I drive an organization with the simple phrase, "What are we best at?"

Stop pursuing every line of business in your portfolio. Own one idea. Complete it. Map the current model of purchase and usage. Change how things are done so that at least some part of the market uses only your product. Extend from that core user to a much broader universe. Describe your concept in a short eight-word story. Answer this question: What is your equivalent of "sexy, glamorous, and comfortable for me every day"?

CHAPTER TWO

Woo Your Biggest Fans (Because They're Absolutely Worth It)

THE CHAPTER IN A BOX

The Main Point

A brand's core consumers define its voice in the marketplace. They are its primary advocates. They can recite the backstory for their friends. They force trial and visitation by skeptics. They see your strengths, weaknesses, and opportunities. If you listen to them, they can define your growth trajectory. You need to pay them back. Little rewards go a long way: an invitation to a special event, a trial of a new product, a free sample with a purchase, a visit to your factory, or a reward for a referral. By our measures, they deliver on average eight times their own value in recommendations.

Why These Stories for This Chapter

Whole Foods Market and The Container Store got their start in life as niche companies. Early adopters either had a greater interest in nutrition or a much higher need to organize. These early zealots set the stage for growth and extension. The first Whole Foods

Markets and Container Stores were shells of what they are today. They had smaller footprints, less extensive offerings, and very dull merchandising. The early fans brought their best friends to the stores, showcased their purchases, and challenged everyone to find something better. They were the apostles. To this day, many of these people swear by the companies' products. They talk about the private labels, the sourcing policies, and the changes both companies made in their lives.

Ask yourself these questions: How do I fill my consumers with pride and a conviction that they have made the right purchase decision? How do I make my guests feel like old friends when they visit me?

Chapter Overview

For most companies, their top 1 or 2 percent of customers contribute 20 to 30 percent of sales through direct purchases. These same customers advocate purchases through word-of-mouth endorsements to their friends, families, and colleagues and indirectly generate the next 50 percent of sales. These customers—your biggest fans—can make the difference between profit and loss. If you can win and hold the top position in their heads, you can drive growth and prosperity. But few companies collect the data needed to see and take advantage of this phenomenon.

We are currently working with a leading luxury department store. It happened to have these data in its customer files. A little analysis showed that 14 percent of the store's customers were driving 50 percent of sales.[1] We then conducted a detailed purchasing and advocacy survey. We found that these fanatical frequent shoppers endorsed the retailer with their friends. They said: "It has style," "It has service," "It has unique goods." They invited their friends on a shopping trip: "Go visit with me next Saturday," they said.

These customers obviously had a different relationship with this retail brand than other customers. So how do you woo such loyal customers?

Headline: Fanatical Fans Create the Bedrock for a Successful Brand

Your most loyal customers set the stage for continuous volume growth. If you listen to them, they can help you define how far afield you can extend. If you track them and induce them to introduce you to their friends and family, they can be your surest route to growth. If you forsake them at any point, they can, like jilted lovers, go from being fanatical fans to fanatical detractors. They will tell you in clear language what is a sin and what is unacceptable behavior. But don't turn away. You need to listen, question, listen again, and test.

How do you capture these people's hearts and minds? The most important element is getting the right salespeople on your selling floor. Those people are your link to them. We found that 10 percent of the luxury retailer's sales staff had a relationship with 90 percent of the best 14 percent of the store's customers. In other words, a small number of staff members knew how to build relationships, while the vast majority had no relationships. So give the people on your sales team the tools, training, incentives, and encouragement they need, and you can win. Earn their loyalty and trust. Understand their motivations. Pay them for superior performance. Help them explain your value. Help them offer details about the technical and functional benefits of your product. Don't leave it to chance that your story is told with enthusiasm, energy, and zeal.

In this chapter, we profile two companies with high concentrations of sales generated by a small percentage of their consumers. One is Whole Foods Market, the natural and organic food retailer. The other is The Container Store, the personal-storage retailer. We look at how they do this, and we lay out the case for concentrating your resources on understanding and catering to the few. We believe this is the surefire road to growth and profitability.

Headline: Texas Boys Made Good

What's the probability that two twentysomething Texans going to the University of Texas at Austin end up as housemates and drop out of college? UT admissions-office statistics suggest that dropout rates could be as high as 20 percent. What's the probability that the two would later start single-site retailers with a superniche focus and turn them into Best Companies to Work For and multimillion-dollar chain stores? Could be 1 out of 100,000. What's the probability that both companies would have a single supplier help them with a third or more of their sourcing and allow them to concentrate their value added on retailing, not sourcing? Could be 1 out of 300,000. And what's the probability that both become multimillionaires and philanthropists and take up the challenge of what each of them calls *conscious capitalism*? Could be 1 out of 1,000,000.

That's exactly what happened to John Mackey and Kip Tindell, both now in their early sixties. Mackey is cofounder of Whole Foods Market, and Tindell is cofounder of The Container Store. They both still lead their "start-ups" and act as the most passionate of apostles for their concepts. From the start, both recognized that fanatical fans would move their purchases to them and that success would reverberate in the market. Mackey needed to reach people who believed that they are what they eat. Tindell needed to reach people who believed that their personal efficiency and productivity could be enhanced by an organized life.

They both intuitively recognized that they needed to sell to the premium segments of the consumer market and that they were not directly substituting for existing consumption behaviors. They needed to create engagement, interest, and learning with their customers. They knew that they needed to do this on the store floor, not with big image advertising campaigns. Coincidentally, they both use similar words and phrases about "purpose," "servant leadership," living wages, worker engagement, supplier loyalty, and consumer advocacy, education, and enrollment. Not every word is the same, but they share the same binding brand insights.

Whole Foods Market

As John Mackey tells his story, he was "just a kid who wanted to open one store and earn a living" when he created the grocery company that would morph into the still fast-growing Whole

Foods Market, the eighth-largest food retailer in the United States, with sales of $14.2 billion.[2] "We were not thinking grandiose," he told us. "We just wanted to survive."

When Mackey started his company in 1978—calling it SaferWay, a play on the name of the big California retailer Safeway—he wanted to help people buy organic and healthy foods. The company became successful beyond his imagination, but only after it abandoned the theory of "holy foods"—that is, of not permitting food that it deemed unhealthy inside its store. Mackey describes this as a compromise aimed at a bigger promise: nudging an informed population to buy better food over time.

"We didn't sell caffeine. We didn't sell meat. And we didn't do any business," he laments. In the end, he "figured out that the best way to go was to offer lots of choices for people and attempt to educate. We made the decision not to be 'Holy Foods Market.'" After this, the company found very engaged consumers and sufficient traffic to expand.

In 1980, Mackey did his first merger and opened a 10,000-square-foot Whole Foods Market.[3] Since then, the company has grown regionally through acquisitions. Its IPO took place in 1992. With shares as currency, Mackey was able to snap up regional healthy-grocery stores. The company bought Wellspring Grocery in North Carolina, Bread and Circus in Massachusetts, Mrs. Gooch's in California, Fresh Fields in Maryland, and Wild Oats Markets in Colorado. "We learn and grow from every acquisition. We've done 22 acquisitions, and 25 percent of our stores were acquired," he says. The secret has been to "inject [Whole Foods's] DNA into the values, mission, team structure, compensation, and empowerment. And . . . leave everything else on its own." The company's 12-region structure allows decentralized decisions on buying, stocking, merchandising, and promotions.

When the company went public in its fourteenth year of operations, when it had 12 stores, Mackey was asked how big he thought the market opportunity was. He guessed about 100 stores. Today, Whole Foods has around 400 stores, and there are more to come: it is starting to experiment with small-footprint stores with a limited assortment for lower-income consumers in urban markets. Mackey says the company is now thinking about 1,200 stores for the United States.

Mackey's success means that a great deal has been written about the company. In fact, like many entrepreneurs, he has written his own book, *Conscious Capitalism: Liberating the Heroic Spirit of Business*, a grand plan for business to do good—to help suppliers, workers, and customers. But the lessons from Whole Foods Market go beyond that theme. For us, the big one is the focus on consumers—and how to woo them.

"We are not oriented to achieving an arbitrary goal," Mackey explains to us. "We are not just trying to have a relationship with consumers. We are a purpose-driven company. We are trying to serve customers as best we can. We believe if we take care of our customer, the business will flourish."

Whole Foods Market is much more than just a grocer. It is a lifestyle provider. It tells its consumers, explicitly and implicitly, that you can learn by shopping.

Headline: Have a Set of Core Principles and Wear Your Values on Your Sleeve

A year after opening, Mackey says, a flood almost destroyed the company. But consumers, suppliers, and employees worked tirelessly to reopen the store. "The flood was a near-death experience. Stakeholders saved us," he says, still grateful for the help. "They pitched in. Team members worked for free. Banks loaned us more money."

Ever since, Mackey has promoted a stakeholder philosophy in which the company balances the needs of customers, team members, shareholders, suppliers, and communities. He can get a little heavy at times, especially when he's talking about balancing the "collective fate and soul of the company."

But, like many of the companies profiled in this book, Whole Foods Market has developed a defined list of core values:

We sell the *highest-quality natural and organic products* available.
We *satisfy, delight, and nourish our customers*.
We support Team Member happiness and excellence.
We create wealth through profits and growth.

We serve and support our local and global communities.

We practice and *advance environmental stewardship.*

We create ongoing win-win partnerships with our suppliers.

We promote the health of our stakeholders through *healthy eating education.*[4]

The values are an important part of the Whole Foods Market brand. Good food, healthy food, education, and the environment are easy messages to remember. When we interviewed staff members in the stores, they got these values—and they could restate them. They said that the company lives by them.

"Businesspeople are mistrusted as selfish and greedy," Mackey says. "Business needs to talk with a new language: create value for all stakeholders, not just investors. It is not a zero-sum game. In business, it is about making trade-offs that are mutually beneficial. Create value for customers, suppliers, communities, people—no one losing."

Headline: Go Beyond Profits, Align with Your Customers' Interests, Pick a Big-Picture Issue, Then Educate Them—For Whole Foods, It's the Health of the Nation

According to Mackey, 50 years ago, Americans spent 25 percent of their income on food and 4 percent on health care. Today, he says, they spend 8 percent on food and 20 percent on healthcare. And the result is that 69 percent of Americans are overweight. We later checked, and his numbers are approximately right—enough to make the point. He says that Americans are fat and sick.

To reverse the trend, the United States needs a different approach. "You need to know how to cook. Cook beans. Eat in bulk. Buy produce in season," he says. "I'm vegan. Spend nothing on health care. It's about consciousness."

Whole Foods Market doesn't follow the "holy foods" philosophy. As Mackey explained: "We need to tread carefully about imposing our own personal choices on our consumers." For instance, Whole Foods Market does stock meat. But it seeks to sell fresh, wholesome, and safe food. Its products are evaluated, and suppliers are told to provide products that are free of artificial preservatives, colors, flavors, and sweeteners and hydrogenated fats.

The company has developed a private-label brand called *365 Everyday Value*. Private labels can be very profitable, and Whole Foods Market has been able to invest in locally grown produce, sourcing from more than 2,000 local farms. It promotes animal welfare on farms and ranches and rates its suppliers of beef, pork, chicken, and turkey. It is perhaps not surprising that the big corporate food and beverage companies are largely absent from Whole Foods Market.

Also, Whole Foods Market is big on customer education. One of its healthy-eating education programs includes a focus on—no pun intended—whole foods: everything that is unprocessed and pure. It's about emphasizing plant-based nutrition for its phytonutrients and fiber; healthy fats from nuts, seeds, and avocados; and nutrient-rich foods, including beans and whole grains.

The program lines up ways in which consumers can "prep for success," such as cooking big batches, roasting vegetables, and preparing dishes like lentil chili. On its website, there are even menu ideas for every day of the week. Also, there are shopping lists for produce, grains, beans, and nuts aimed at making healthy choices fast and easy.

Historically, Mackey has not been a big believer in using conventional paid media to engage consumers. Marketing is 0.4 percent of sales. Whole Foods Market has focused primarily on earned media and community nonprofit partnerships. It publishes 1,000 messages per day, and it has 4 million Twitter followers; this makes Whole Foods Market the number one retail brand on Twitter.[5] Also, most stores have community meeting rooms and cooking schools for events. In these spaces, it stages brand development events to bring people to the store—but *not to shop.* The goal is to encourage consumers to become part of the Whole Foods Market family. As the company hit its thirty-fifth anniversary, it turned to advertising to complement its public and community relations tactics and to take control of its own message as it continues to grow.

Now Mackey is coauthoring a book on diet and nutrition along with a couple of medical doctors who are on the staff of Whole Foods Market. Mackey himself has adopted the so-called Engine 2 Diet philosophy. This is a diet devised by a former Texas firefighter who wanted to help those in his unit become fitter and stronger and avoid heart disease. It emphasizes fruits, vegetables, whole grains, beans, nuts, and seeds; plant protein; healthy fats; complex carbs; vitamins and minerals; and fiber. It calls for no animal protein, no extra oil, no added sugar, and low fat.

The new book will go beyond the elaborate website where you can download recipes, learn about the "dirty dozen" most important organic vegetables, and receive promotional offers. It is a how-to book on how to shop and eat in a healthy way. "We've cracked the code, and we'll wake people up," he says. His target is to lower the incidence of Type 2 diabetes and cardiovascular disease.

Headline: Make Your Stores Come Alive: Whole Foods Market Does This with Fresh, Prepared, on-the-Go Lifestyle Food

Before the glorious merchandising of Whole Foods Market, health food stores were often dull and dreary. Whole Foods Market changed this. If you shop its flagship store in Austin, Texas, you have a full 80,000 square feet to wander. Customers call it *Foodie Heaven* and the *Holy Mecca of Whole Foods*.

In the store, there is a wine cellar, a glass walk-in beer freezer, a sushi bar, a sit-down Italian trattoria that serves shrimp pasta, a BBQ stand, a 72-variety cookie bar, a sweets area serving gelato, a taco bar, a sandwich stand, an opulent selection of salads, a create-your-own bulk trail mix section, a chocolate fountain, and extensive indoor and outdoor seating. At lunchtime and most weeknights around dinnertime, the store is packed.

Mackey is very proud of the store design and the "beauty" of the latest-generation stores. "The cost of beauty is a little bit more expensive. We create beautiful and wonderful experiences for consumers. We need to nourish our bodies with healthy foods. We need to nourish with things that are beautiful. Plato had it perfect. We nurture our souls."

During a pre-Thanksgiving store visit, you could take free samples of food and wine, including pricey Veuve Clicquot champagne, shrimp, hot vegetarian entrees, cookies, cakes, and gelato. People were having a party in the store and using the sample day as a "free meal." But for Whole Foods Market, it probably was not just a free meal. Few people were just sampling. Most of them were using the "trial" product to test a menu for their actual Thanksgiving feast.

Some 66 percent of total sales are perishables. This is a substantially different mix from a normal grocery store's. In an expansion of its "fresh" strategy, Whole Foods Market recently began stocking "fresh" brewed beer. It is looking to take share from brewpubs, craft beers, and global brands such as Budweiser. It's a classic Whole Foods Market move: the niche attack. It takes the premium market in a category and delivers best-in-class product.

The economics of high service are greatly enhanced by high-volume sales. The Austin store, with more than $80 million in annual sales at a single site, is an economic miracle in grocery retailing: such big, beautiful, high-velocity stores are a brand trademark. In the Whole Foods Market world, consumers rate the company every day on its selection and the freshness of its avocados, apples, bananas, blueberries, blackberries, leeks, mushrooms, fish, meat, bread, and—most important—prepared food.

Headline: Get the Right People on Board, Hire Full-Timers, Promote from Within, Teach Collaboration and Cooperation, and Emphasize Engagement and Values

"This is a cool place to work," said one checkout person, a long-haired, slender young man in his early twenties with a ponytail and tattoos down his arm. "I make suggestions to people based on what they are buying. I hear what they need and want. Good people shop here. I feel like I am making a contribution to their lives."

This same checkout person suggested that our mix of prepared foods was "too green." Next time, he said, we should throw in a slightly different vegetable mix, including red, orange, and purple vegetables. "The more you mix it up," he encouraged, "the healthier you will be."

Having the right people in the store is critical to Whole Foods Market's success. How does it recruit?

Mackey says that his culture attracts its own kinds of people. "We are a meritocracy. We post all positions. We do group interviews. How do you get ahead at Whole Foods? You start off as a cashier, then you become an associate team leader, then you transfer to another team. If you are good, you become a team leader, then a store team leader. Next step up is a regional VP and then a regional president."

Mackey says that hiring is done by the team. "You can always fool one person. At the senior level, I am involved in promotions. We are looking for people who have a high degree of emotional intelligence. In our company, relationships really matter. We want people with empathy and self-awareness—servant leaders."

He continues: "If you answer the question, 'Why do you want this job?' by saying, 'It's the next place to go,' that's a bad answer. The right answer is about helping Whole Foods [and] servant leadership. The best leaders are not trying to line their pockets. Compensation should not be the primary driver. Top jobs pay better at Walmart."

The company says it has a salary cap that limits total cash compensation for any team member, including executives, to 19 times the average annual wage of all full-time employees. This translates into an effective cap of $750,000. That's a lot lower than the ratio at any peer Fortune 250 company, where the ratio can be as high as 400 or more to 1. Mackey himself takes a $1 annual salary and no cash bonuses or stock option awards. Nevertheless, he still holds 800,000 shares worth around $40 million after substantially reducing his total holdings over the years.

But if Walmart offers higher wages for the upper-level jobs, Whole Foods Market does pay above market to get better people, retain them, and prevent unionization. Mackey is a big believer in taking care of employees. He commits to full-time work hours: more than 70 percent of the company's staff members are on the full-time payroll. Also, there are good benefits: health care is free for 10-year veterans and $10 per paycheck for employees after a half year of full-time employment. Employees who opt in to testing low for cholesterol and blood pressure and using no nicotine receive higher store discounts on purchases through the company's "Healthy Discount Incentive Program."

Whole Foods Market's recruiting materials underscore Mackey's messages: "Whole Foods Market attracts people who are passionate—about great food, about the communities they live in, about how we treat our planet and our fellow humans—and who want to bring their passion into the workplace and make a difference. Our Team Members make us who we are by being who they are. Not only are our Team Members the secret to our continued success, they have also made us one of *Fortune*'s '100 Best Companies to Work For' every year since the list's inception. As the saying goes around here, without our Team Members, 'We're just four walls and food.'"[6]

Headline: Get It Right and Your Apostles Will Articulate the Concept and Spread the Word

We asked one particular consumer who participated in our omnibus survey to describe Whole Foods Market and healthy food in a staccato riff—with a ring of discipleship and a tone of confidence. Without batting an eyelash, Andy, a sophisticated fiftysomething single New Yorker, fired off the following:

> Healthy food delivers all your needed calories, balanced protein, carbohydrates, and fats. I had a midlife health crisis and Whole Foods helped me come back. They taught me that healthy food is nutritious and appetizing. It is composed largely of fresh foods, not processed, without added sugar and salt. It delivers the right combinations of antioxidants to prevent disease. It is composed of fats that are not saturated and not high in cholesterol. It gives you a sense of fullness and leaves you light and active. Virtually anything I buy at the prepared foods bar at Whole Foods qualifies. I eat it at the store in the upstairs café. Healthy food leaves you

slim, happy, and feeling good about yourself. A healthy food is natural, has no additives, and is free of pesticides. Examples of healthy foods include all fruits, vegetables, lean meats, beans, whole-grain wheat, and exotic unprocessed carbohydrates like quinoa and whole-grain pasta.

This consumer credits Whole Foods Market with helping him make a lifestyle shift.

"All my adult life, I worked hard," Andy says. "I traveled a lot. I ate what was available. Whole Foods opened my eyes to better nutrition. Now when I travel, with their network of stores, I can get good food fast. I can choose what looks good to me. And I can do it for well under $25. Cheaper than any restaurant with a wait staff. And if I buy it and eat it at Whole Foods, there are no dishes and there is no one waiting for a tip."

Other consumers in our survey offered similar praise:[7]

- ► "I enjoy the organic and non-GMO brands they have stocked. I love that they have a juice bar and healthy ready-to-eat meals."
- ► "Whole Foods does not allow [just] any type of product to hit the shelf. They actually consider what is in the product."
- ► "I like the variety of environmentally sound, gluten-free products."
- ► "There's a lot less junk food [than at other grocery stores]."
- ► "There's an integrity and honesty about its offerings."

In our survey, Whole Foods Market was rated as providing "high-quality produce and prepared foods." Its other top attributes are "trust," "clean stores," and "a knowledgeable and friendly staff." Also, consumers eagerly acknowledge the company's social responsibility. Whole Foods Market is lauded for making consumers feel healthy, helping them do something good for themselves, and making them feel smart for making good decisions.[8]

These words are important. This is because the apostle connection is almost always spread by word of mouth.

And they are evidence that Whole Foods Market has effectively wooed its customers.

Headline: It Doesn't Matter Whether Someone Is Rich or Poor—Every Consumer Has the Potential to Be an Apostle

Most Whole Foods Market consumers are not poor. They are, overwhelmingly, female and top-tier in income. Also, because many Whole Foods Market stores were built near college campuses, many consumers are 18 to 25 years old. The typical apostle customer spends a whopping $3,643 per year—and converts an average of six consumers who spend about two-thirds of this amount.[9]

But Mackey does not want his company to be nicknamed "Whole Paycheck." He maintains that all kinds of people can do all their grocery shopping at Whole Foods Market. He says that the healthiest diet in the world is not very expensive— "$3 to $4 a day."

For this reason, Mackey and co-CEO Walter Robb are on a quest for better value, more accessibility, and price competitiveness. The company is also on a quest for new consumers: single households with boomers, single millennials, and young families on the go.

Whole Foods Market has pioneered a new urban-market format with lower prices on high-visibility goods. It has taken this proposition to markets such as Detroit and Broad Street in New Orleans, and will soon take it to the south side of Chicago in Engelwood. In these inner cities, Whole Foods Market has value-engineered its stores, investing less capital, scheduling less labor, and seeding cooperation with the local community while maintaining the same strict quality standards.

The idea, which Robb has championed, is to bring high-quality, healthy, affordable food to lower-income communities with limited access to fresh food, to offer educational resources on diet and nutrition, and to put a new platform for growth in place. There are no $400 bottles of wine in these stores.

If they are successful, these stores could provide another few hundred locations for Whole Foods Market and really increase its chances of achieving broad-based nutritional improvements. If they can do it without margin degradation, then they would substantially increase the company's share value.

It won't be an easy challenge. As part of our research, we talked to inner-city Whole Foods Market consumers. They understand the concept—but they still think the lower-priced product mix is pricier than that of traditional grocery companies. "I get that it's more expensive to have natural chicken and organic products," said Stacey, a 32-year-old African American woman. "But it hurts my pocketbook. I have to make trade-offs. There are no bargains here. But it is fresh and we know they care about us."

Headline: The Lessons of Whole Foods Market

As with all successful companies, competitors have put Whole Foods Market in their firing sights. Most of the top 10 grocers in the United States have increased their organic, natural, and "healthy" eating selections. They have amped up prepared foods. They have pointed to lower prices on popular baskets of goods. They have increased communication budgets and efforts at "emotional" connection.

But none of them has been able to duplicate the brand aura of Whole Foods Market. They have been unwilling to reject suppliers for bad natural practices. They have been unwilling to impose salary caps and force "egalitarianism" as a company philosophy. Their efforts at food health education and breadth of assortment have largely fallen short. Whole Foods Market's stores have advantages in several areas:

- ► Frequency of shopping by core consumers
- ► Velocity of goods in its prepared foods sections
- ► One-stop shopping for healthy products
- ► Advocacy by core consumers
- ► Seeding of behaviors from the college population when people graduate and move on to become "young family/heavy grocery" consumers

Expect to see continued innovation at Whole Foods Market, including advanced home delivery options, a loyalty program, and emphasis on mobile apps with shopping lists, recipes, meal plans, and electronic coupons. If Mackey is right and lower, more competitive prices lead to volume growth, expect to see more direct competition with traditional grocers.

Whole Foods Market delivers high profit and high cash flow as a result of its price premiums. It has a superior mix of prepared foods sold at a higher-than-average grocery margin. This formula is driven by the strength of its brand. Consumers trust Whole Foods Market, and they swear by the various private-label products, especially 365.

There are three types of consumers at a Whole Foods Market. The most valuable is the full-service shopper, who buys 90 percent of her groceries and prepared foods at Whole Foods Market and spends a lot—$250 a week or more. The second most valuable is the single "no cook" consumer, who uses Whole Foods Market as a caterer, shopping for dinner and other food items several times a week. This consumer spends $100 a week or so. The last segment is the occasional user, who might prefer the company's quality and reputation, but is unwilling to pay the price premium to get Whole Foods Market's products on a regular basis.

Whole Foods Market has enjoyed steady same-store sales growth of 6 to 15 percent for every year in the last decade except the Great Recession years of 2008 and 2009, when even affluent consumers suffered a substantial decline in wealth.

Operating margin is now close to 7 percent—four times the amount of other grocers'. Sales per square foot are close to $1,000 per year—more than twice as high.[10] These economics allow Whole Foods Market to pay more, dress up its stores, sample new high-margin goods, invest in new recipes and demonstrations, and carefully expand the range of goods it carries.

Growth of the Whole Foods Market brand is dependent on increasing consumers' food IQ—and encouraging consumers to spend 20 percent of their income on healthy, longevity-inducing fresher foods. If the food IQ revolution continues to catch fire, Whole Foods Market has a long runway for growth.

The Container Store

The Container Store is the place where you can get your life under control—organize your clothing, your kitchen, your paperwork, and your children's toys; find wrapping paper for your gifts; learn to save time; and know where everything is. When launched in 1978, it was a category killer against a class of trade where competitors had small sections. CEO Kip Tindell's first store was 1,600 square feet, with stacks and stacks of products to help people organize their closets, kitchens, baths, offices, garages, and laundry.

"We were scared," Tindell tells us. "We were wondering what would happen if we opened and nobody came. People were very skeptical before we opened. They asked, 'Who would come to a store to buy empty boxes?'" The company was a bit of a family affair. Sharon Tindell, the chief merchant, is Kip's wife. His former boss at a paint store, Garrett Boone, was cofounder. Friends and family members invested around $35,000. Nobody believed he was making an investment in a business that would deliver close to $1 billion in sales. Most of those who invested did so grudgingly. They did not believe that a store that sold "empty boxes" would really be successful. But Tindell's contagious enthusiasm and relentless asking convinced them to say yes to his request for funding.

Tindell focused his marketing on the top-tier social elite in Dallas. It was an unexpected success. First-day sales were $550, according to Tindell, although one-third of the takings came from Boone's sister.

Early on, growth was hard and the rollout was slow. The young entrepreneur had limited capital, and expansion was largely self-financed. Hundreds of competitors sold storage products, including Sears, Macy's, and the local hardware store. But The Container Store flourished. The market "got" it.

Over time, by word of mouth, wealthy suburban and urban women told their friends, "Get your life in order at The Container Store; let them help you get organized." And a brand built on a modern need was created.

Tindell's plunge opening was in New York City, where success proved the applicability of the concept in tight urban markets as well as in spacious suburban America. Today, he believes that the brand value proposition is even more valuable when space is expensive and time is constrained. Consumers have more goods to store, and when they get good organization, they can squeeze in even more.

In this way, Tindell has wooed his customers. They now go to The Container Store en masse to organize their lives.

Headline: Build a Culture Your Customers and Employees Can Identify With, and Write Down and Memorialize a Set of Foundation Principles

Tindell says that The Container Store's goal is to become the best retail store in America. That's audacious.

At the start, he decided that the brand would stand for dramatically better service, one-stop shopping for storage and organization solutions, and a sales force that would be able to understand customer needs and translate them into relationships built on value. He was intent on generating a virtuous circle in which consumers got pleasure and time, he delivered high velocity per square foot, and the product had enough uniqueness to be a draw.

But Tindell, like many other founders in this book, attributes The Container Store's success to the "culture" of the company. About 10 years after he launched the company, Tindell found himself in a position where he could no longer personally drive decisions at every store. He needed to provide his new organization with a framework on which people could base their decisions and that would facilitate bringing new associates on board. The company had grown so large that he no longer knew everyone personally. He decided that he needed to write down and memorialize the principles for which he wanted the company to be known. One night, he called all the employees of his new Houston store to the manager's house for a brainstorming session. The output of that session later became the feedstock for the company's Seven Foundation Principles.[11] These principles are intended to guide employee behavior. They substitute for the thick books of regulations that look like telephone directories that some retailers use to regulate employee behavior.

Here, we provide these principles and annotate them with our interpretation:

1. **One great person equals three good people.** If you find a
    single great employee and can train her, her productivity and

performance can equal the power of three other good employees. You can pay this employee twice as much as someone else and still have lower labor costs. If she knows she is making top dollar and having fun while working in an environment that respects and cares for her, you will enjoy turnover as low as 10 percent per year. (That's a tenth of the turnover that many retailers experience in floor-level sales positions.)

Tindell says, "Talent is the whole ball game." How do you get employees to engage? He says it comes from hiring, training, and incentives. The Container Store looks for people who can sell a solution—and that requires listening skills, creativity, imagination, and resources. Only 3 percent of applicants are hired. Then, each new employee is given 80 hours of training before being allowed to sell anything. In their first year, full-time associates receive a total of 263 hours of training.[12] There is a full development program—skills assessments, performance reviews, training videos, and coaching. Finally, associates make twice as much money as salespeople working elsewhere.

2. **Communication is leadership.** Leaders lead by talking and engaging. They are visible and present. They share facts and engage employees in challenges. Tindell says that you need to empower people, give them tools, ignite their talent, and explain goals.

3. **Fill the other guy's basket to the brim—making money then becomes an easy proposition.** This one says: "Don't try to take the last dime from your suppliers. Get them on your side. See how to create win-wins." More than half of the goods sold by The Container Store are exclusive merchandise. That is the result of custom manufacturing—which comes from positive interactions with suppliers. Tindell talks about trying to enrich everyone in the entire supply chain rather than squeezing vendors dry. He calls this "creatively crafting" a mutually beneficial relationship.

4. **The best selection, service, and price.** The Container Store has pursued this principle by offering 10,000 products, the best sales advice on the floor, and "better, best, exceptional" pricing (as opposed to the retail industry standard of "good, better, best"). Tindell likes to say, "We sell the hard stuff," meaning that most of the goods sold at The Container Store require explanation, customer engagement, and encouragement. He has an uncanny

way of avoiding direct competition. "You can't showroom solutions and proprietary products [when consumers price them on the Internet]," he says.

5. **Intuition does not come to an unprepared mind—you need to train before it happens.** As already noted, The Container Store provides first-year sales employees with almost 300 hours of formal on-the-job training. Most retailers provide less than one day, and most of that is simply the mechanics of checkout. This company has a huge investment in associates' learning from day one.

6. **Man in the desert selling.** Tindell says that employees are there to discover the customer's problems. As a result, they are expected to go way beyond providing a glass of water to someone who just came in from the desert. He likes to illustrate this by saying: "They need a hat, an umbrella, some lotion, some slippers, a chair, an ice machine—and maybe even a margarita!"

   Tindell calls this a "solution-based," not "items-based," form of retail. It's aimed at solving the entire problem and thinking beyond the immediate need. It demands a different kind of salesperson—and this sets The Container Store apart from its rivals. Tindell says that no competitors want to engage in this personnel-intensive form of retail.

7. **Generate an air of excitement.** Tindell says that the goal is to entertain and engage customers and create memorable shopping experiences. "We make shopping fun—like going to Disney World, the time of their life." He says he knows customers who are "dancing in their closets [because] they are so happy with their products."

Headline: Create a Sense of Theater, Make Your Concept Visible for All to See, and Provide Your Customers with an Oasis

If you go into The Container Store, you will immediately understand how the concept has developed over 30 years. Just before Christmas, we visited a flagship store in Manhattan immediately south of Bloomingdales. On a cold midweek December morning, the store was packed. Brightly colored gift wrap and packing materials dominated half of the first floor. The rest of the floor was dedicated to Elfa closet designs, to which consumers could just say, "I'll take it."

Closet price points varied from under $1,000 to $4,000. Each model closet was fully furnished with neat clothing, socks, and shoes and used The Container Store's value-add storage accessories—racks, shelves, doors, hooks, and sliders. It was obvious that you could buy pieces or mix and match, but the brand was presented as a visual takeaway. In a single second, busy New Yorkers could imagine their own closets before and after The Container Store treatment. The staff members on the floor are happy to come to your home to take exact measurements and design your closets or storage areas for any need. The Container Store gladly provides turnkey solutions.

One consumer who was shopping the gift wrap section could not keep herself from smiling ear to ear. "This is the best selection of wrapping paper I have ever seen," she told us. "All my gifts will be beautiful and perfect. I came in to browse kitchen gadgets and storage, and I'm walking out with 10 rolls of gift wrap, ribbons, and bows. I'll come back and maybe buy that dream $3,000 closet. That's what *I* need for Christmas."

According to Tindell, his customer is busy and educated. She has a household income of roughly $130,000. He says that 30 percent of customers deliver a full 83 percent of sales. Also, she spends much more when she shops without her husband or partner. "Husbands are bad for The Container Store," he says with a grin. "When they are present, 'dwell time' is lower." He claims that husbands make it a directed shop, and after the immediate need is satisfied, the couple is walking out of the store.

The Container Store tells customers that they deserve an organized oasis that is easy to maintain—"a solution that is beautiful and functional." For $75, you can get a "Contained Home" consultation directly in your home.[13] Staff members provide a personalized organization plan. They will sort, stage, and organize space for $75 per hour. If you spend $500, you get a $75 credit. The Container Store is happy to provide an installer, who will also paint. It's a big and appealing promise for people on the go: "Organize, transition space, downsize, unpack."

Headline: The Lessons from The Container Store

Invent in a category where you are passionate. Become the category expert. Continuously build out your offering. Deliver at multiple price points. Improve your initial offering: "value engineer" and deliver premium product. Weed out everything that's not moving—or improve it. Engage suppliers in your success and show them that an alignment with you delivers growth beyond anything they can get with all their other partners.

The Container Store's value proposition is simple: under one roof, you can buy everything you need to get organized at home. You can get advice from highly trained and motivated salespeople. They will take you from chaos to organization with the click of an order book.

The company focuses on affluent, busy, space-constrained adults. The target customer is 30-plus, with money to spend on saving time. Closets, kitchens, and garages—these are the starting spaces. But everything in the home is a potential target for The Container Store.

Typically, customers spend a lot of money when they first seek The Container Store's help. After that, they visit periodically to get updates and improvements. A great customer will spend upwards of $2,000 on that first big step. If they are satisfied, customers become fanatical fans—apostles—and then systematically work through the rest of their home. They rely on The Container Store for other services as well, including seasonal and personal gifts.

Tindell says that you need to give customers a reason to come to a brick-and-mortar store, especially in this digital age. If you don't, they will rely on online purchasing. "That's the best protection against large online merchants. It's hard to sell solutions over the Internet. It's easier to design a closet in a store. Most people don't want to create a solution online."

The Container Store landed on a concept that has a big-ticket initial sale followed by a stream of ancillary purchases. The "organization addicts" concept can be duplicated in other businesses. Look for a way to lock in a broader category definition of what you do. Understand the challenges your consumers are facing in a more holistic way. Solve the underlying problem, not the symptom of the day. Build a service function that continuously provides input into unrealized new product opportunities.

Great brands like The Container Store and Whole Foods Market are founded on the following:

- ▶ A unique value proposition.
- ▶ The needs of a tightly defined target consumer.
- ▶ The apostle model, in which success with a few consumers drives the base load volume: the net present value of the purchases of apostle consumers is very high, in excess of $10,000, and they are likely to influence others.

Your biggest fans can become your greatest source of value. Identify them. Serve them. Ask deeply and with meaning, "How are we doing?" Do it every day. And do it quantitatively. Talk to your critics and work like mad to woo them back. Every complaint is a gift—but only if you respond to it. Every compliment is a chance to drive a referral and an endorsement. Every employee should be encouraged to close out his shift with answers to a simple question: "What was the most memorable suggestion, complaint, or point of praise from customers today?"

*****

One Conclusion

Innovate, don't follow. Create the enterprise with the tremendous engagement of your consumers and your store team from day one. Build loyalty through a magnetic supply chain in which all links are aligned—suppliers, employees, and consumers. Build the brand value proposition on the basis of offering unique value and exclusive goods, saving consumers time, and providing them with emotional benefits. Fearlessly compete against bigger, incumbent companies, because the chances are that initially they will *not* see you. Never rest on your laurels. Eventually other companies will see your success and try to imitate a few elements of your innovation. But if you are ahead, you have time and can create layers of advantage. Stay true to your heart: compromises are brand dilutive. Create beautiful stores and products that capture your consumers' imagination and surprise them. Aim for complete consumer delight.

Three Takeaways

1. **Your core consumer is crucial.** At the root of every successful brand is a core consumer who really "gets" it. These consumers are willing to live and die by what you produce. They are willing to tell their friends about you—and they do this in their own words. Assuming that they are a substantial population, they will be at the heart of your future as a retail empire. You must cater to their needs and understand their new requirements.

2. **Set the price to earn a decent return.** When you create—or re-create—a category, the pricing rules are open. You can set them. You need to establish a target total velocity of sales per store and revenues per square foot. Your average margin has to deliver economic success. Don't look at wannabe brands that sit in your space for pricing guidelines. Be ruthless in getting pricing premiums for superior products. Be careful to articulate the value you add and the differences you offer, in terms of emotional and technical features. Consumers will pay for technical, functional, and emotional benefits. Give them hooks and explanations, and they will repeat your messages.

3. **Expand relentlessly.** Once you have a successful business model, your job is to fill the space quickly and expand geographically—into every possible market, with every possible consumer. Whole Foods Market and The Container Store demonstrate that your physical presence can create market expansion opportunities. Stores in overlapping geographies actually build the brand. Store density establishes you as a player. You can have years of runway ahead of you. Think expansion, not cannibalism.

SOME KEY ACTION POINTS

1. Work the first store to produce a replicable model.
2. Go beyond an initial set of product ideas to a more expansive market.
3. Hire the best workers you can. Train them relentlessly and cheerfully, and pay them more than the competition.
4. Share the wealth with workers and provide benefits to core consumers.

5. Regionalize and adapt locally for taste, function, and need. Don't force national stocking policies.
6. Don't be shy about pricing to achieve profitability. You will sustain higher prices if you offer better products.
7. Don't fear competitors; beat them with your depth and your in-store knowledge.
8. Create an innovation cycle that drives trial visitation. Aim for major news every quarter.
9. Never feel as if you have overcommunicated your mission, vision, and social objectives. Tell your employees again and again; have them replay your words in their own way.
10. Push share ownership as deeply and widely as possible. "Think like an owner" generates incredible energy and oomph.

Explore uncharted territory. Catch a trend early. Let it be something where you are a passionate consumer. Don't worry about a few little competitors. Learn from them, imitate what is worth copying, and go beyond where they are. Hold on to specialty knowledge. Use design to deliver merchandising.

Don't wait for the right moment. Today can be your new beginning. Sketch your prototype, raise money for your first build-out, and recruit a diverse and passionate team. Small is beautiful. It gives you speed and adaptability. If you are embedded in a big company, stretch the rules, feed your instincts, beg for resources, and make promises on the basis of early research. Dream big.

CHAPTER THREE

Always Welcome Your Customers' Scorn (Because You'll Come Back Stronger)

THE CHAPTER IN A BOX

The Main Point

Brands and companies go through life cycles. The initial years are the most exciting. There is a huge fear of failure among the founders. But after that, the second generation of employees frequently has not heard the stories of the company's creation. By the third generation, management often relies on old frameworks for success. Barnacles attach themselves to the infrastructure. Deep down in the organization, those on the front line see, know, and can recite the company's failings, but no one is listening. They can tell you about misguided value-engineering efforts. They can tell you about product failures. If you reach the consumer, you will learn every detail of the company's failings. If you listen very carefully and really respond, you can drive a third-generation renaissance. Meeting scorn and dismissal with a comprehensive and deliberate response is the key to revitalization.

Why These Stories for This Chapter

Frito-Lay was the dearest business inside PepsiCo's portfolio. It had been a 40-year wunderkind. Its growth had been legendary, and it had demonstrated proof of scale, an advantageous route network, and breadth of distribution. But by the early part of this decade, its growth had slowed considerably. The snack category was still growing because of both demographic factors and time pressures on consumers. Yet the majority of this growth was going to small start-up companies. These companies were pursuing the kinds of strategies we have highlighted in this book. They had resolved to change the world, to provide better options, to capture new consumers. Frito-Lay had a framework for new products based on current product profitability. If you are used to producing gold, it is hard to get excited about tin. But then it discovered a new tool called demand spaces. As Indra Nooyi, PepsiCo's CEO, says: "Demand spaces opened our eyes. It gave us a lens for growth. It gave us a way to spread our brands, to target new users."

Hilton has a story similar to Frito-Lay's. It had pioneered premium hotels and had the lure of history. But its product required constant refreshing. It required a level of reinvestment in physical assets that the company was willing to defer. In many markets, the properties within its portfolio—ranging from Hilton to Hilton Garden Inn to DoubleTree—overlapped one another. The demand-space approach permitted modernization, the identification of a set of table-stakes requirements, and a set of differentiators that would change the game.

Chapter Overview

Every company goes through transitions. In the early years, the company's concept is obvious to everyone. The point of differentiation is glaring. At every level, you can ask, "What do we do best?" and get an unambiguous answer.

But over time, almost every company experiences staleness and sometimes a loss of momentum. The original proposition is imitated. The blinding differences between the company and its rivals become subtle. High profits get competed away. Executives respond to Wall Street pressures for an investor thesis by creating business-speak—lots of words and many graphics, but little clarity about priorities, return on investment, growth commitments, and how current efforts will generate new value. The founders and their history become a corrupted myth or totally misunderstood.

The rise of the activist investor has made things much worse. Companies do not have the leisure to "bake" a new strategic initiative. As a result, untested and hypothetical ideas are often wheeled out as the next golden goose. Within months, the analysts are questioning and negating.

If you find yourself in this situation, what do you need to do?

Headline: Search for What Really Drives Consumer Choice

You need to find out not only *what* your customers really, really want, but also *when* and *why* they really want it. Conventional market definitions often put blinders on your company and you. As we noted in the Introduction, the demand-space approach opens your eyes and your imagination, expanding your definition of the market in which you compete. You can earn your growth by serving each demand space with power, precision, and direct response; establishing a two-way dialogue; and thus bringing new excitement to the category.

In this chapter, we profile two companies that have come to understand consumer needs in a powerful new way. One is Frito-Lay, the salty snack business owned by PepsiCo. The other is Hilton Worldwide, one of the world's most iconic hotel brands. From their experience, you will learn how to think about consumers in terms of need and occasion. You will learn how they overturned decades of history, erasing their marketing rules of thumb and reinventing themselves.

Frito-Lay

What do you do when you become the division CEO of a business that used to be the jewel of the parent company but has not grown volume in three years? How do you energize an organization that has $14 billion in revenues and is making the highest profit of virtually any major food and snack company in the world? How do you take a market share of more than 60 percent and try to squeeze it higher?

That was exactly the dilemma facing Tom Greco when he was made head of Frito-Lay, the salty snacks business owned by PepsiCo, in 2011. Greco is an outgoing, gregarious Canadian. He gained valuable experience at P&G and built a blue-chip résumé at PepsiCo.

Frito-Lay's North American business is one of the treasures in PepsiCo's portfolio of businesses. Its iconic brands include Lay's, Doritos, and Tostitos. Most children in America grew up on Frito-Lay's Cheetos brand. Most of us can almost taste the cheesy orange flavor on our fingers when we say *Cheetos*. When PepsiCo first bought Herman Lay's snack company in 1965, it was just a regional potato chip player competing with scores of other companies.

This is widely considered to have been one of the best food acquisitions of all time, masterminded by Don Kendall and Herman Lay in 1965. In the early 1990s, PepsiCo legend Roger Enrico took over. He invented the Pepsi Challenge, a highly advertised taste test that brought Pepsi Cola, the company's flagship branded drink, to within a hair of Coca-Cola's market share in the United States. Enrico was the marketing whiz kid who realized that a sweeter flavor would win the vast majority of the time in a single taste test. Under his leadership, Frito-Lay broadened distribution, built dozens of regional manufacturing centers, added thousands of route drivers, and heavily branded Lay's, Tostitos, and Doritos. As a result, the company had a manufacturing cost advantage, brand price premiums, and a virtual hold on the most valuable retail real estate in stores. It made a fortune selling single-serving snacks in convenience stores.

The company's store-distribution system remains a formidable competitive advantage. It has the world's largest fleet of trucks, with 18,000 route drivers[1] who make up the most aggressively managed driver army in the world. Every day at 3 a.m., they go to hundreds of Frito-Lay depots and begin their routes. They follow a well-engineered route map, dropping off cases of snacks at thousands of outlets. This army promotes Frito-Lay's face to consumers. It puts products within arm's reach of anyone who wants a snack. It gives Frito-Lay a freshness advantage over competitors. And because of its scale, it delivers this benefit at a lower cost than other salty snack companies.

Headline: Create a Highly Advantaged Business by Focusing on Cost, Visibility, and Scale

With its size, brand power, and cost advantage, Frito-Lay earns more space on retailers' shelves and concentrates its efforts on growing the highly profitable single-serving snack products. In stores, Frito-Lay's reps give the bags an identity. If you walk into a 7-Eleven, the Frito-Lay rep has probably just been in the store. Bags of the salty snacks are neatly lined up—"snapped, popped, and laced," as they say. Throughout grocery stores, a great Frito-Lay rep will introduce as many as 20 points of interruption—displays that consumers and their children can't miss as they do their shopping. The chances are that if you don't buy a Frito-Lay product on a shopping trip, it is because you are determined to avoid temptation.

As Frito-Lay discovered, good things can run out of steam. It needed to find an encore. The company had consistently driven growth in pounds per capita. At some point, however, incremental pounds get to be impossible. There are only so many salty snacks that one person can consume.

Also, Frito-Lay was facing a new competitive environment. In the past five years, consumers have increasingly been looking for a wider variety of snacks. This is what industry specialists call the *fragmentation of taste*. Many big food companies have been shanghaied by this trend. Many new companies have been launching "better for you," "all natural," and specialty snacks. That clawing sound in the market is entrepreneurs targeting Frito-Lay's volume.

Companies such as Chobani, Monster, Wonderful, KIND, and Amy's Kitchen have launched innovative "new to the world" snacks and beverages. They have avoided traditional scale disadvantages by using food brokers, contract manufacturers, rental merchandising forces, and agency brand intelligence. They have been successful thanks to their zeal, focus, unambiguous positioning, and relentless drive for growth.

Most often, the founder is on site and holding up the new company's truth for all employees. He has the belief set of a zealot and is personally involved in every decision. For instance, during the early years, Hamdi Ulukaya, the Turkish American founder of Chobani, the top-selling Greek yogurt brand in the United States, slept in his beloved factory. He was obsessive about teaching Americans about the benefits of Greek yogurt—high protein, better for you. Ulukaya and others in this new breed of founder-entrepreneurs have a visceral sense of their markets. Their backs are figuratively to the wall; they have their life investment on the line and no sources of cash for subsidies. There is no rich parent company that can bail them out if they don't make their weekly sales targets.

In the face of such competition, almost all the major food and beverage companies have experienced share loss and loss of momentum in the past half decade. This is because they have lost three things: their position in the minds of consumers, their share of eating occasions, and consumer preference. According to BCG analysis, the small-company universe (under $500 million in sales) is growing four times as fast as the large-company universe ($5 billion or more).[2] Part of the loss comes from the tendency of big companies to be internally focused, do poor market research, and rely on traditional television media for vibrancy. Too often, in these big companies, PowerPoint presentations rule. The CEO sits at the back of the room, listens to one anxious brand manager after another, and asks questions. Only rarely are fresh perspectives—"new truth"—brought to the table.

Also, the hurdles for innovators in larger companies are much higher than for those in smaller companies. In effect, the big companies become victims of their own success. They use profit margins on historically created businesses to judge start-up businesses. They have narrow windows for measuring launch success. And the "owner" of an idea may stay in her job for only 18 months—an inadequate amount of time to achieve enduring success. If they stayed any longer, they would no longer be on the company fast track. So, since everyone is always trying to impress others in the shortest possible time, there is little continuity.

In such a corporate environment, long-term business building is a back-burner activity. The winners are those who do promotions. They introduce value packs in order to increase volume, even if this reduces price realization. They drop coupons even though redemption rates are low. They add a new flavor, even if this cannibalizes 90 percent of current volume.

Headline: Want to Know How to Respond to Your Consumers' Scorn? Look at Their Demands, Not Just Their Age or Sex

Frito-Lay was suffering from this same malaise when Tom Greco stepped up to the challenge of recapturing the glory days of Roger Enrico. "Our job was to help find new pockets of growth," Greco tells us. "They are not staring you in the face." In mature markets like the United States, if one food company is to win, another company has to lose. So food companies have to battle to take a bigger share of that calorie intake. As Greco explains: "Food is a zero-sum game. Calories are flat. In order for someone to eat more of what we make, we need them to eat less of what someone else makes."

To discover growth, Frito-Lay took a very different path from the one taken by other packaged-food companies. Al Carey, Greco's predecessor, had already turned to sophisticated new market research to redefine the boundaries of Frito-Lay's business and brands. He used BCG's pioneering approach, which we call *demand-centric growth transformation,* to understand what really, really drives consumer choice. Upon taking over from Carey, Greco endorsed the power of this approach to unlock growth, and so did his full leadership team.

Everyone knows that consumers use products in different ways, depending on when they consume them and whether they are by themselves, with their friends, or with their family. Depending on whom they're with and what they're doing—and what time of day it is—they give priority to different products with different features.

The conventional view is that consumers are fickle and inconsistent, hard to understand and predict, and therefore unmanageable.

We disagree. We think they are perfectly consistent, perfectly understandable, and quite predictable.

The secret is to do the right kind of research. The secret is to ask the right kinds of questions: Whom were they with when they last used the product? What was the occasion? What were the benefits they sought? What were the trade-offs they made? Did the product make them feel satisfied or good about themselves? Or did it make them feel upset, guilty, or angry?

Ask these questions, and you will start to understand what really drives consumer choice. You will be like Zeus on the top of the mountain, with a lightning bolt in your hand, able to aim your products at consumers like these:

▶ Mary, the 18-year-old schoolgirl who comes home at 3 p.m. and wants something to eat

▶ Joe, the 45-year-old office worker who looks at the clock as it strikes 3 p.m. and reaches into his desk drawer for something to mindlessly chew

▶ Eleanor, the stressed mother of two whose kids have just walked through the door and who wants a snack for the babysitter to give them

Across the country, 3 p.m. is the witching hour. Viewed properly, it is made up of many different eating occasions. If you understand this, you can begin to understand what really drives consumer choice. You can start to fashion products and services that satisfy consumers' hopes and dreams. You can deliver what's really on their wish list.

Too often, companies do not understand this. They commission the wrong kind of research. They ask the wrong questions. They base their conclusions on syndicated data—the historical purchases by category reported by Nielsen and IRI.

Our approach focuses on consumer needs and wants and what we call *demand spaces*. If you ask the right questions, you can create a map of different kinds of demands, or different demand spaces. A "space" is an occasion or an emotional moment, and each unique space has a unique demand.

Greco used this approach because he wished to establish not only *what* customers really want, but also *when* and *why* they really, really want it. He wanted to understand snack "occasions": how different customers consume snacks in various situations—alone, with friends, on the go, in the morning, at lunch, in the afternoon, or after dinner.

With the demand-centric approach, Frito-Lay could do three things. First, it could get a clear view of the various demand spaces in the snacking market. The tool enabled the company to do the following:

▶ Look at the customer's last consumption choice in the defined category and compare it with the choices of thousands of respondents to provide statistical accuracy and forecasting ability.

▶ Establish the emotional and functional drivers of choice. (Most research today focuses on functional drivers—the engineering attributes of products—and assumes that customers do not make an emotional choice.)

▶ Cluster similar responses to find common need bundles—a demand space.

▶ Compile a set of distinct spaces, each defined by a clear-cut (emotional and functional) need bundle. Spaces should not overlap.

▶ Identify the reason for the choice. For instance, is it primarily because the customer is a thirtysomething woman or a first-generation Hispanic, or is it because it's morning?

Second, Greco and his team could discover which of the Frito-Lay brands had a "right to win" in each of the different spaces. Each space has a unique set of demands. These can be described prescriptively. He found out where his competitors were strong and where they were weak.

Third, they could establish the commercial opportunity for each demand space. They could know the size of the prize.

When put together, these three elements constitute a killer application. The demand-centric approach "closes the loop" by demonstrating that the brands that own the relevant emotional attributes (element two) of a demand space (element one) can win a differential share of a properly sized market (element three). In other words, this is a consumer-grounded model that can predict share and growth in the category. You can create a bull's-eye product to match exact needs in the space and predict—if you make the product available and consumers aware of it—how much you will grow the business.

That is the "wow" of demand spaces.

Headline: Frito-Lay's Search for Demand Spaces

A company with a clear map of demand can expect to be able to clean up. But, as we've seen, success requires the right research. As Greco says: "Analytics are where you can find growth. Most consumer products companies are superficial about their research and their understanding of their markets. We have gone through an absolute dentist drill to understand the drivers of demand at a deep and profound level."

Demand-centric research puts into management's hands the answers to five key questions:

1. What fundamentally drives choice in different consumer categories? And, more important, what does not?
2. What are the consumer needs that are shaping market demand, and what is the relative size of these needs?
3. What categories and products do consumers use? When, where, with whom, and how do they use them?
4. What is the company's right to win, and for which needs? Where is it vulnerable to competitive attack? Where is the white space or unfilled universe of demand for the company?
5. What needs are competitors satisfying, and how? Where are they sourcing share today, and why?

Frito-Lay commissioned a survey of consumers in different regions across the United States. For the first time, the company had a clear view of the American snacking market and Frito-Lay's room for growth.

Until then, the company had conceptually thought of itself as competing in salty snacks. The new model has it competing fully in a macro snack market that includes biscuits, nuts, chocolate, candy, ice cream, yogurt, and adjacent categories.

"For us, demand spaces is about reframing categories," Greco states. "We no longer think of ourselves as a mid-sixties-share player in salty snacks. We are a mid-teens-share player in macro snacks. This includes crackers, nuts, candy, and chocolate. We define our market as macro snacks, not just salty snacks. That opens up many more growth opportunities."

The research divided the snacking market into 10 different demand spaces and attached a value to each of them.[3] The largest was "Fun Times Together." The next largest was "Enjoy & Indulge." Other big spaces were "Young & Hungry," "Couples Unwind," and "Family Fun." Each of these has distinct emotional needs. In "Fun Times Together," where snacks are enjoyed among friends, the emotions include "Flavors everyone will enjoy," "I enjoy eating with others," and "This helps to enhance the moment."

But Greco also found that he wasn't just competing against other salty snack providers. He learned that salty snacks were not a category: consumers buy a variety of products to deal with their snacking needs at any given moment. So the issue is not salty snack versus salty snack, but instead the time of day, who else is eating, and where the consumer happens to be. Consumers in the "Fun Times Together" space ate not only Lay's potato chips, but also yogurt, Hot Pockets, food from McDonald's or the local pizza shop, cookies, and Snickers bars.

Above all, Greco learned that his three big brands—Lay's, Doritos, and Tostitos—were overlapping each other in the market. They were cannibalizing each other. He needed to make each one distinctive and focused on a particular set of customer needs—a demand space.

Headline: A New Map and a New Battle Plan: Don't Waste the Insight, Make Sure You Implement It

The team concluded that Frito-Lay, a $13 billion business at the time, could grow its volume and units much faster. It also concluded that the company had to reinvent itself. Greco and the leadership team needed to completely overhaul the company's rule book. With the findings from the demand-space work, Frito-Lay had a bible for innovation, for guiding what was spent on marketing, for establishing point-of-sale merchandising, for consumer targeting, and for helping to set growth objectives. Instead of doing the same old thing again and again, the company would have a new map and a new battle plan.

Demand spaces turned Frito-Lay's marketing paradigm upside down. This technique separated the positioning of the various Frito-Lay brands—in particular Tostitos, Doritos, and Lay's—and pushed consumers to choose one product or another for a particular occasion. This provided a road map for the company's massive sales force.

As Greco explains: "We have been targeting a space we call 'Fun Times Together.' It's about what you eat when you bring people together. You need to understand the occasion. This one is about fun, youth, and energy. For higher incomes, it is about premium products."

Frito-Lay introduced Tostitos Cantina for this situation. Cantina is actually four products—chips and dips combined for parties. They are marketed and activated together. Frito-Lay gained volume from parties at home and group get-togethers. "We sold more than $100 million, and Cantina was an IRI Pacesetter for new products in 2013. It was a very big first year," says Greco. "Demand spaces defined the technical specs needed to win along with the emotional benefits important to consumers. We gained share in the relevant demand space for Cantina. It was exciting, restaurant-inspired, and fresh."

Another brand that Frito-Lay reviewed was Doritos. "Doritos is in the 'Young & Hungry' demand space. It competes against many products, including heated snacks," Greco explains. "When a teenage boy comes home from school, he is hungry. He wants immediate satisfaction. So we formed a relationship with McCain's [a Canadian frozen-food manufacturer] to create Doritos Loaded, a heated cheese-filled triangle. McCain is a great partner. They make it and move it. We sell and market it. It is a great new product for an on-the-go occasion." During the launch period, Doritos Loaded was the number two stock-keeping unit at 7-Eleven convenience stores. It is totally new-to-the-world volume for Frito-Lay.

The biggest brand transformation has been Lay's potato chips, a 75-year-old baby. It had been stagnant for five years when Greco and his team applied the demand-centric approach to growing the business. The goal was to get consumers thinking about Lay's differently. They call it the *Do Us a Flavor* contest.[4]

"Lay's was boring," Greco admits. "We needed to make it topical. We engaged the Facebook Leadership Team. We knew we could import a successful program from the UK and sharpen it with the specifics from our U.S. demand insights. We invited America to name their favorite flavor, and consumers voted. In the first year, 4 million consumers submitted flavor ideas. In the second year, 14 million took the time to figure out a new flavor for Lay's. They designed a package, shared it with friends. The four products launched in 2014 were cappuccino, wasabi kettle, salsa, and bacon Mac and cheese. America votes for the winner, who gets $1 million."

In 2013, the finalists were chicken and waffles, sriracha, and cheesy garlic bread. They were produced and distributed, and Facebook changed its "Like" button to "I'd Eat That" just for Frito-Lay. The products became collector's items and were sold on eBay for $45 for one bag of each flavor. The garlic bread entry ultimately won. For old-time Lay's consumers, garlic bread Lay's were an anathema. But garlic bread turned millennials into fans who voted in the millions that "I'd Eat That."

New business. New consumers. New tastes. A new vision for the brand. A potential five-year play. Frito-Lay's brand transformation of Lay's has been big and expensive, requiring scale to master. Its success has been almost impossible for competitors to respond to. The effort has ignited Lay's. This 75-year-old brand grew 6 percent in measured U.S. channels from 2012 to 2014.

Greco says that after three years of very hard work, Frito-Lay is delving deeper and deeper into what drives choice and going outside the bounds of convention to meet consumer needs. The company can recount the snacking habits of very tightly defined demographics.

Frito-Lay's goal is to take demand-space thinking from the product all the way to the shelf. The company has boosted spending on digital media from 9 percent in 2011 to 32 percent in 2015.[5] It has invested heavily in point-of-sale advertising. In prior years, when Frito-Lay launched a product, it provided money for first-year advertising, but saved only limited funds for in-store activation—that is, getting the consumer to buy. Now, Greco says it must be all in or nothing: advertising *and* point-of-sale promotion, not just advertising.

This is a massive departure for a big food company. The normal math in a packaged-goods company is to lose money in the first year, withdraw support in the second year, and make money in the third year. The thinking is this: overall, the net present value is positive, so if you need to skimp on one element of the marketing mix, that's all right. But Greco is saying "No!" to this approach. It's all or nothing.

The demand-space tool has provided the entire organization with a common language to align its activities. When planning for capital investments in manufacturing, the supply and finance organizations will identify which demand spaces are growing fastest and which offer new opportunities for growth. The sales organization has translated the consumer insights into retailer opportunities, designing customized programs by retailer and by region. For example, Frito-Lay is using decentralized print programs to come alive in local markets. It's Frito-Lay promoting Bears' football in Chicago and Jets' football in New York to drive share in the "Fun Times Together" demand space. "This hasn't replaced Frito's advantage in-store, it has strengthened it," says PepsiCo Global Snacks president Ann Mukherjee.

Tom Greco is boldly targeting mid-single-digit growth, and he sees Frito-Lay doubling in the next 10 years. He says that demand science has helped the company unlock growth by (1) providing the facts about demand spaces, (2) identifying the growth terrain, and (3) driving media to shelf execution and excitement. The next part is about shaping the future of demand.

He says that demand spaces have opened and expanded people's minds. "We went from losing market share to gaining share and, importantly, growing volume and units. We've now reached capacity on several platforms and are putting in new lines. That's a good problem to have." But Frito-Lay is not declaring victory. It is too busy working on the next generation of innovative products, programs, and capabilities. "We are now focused on sustaining and, in fact, accelerating growth."

REFLECTIONS ON FRITO-LAY'S USE OF DEMAND SPACES: AN INTERVIEW WITH ANN MUKHERJEE, PRESIDENT OF THE GLOBAL SNACKS GROUP AT PEPSICO

Ann Mukherjee is considered the original champion of demand-space analytics within PepsiCo. Now the president of the Global Snacks Group and PepsiCo Global Insights, she is a double graduate of the University of Chicago, with an economics degree and an MBA. Her job is to drive accelerated growth in PepsiCo's brands, 22 of which generate more than $1 billion in sales. She lives by the slogan "Transform tomorrow today."

"We [took] a very efficient operating supply-driven company and made them converts," Mukherjee states. "They are now leaders who are passionate about demand-driven, consumer-brand-oriented growth. At Frito-Lay, we had lost our way. We had gotten too comfortable. And the world around us was changing. We were the best sales company, but we had lost the war with consumers. They were no longer willing to accept limited choice.

"Frito-Lay had to play a different game. The market had fragmented; the cost of entry had fallen. We had priced business up and had created a price umbrella. It created an opportunity for people to compete with us. They were smaller, nimbler players. They figured out a niche business that would give them enough scale to be a viable business. We were losing share.

"We had to do fundamental work on the business. That was the birth of demand spaces. We needed to understand the strength of our portfolio of brands. We had operated in a silo fashion. Brands and functions did not operate in an integrated way.

"The first step was to quantitatively understand what drives choice. In categories like macro snacks, the *context* was the driver of choice. You snack differently by yourself [than you do] with others. We wanted to find spaces that were mutually exclusive.

"Strategy is about choice. The demand-space framework gives choices. I could position brands depending on their incremental growth opportunity. It's a broad range of choices: How do we position brands, how do we communicate them; how do we innovate brands; how do we decide on pack size; where in the store do we put them?

"For Tostitos, our demand-spaces work identified the space when it was most relevant—when young consumers are having fun together.

We wanted to bring restaurant fun to the home. We created Tostitos Cantina. In the year of launch, it was the largest innovation in food—nothing bigger.

"We then went about the task of organizing to unlock the growth. We had the seal of approval at the top. We focused on the top 300 people across functions to make it real. We educated them on demand spaces by giving them an assignment. We had a video of a consumer named Suzy who was organizing a party. We sent them shopping. And when they came back, they met the real-life Suzy. They learned that she is on a budget but does not want to skimp. As she said, 'I want my guests to come to my next party.' It was eye-opening how she configured the snacks. That defined our arena. It was an [aha] moment for the organization. We compete in a bigger ocean. The experience showed that everyone in the organization needs to be lined up together to meet the needs of our consumer. And that's what we did. The true power of demand spaces has been its ability to galvanize our powerful business system."

Headline: Insights Accelerate Growth

"We accelerated Frito-Lay's growth," she says. "We did it based on rigorous analytics and science. We changed the way we do innovation. Now, supply chain [and] finance are talking demand spaces. We have continued the journey and made the demand spaces longitudinal (capturing the data annually and updating the size and growth of each space). We linked it to shopper data. We united the marketing, sales, and operations sides of the business and now work 'media to shelf.' The longitudinal data was the coup de grâce. As a result, we united operations and sales on the future needs of the business.

"What's a good example of the success? We were very keen to pursue the 'Young & Hungry' demand space. We knew they wanted brands with badge value. That led us to Taco Bell and the Doritos taco at the restaurant chain. We've just sold our billionth taco! Wow. We made the taco better. It had the Doritos crunch and the intense, bold flavoring of Doritos. It delivered the gorgeous cheesy-flavor dust on your lips and took the taco experience to a whole new level. Taco Bell charges a 30-cent-per-unit premium—$1.29 versus 99 cents. It makes their profitability sing. It's great for Taco Bell and for Frito-Lay."

"As a result of demand spaces," Mukherjee continues, "we took up the work-school-break underserved space. We configured a full convenience-store format. This is aimed at adults. It's all 'ready to go'—Sun Chips, Kettle Cooked chips, a line of munchy crackers, Grandma's Soft Baked Cookies.

"[The concept of] demand spaces is not a magic bullet. But it adds comprehensive data. If you get sponsorship from the top, you can mobilize an organization. You need to keep it simple. It is pervasive and comprehensive. You give people a stake in the game. It creates a mentality of evangelism and inspiration. You can rally a core group who are zealots and evangelists. Don't try to do everything overnight; get quick wins and build momentum. It has turned out to be the most rewarding thing in my career."

Headline: View from the Top: What Indra Nooyi, PepsiCo's CEO, Thinks About Demand Spaces

"Demand spaces is the perfect tool for managing a portfolio of brands," says Indra Nooyi, CEO of PepsiCo. "In the normal course of business, brands drift together. You end up with overlapping positions and new products that deliver little incrementally. All advertising looks alike.

"But demand spaces opens up your eyes to new opportunities. You begin to look at new competitive spaces. You understand the implications of consumer behavior. You can imagine differently," she says.

Nooyi points to the snacking space "Fun Times Together." She says that this space is a rich mine of opportunity for her snack-and-beverage behemoth. "It's a space that is different for young males, Latinos, [people of] lower income, all the demographics. If you target with users in mind and [specific] occasions, you create solutions to real needs.

"We are at the beginning of our growth cycle based on this tool. We have found there are big vacant spaces. It will drive our innovation. It allows us to think differently about our markets. And because we are both a snack and a beverage [business], we can think about pairings. This is a distinct competitive advantage. We have been [using the tool] for three years, and we are just beginning to scratch the surface and commercialize to the opportunities."

Headline: Lessons from Frito-Lay

After many successful years, Frito-Lay's brands had started to lose ground to smaller competitors. Customers were unhappy with the limited offerings from this great company. Rather than ignore its customers, Frito-Lay listened to them. It welcomed its customers' scorn. It turned to an original approach—demand spaces—to understand what really drives customer choice.

The company conducted a survey that led to the development of a demand map containing a range of demand spaces. This is the first lesson.

The second lesson is this: the company ensured that it integrated the findings from this survey across its portfolio of brands.

Third, it did not do this just once, but made it an annual or biannual exercise. Customers' needs change, so you have to keep up with their every move.

Fourth, the company used demand-space thinking in an expansive way. Use it not just for product innovation, but for a root-and-branch review of your organization. Make sure you are demand-centric, not just consumer-centric.

Hilton Worldwide

Stunning growth is possible in most consumer categories. There are few businesses that cannot discover the points of light that consumers crave. But most organizations have an immunity to new ways of going to market. They protect instead of attacking.

Hilton Worldwide was one such company.

When Chris Nassetta, a 30-year veteran of the lodging business, was picked to run Hilton Worldwide by Blackstone, the private-equity business that had acquired the company in a $26 billion leveraged buyout in 2007,[6] he knew that he had a job on his hands. The venerable lodging business—the world's most recognizable hotel brand—was a shadow of its former self.

It was started in 1919 by Conrad Hilton. The son of a Norwegian immigrant, Hilton established a high-rise hotel in Dallas, Texas. Before long, he owned a string of premium hotels. They were frequented by the famous and the fashionable. They were the place to be seen. They came to define how hotels delivered services and created a luxury experience.

In the roaring 1940s, Hilton became the first coast-to-coast hotel group in the United States when it acquired the Roosevelt and Plaza Hotels in New York. In 1947, the Roosevelt claimed a memorable record, becoming the first hotel in the world to install TVs in every guest room.[7] By the end of the decade, Hilton had sealed its reputation as the world's most luxurious hotel group, buying the Waldorf Astoria in New York and opening the Caribe Hilton in Puerto Rico, its first international hotel.

Through the 1950s, Hilton continued to be a magnet for the glamorous. It defined the *Mad Men* era. It opened the first modern hotel built from the ground up in post–World War II Europe in Istanbul, hosted a dinner for Queen Elizabeth II in Chicago, and attracted film stars such as Marilyn Monroe. It was at the Hilton in Puerto Rico that Ramon "Monchito" Marrero, a legendary barman, created the Piña Colada, the cocktail of choice among high society and the Hollywood set.[8]

But by the 1960s, Hilton was starting to lose its Jazz Age luster, even though the fashionable still chose to stay at the most famous Hiltons. John Lennon and Yoko Ono staged their "bed-in for peace" protest against the Vietnam War at Hilton Amsterdam. Elvis stayed at Hilton Hawaii Village on Waikiki, where Michael Jackson would stay some 20 years later.

In September 1999, Hilton acquired the Promus Hotel Corporation for $3.1 billion, creating one of the largest hotel companies in the world at the time. It was a significant move that added Promus's DoubleTree Hotels, Embassy Suites, and Hampton Inns. This gave Hilton additional winning and differentiated brands in new territories within different market segments.

Yet, as a whole, the Hilton brand itself was becoming tired and worn. It looked as if its best days were behind it. As the *Washington Post* observed: "The company had become a byword for poor, Balkanized management." For too long, the executives at its grand Beverly Hills headquarters had taken things for granted. "There was no culture of innovation," recalled Nassetta. "It was more a culture of 'do it at a relatively slow pace' and 'do it the way we've always done it.'"[9]

For the inventor of the original modern premium hotel, this was a sad decline.

To get back on track, Nassetta and his team focused on three main brand-related issues: repositioning the flagship Hilton brand, which was widely seen as ailing; reviving the full-service portfolio, including DoubleTree by Hilton; and recasting the loyalty program, Hilton HHonors, as a brand on a par with the hotels.

They knew that the Hilton brand had to reconnect with customers in an emotional way. It had to recapture its zest. It had to rediscover the essence of its success when it was *the* place to stay for royalty, rock stars, and the cream of high society.

Headline: Reshaping the Brand Portfolio: Get to the Heart of What Really Drives Consumer Choice

When Tom Greco looked at Frito-Lay, he realized that he had a bunch of brands that overlapped each other. This was not good. It meant that they were competing with one another for the same customers. Nassetta realized the same thing at Hilton Worldwide. When Blackstone bought the company, there were nine different hotel brands. The most luxurious were Waldorf Astoria and Conrad. Then came the "full-service" hotels: Hilton itself, DoubleTree, and Embassy Suites. After these were the "focused-service" hotels: Hilton Garden Inn, Hampton Inn, and Homewood Suites. In addition, there was the timeshare brand Hilton Grand Vacations.

Some of these were undisputed champions and category killers: Hampton Inn was one; Embassy Suites was another. Four times between 2011 and 2015, Hampton Inn topped the Franchise 500 list published by *Entrepreneur* magazine. Embassy Suites has won the J.D. Power customer service awards nine times.[10] But many of the full-service brands—not just Hilton— were underperforming. They were starting to lose out to the focused-service hotels, which offered fewer—but always the most essential—products and services at the right price levels.

Two of Hilton's full-service hotel brands were struggling to deliver all the many and varied service and quality features on a consistent basis. This was reflected in their quality assurance and customer satisfaction scores, which were all trending downward when Nassetta looked at them—DoubleTree's by 3 percent in the course of one year, Hilton's by 2 percent. Also, it was clear that the hotels were not sufficiently distinctive or different from one another. As at Frito-Lay, the brands were all targeting a similar demographic.

As Jim Holthouser, global head of Hilton brands, explained to us: "In 2008, we were still struggling with how to think about DoubleTree relative to Hilton. It needed to be a stand-alone brand with its own swim lane, but we hadn't defined it yet." So Nassetta turned to a team of Hilton's dedicated data-driven brand and commercial-products executives, including Holthouser. Like Greco at Frito-Lay, he asked them to experiment with new market research techniques that placed great emphasis on emotional connection. As we saw earlier in this chapter, conventional market research is based on syndicated data and industrial segmentation, which group people broadly by age, income, and occasions, such as "leisure versus business" or "long-stay versus short-stay." The new approach, however, is much more granular and indicates what different people want on different occasions and at different times of the day. It tries to get to the heart of what really drives consumer choice.

To get answers, Hilton conducted hundreds of interviews and surveyed thousands of consumers in the United States, Canada, the United Kingdom, Germany, China, Japan, Brazil, and Egypt. People were asked to describe what they wanted and—this was especially crucial—when they wanted it. The results were startling. For the first time, Hilton had a map of what really mattered to consumers. It could separate the hospitality market into a rainbow of different categories—demand spaces—based on what consumers really, really wanted when they stepped over the threshold of a hotel.

The categories are expressed in common language. One demand space was "feel at ease," from customers who want to have a "worry-free experience." Another was "rewarded," from customers who want to "feel on vacation even when they're on business because they work so hard." In all, Hilton's branding team identified 12 demand spaces. It then allocated each of the brands to one or more of the demand spaces.

The consumer work led to distinct positioning for each brand. Hilton was allocated the "recharge and refresh" space, and DoubleTree was given the "personal connection" or "personalized" space. This allocation was reinforced by rules about what the hotels could and couldn't offer, to stop one hotel from drifting into the so-called swim lane of another hotel.

As we show in greater detail later in this chapter, Hilton and DoubleTree were targeting very similar consumers. By bringing clarity to their positioning, the company was able to unlock growth and customer opportunities. The "recharge and refresh" space was very large. It was a perfect complement for the Hilton brand, with its diverse property portfolio ranging from meeting and convention hotels to resort destinations. It has a wide range of business and leisure customers. It needs a big space to grow.

Likewise, the "personal connection" or "personalized" space was perfect for DoubleTree. The brand is skewed toward business travelers who are looking for decent service but don't need consistently top-quality accommodation.

Headline: Resurrecting the Hiltons: Search for a Distinctive and Differentiating Brand Position

Anyone staying at a Hilton brand hotel before 2007, when Blackstone bought the company, would have been shocked at just how far the great brand had fallen. Take Hilton McLean, in the suburbs of Washington, DC. It was the epitome of the Hilton brand gone wrong: old, shabby, and out-of-date.

But Nassetta knew what he had to do to resurrect an iconic American brand. He needed to make it more consumer-focused, just as it had been in the 1940s and 1950s. He asked his branding team to rethink the way Hilton engaged with the customer. His team's recommendation, reflecting the conventional wisdom, was to make Hilton "cool and hip" again. In one sense, this was perfectly logical. In its heyday, Hilton had been cool and hip. If Hilton were to recapture its earlier success, why not go back to this great heritage?

But Nassetta was unconvinced by this pitch. He instinctively realized that the cool and hip market was no longer right for Hilton, given its size and its global reach. Following this instinct, the branding team used the detailed data-driven demand-space research, which had elicited information that was very different from the kind typically produced by market research. The researchers asked customers about their real choices. What are the must-haves of your experience? How do hotels in general and Hilton in particular make you feel today? How would you like a hotel to make you feel tomorrow? Look at evocative pictures: which best describes the Hilton brand?

One typical customer was John.

John is an account executive for an IT services company. He is married, with two teenage boys. He spends 22 nights a year on the road. Typically he stays at full-service hotels. He likes the "extras"—the high-touch service and room service. He characterizes himself as a "somewhat loyal" Hilton customer.[11]

When we first started talking with him, we asked him about his must-haves. "Number one, I have to have a clean room," he said. "It sounds so simple, but you'd be surprised how hotels screw this up. I can walk into a room and instantly know if I'm going to have problems. First, I'll look at the air vents. If I see black dust on the vents, I know there'll be problems, and I instantly start to smell mold, whether it's there or not. Then, in the morning, when I use the bathroom, I look for how quickly the water drains. If slowly, then I know there's hair in the drain. Hilton usually doesn't have those problems, but I have seen a few that have. When you miss here, it's hard to recover."

John then spoke more about the brand as a whole. "I'd say Hilton's a fairly reliable business-hotel chain. Now, I will say they are a bit out-of-date. The buildings are not up-to-date anymore. The old stuff has to go! This may sound bad, but it's like an old woman wearing a lot of makeup. It's so obvious that she is not able to afford the plastic surgery that she desperately needs. When I walk into the room, I go straight to the bed and strip off Grandma's bed cover that has all those dated colors. It's like it's trying to hide something."

So, if he didn't like the antiquated look, what did he want? How did he want to feel after a night in a Hilton? "Ultimately, I want to wake up the next morning and feel recharged and ready for the day ahead. I want to know I'm going to nail my meeting. I want to know I won't have bags under my eyes because I had a great night's sleep. I want to know I had something reasonably healthy to eat when I checked in at 10.30 p.m. That's what I want to feel like when I go to a Hilton."

As we talked more, John started to open up more. He soon became quite opinionated. "The more I think about it, Hilton really has lost its way. You may not know this, but in the old days, Hilton was quite luxurious. Twenty years ago, it was brilliant to say that you were staying at a Hilton. Now you need to differentiate between the nice ones and the horrible ones. Hilton is a big name, but it does not stand for quality anymore. It is not living up to its image."

Hilton talked to many other people like John. It conducted a survey of more than 10,000 consumers to size up the opportunities, framed around "travel solutions." As Holthouser explained: "Traditional segmentation approaches, like those around demographics—I threw them out the window. Demographics tell you little about lodging customers, who all look relatively similar. What I can get my head around is thinking about these brands that target specific trip occasions, emotional needs, and price points. I can get my head around that all day long. When you start looking at our particular portfolio and you start thinking about travel solutions, it starts to make a heck of a lot more sense than demographics."

First, the results confirmed Nassetta's hunch that creating a cool and hip Hilton was the wrong thing to do. The analysis showed, in a very data-driven way, that the emotional space of "cool and hip" was small. It accounted for just 2 percent of the market. This was far too small for a global brand such as Hilton, which has more than 550 properties and is fast approaching its centenary.

If the team had taken the advice of the advertising agencies, it would have had to make Hilton look and feel more like W, the trendy cosmopolitan boutique brand owned by Starwood, one of Hilton's competitors. But even if Hilton could have delivered this perfectly, it would have been impossible for the brand to grow and connect with customers.

Second, and most important, the results revealed an emotional space that Hilton should target—namely, the "recharge and refresh" space. This was perfect for the brand because it embraced both leisure and business travelers. From its earliest days, Hilton had sought to be the hotel of choice, whatever the traveler's purpose. For instance, in 1959 it had pioneered the airport hotel concept by opening the 380-room San Francisco Airport Hilton for the business and leisure traveler.

From the detailed consumer feedback, the Hilton team established that the "recharge and refresh" space was large and growing, accounting for 25 percent of the market. It reflected the second most popular emotion that was tested, after "worry free." Also, the team established that the company had a "right to win" in this space. But it did not have a "fair share" of the market.

Armed with this information, Hilton set about repositioning its flagship brand. As a start, it brought back the founder's motto for the overall company, "To fill the earth with the light and warmth of hospitality." This became the "vision" in a carefully crafted "brand architecture." The centerpiece of this work was the development of a brand "personality" for Hilton. This included five "personality traits," the things that customers say they see when they check into a Hilton. These were "authentic," "worldly," "generous," "refreshing," and "competent." It also included a set of values adopted for the company: "hospitality," "integrity," "leadership," "teamwork," "ownership," and—significantly—"now." Hilton had once defined an era, but that era had long gone. Now, it wanted to reflect a new age.[12]

After defining Hilton's personality and values, the branding team developed some functional and technical features. It introduced what the team members referred to as *sacred cows*. These are features that are unique to the Hilton flagship brand. No other brand in the company's portfolio of full-service hotels is allowed to offer them. One is high-quality food and beverage on a 24/7 basis. Another is a connectivity station, located in the lobby, allowing complimentary high-speed Internet access to conduct meetings or simply print boarding passes.

Second, Hilton unveiled some "unique delighters." Customers were provided with an executive lounge, a bar in the lobby, and updated rooms that were spotlessly clean and featured large, white, comfortable beds and new flat-screen TVs. Also, they were offered "fair pricing." Until then, Hilton had often been accused of nickel-and-diming its customers. Now, it needed to be seen as "generous." In this spirit, it made strenuous efforts to answer complaints and resolve problems as quickly and painlessly as possible.

At the McLean Hilton, the difference is stark. You enter the lobby and see the technology lounge, with a video wall and computers that have complimentary Wi-Fi and printing. If you attend a meeting, you may find yourself in a 67-seat amphitheater or a ballroom that holds 1,300 people. In your room, you have a high-definition flat-screen TV. To eat, you can walk downstairs to the härth restaurant, which serves farm-to-table American cuisine, cooked in a wood-burning oven as you sit by the fireside.

As one customer commented: "The McLean Hilton is a first-class hotel. The staff are great from the front door on the way in to when you check out. The accommodations are very comfortable—very nice and completely updated. The public space, bar, and restaurant are beautiful. It's a great place to hang out and relax. If you need a place to stay, this is it!"[13]

Headline: Reviving DoubleTree: Deliver the Emotional Promise with the Right Functional Features

When you enter a DoubleTree at Hilton, you will be greeted by a friendly face at the reception desk and offered a warm chocolate chip cookie. It's an established tradition. Say "DoubleTree" to an American, and he will probably think "cookie." The two just go together.

Every year, DoubleTree gives out more than 28 million of these snacks as a "welcome" gift to guests. "In the early 1980s, most hotels reserved treats like these for VIPs," says its marketing literature. "We started handing them out to everyone because we think every guest is a VIP."[14]

No other hotel in the Hilton chain offers this little touch: it is one of DoubleTree's icons. It has come to symbolize the hotel's unique place as the Hilton Worldwide brand that targets the "personal connection" or "personalized" space: rewarding hotel experiences where the little things mean everything. DoubleTree became part of the Hilton portfolio in 1999, with Hilton's acquisition of Promus Hotel Corporation. But, like the Hilton brand, it lacked a clear identity. Founded in 1969, it was a "me too" brand that was one notch below the flagship Hilton brand.

In the course of the demand-space research, the members of the Hilton team realized that they could not forge a clear identity for the brand on the basis of the actual hotels. Every one was different. What they found, however, was that DoubleTree was perfectly placed to meet the needs of people who say, "I want to feel like I'm being treated in a personal and individualized manner after what has been a long, tiring, and rather impersonal travel day." In this space, it had a clear "right to win."

As it had done with its flagship brand, Hilton set about crafting DoubleTree's brand identity. Its promise was to "restore the human touch to the travel experience by really understanding the individual preferences of its guests." This meant that it would have to "provide the special comforts and personalized acts of kindness that treat the traveler like a valued individual."

With its signature cookie, DoubleTree had a perfect "act of kindness" that was deeply rooted in its culture. But this was not sufficient to guarantee its success. Yes, the insight into what drives consumer choice is essential. But the effective implementation of the functional and technical features is equally important.

This is where DoubleTree tripped up. Its targeted customers were willing to trade down on some of the hotel's physical features, so long as the quality of the service remained high. But when the service fell below an expected threshold, they rebelled.

Hilton's branding team discovered this after comparing the quality assurance scores of its DoubleTree hotels. The team members asked customers a very straightforward question: "Did you get a cookie when you checked in?" For some hotels, the answer was yes just 75 percent of the time.

This concerned the executives at headquarters. It also puzzled the managers of the hotels, who claimed that they always handed out the signature cookie. What was really happening?

To find out, Hilton sent a team of researchers to all the hotels with very low or very high scores. It turned out that the managers of the low-scoring hotels were telling the truth: every customer *was* handed a cookie at the reception. But there was a telling difference in the way the receptionists handed out the cookie.

At the low-scoring hotels, the receptionists typically kept a bag of cookies under the counter and distributed them when customers checked into the hotel. It wasn't an act of kindness. It wasn't a genuine gesture of hospitality. It was an administrative duty: "another thing to do," and a box to be checked. By contrast, the high-scoring hotels transformed the cookie into a piece of theater. The receptionists put on their white gloves, walked over to the warming tray, selected a cookie with a pair of tongs, and presented it to the customer before the check-in took place. It was part of the welcoming experience, as opposed to a transactional act. It was a memorable occasion. There was a sense of drama. There was an emotional connection with the guest.

"What I have learned from brands like DoubleTree," says Jim Holthouser, "is that consistency doesn't have to mean having the same identical product. Consistency ultimately means delivering a promise. So with DoubleTree, we have entrenched a culture of CARE. CARE stands for Create A Rewarding Experience, which helps bring consistent and unique acts of kindness to the brand."

Headline: The Loyalty Factor: Rewarding Converts with Experiences Worth Sharing

The Hilton team used the customer-demand-space approach to create a portfolio of very distinctive brands. No longer was there a fuzzy line between Hilton and DoubleTree. But the team members also saw the potential of the approach to revitalize something else: Hilton's loyalty program, Hilton HHonors. They realized that if they took care of Hilton's "apostles"—the guests who returned time and time again—the converts would take care of Hilton by being loyal and telling their friends and family about the chain.

The program, launched in 1987, boasts 44 million members.[15] This represents 50 percent of global occupancy, generating $13 billion in hotel revenue in 2014. The Hilton team commissioned a new round of demand-space market research. What really drives the members' choice? Why would they stay with one hotel group—and get the benefits of loyalty—rather than another hotel group?

To find answers, Hilton spoke to thousands of consumers. One of these was Bob, who by any measure is an "elite" business traveler, a true road warrior. He spends 170 nights a year away from home: away from his wife and away from his two teenage kids. Traveling for business has taken its toll on Bob and his family. Over the years, he's missed many parent–teacher conferences and kids' sporting events. His wife is very understanding. She knows the demands of the job. Even so, on many occasions, she has taken her frustration out on him for not being there. He tries to be a dutiful husband. He calls home every night he's away. But that's not always enough.

Most of those nights are spent in one of the Hilton brand portfolio hotels, mainly Hampton. This is why Bob joined the HHonors program. "If you travel for a living, you might as well take advantage," he said. "It's nice to be treated special. Of course, all the hotel companies talk about points. But honestly, I have no idea which one has a better deal."

So why does he stay loyal to Hilton and use the HHonors program? "I guess the points are important to me. It's about what I can do for my family, to make up for all the stuff I miss at home, to do something special for them. I thank HHonors for that. I couldn't have done this without the program."

Bob spoke volubly about the program, not least because a fantastic trip was fresh in his memory. "My points balance is pretty low right now because we've just got back from Hawaii and stayed at the Grand Wailea," he said. "My wife was so grateful. It was the nicest hotel we've ever stayed at. Staying in an $800 room for free was cool. It kind of makes up for being gone five nights a week."

After gathering Bob's testimony and the testimony of thousands of other consumers, Hilton discovered a glaring fact: the loyalty program should really be a brand and not a program. It should connect emotionally with the customer. In this way, it could differentiate itself from other loyalty programs, in which the goal seems to be simply to collect as many loyalty points as possible.

As Hilton's branding team searched for what drives choice, it soon found a large emotional space that the team members decided to call "experiences worth sharing." Here, customers wanted to earn loyalty points so that they could take their loved ones on an aspirational trip—the trip of a lifetime, a trip they might not otherwise be able to afford. It wasn't about the points; it was about the experience. It was about the connections they made with their families and, in turn, the connection they felt to Hilton.

Without knowing it, this is exactly the demand space that Bob had been talking about. And eventually, by having HHonors cater to people who wanted experiences worth sharing, Hilton was able to develop an emotional connection with consumers, create some functional products, and get out of the points arms race.

Headline: Demand Spaces, Real Results

The strategy of focusing on the needs or "demands" of the customer has delivered strong results for Hilton Worldwide. Its brands have been rejuvenated. There are real distinctions.

Jim Holthouser said: "For DoubleTree, you can look at it now, and you know it's differentiated. We've identified swim lanes. There are clear physical, service, rate, and consumer differences between the two brands." The results testify to the transformation. In 2012, DoubleTree became the fastest-growing brand in the portfolio, with the number of hotels rising by 60 percent, from 184 in 2008 to more than 400 today—plus 150 in the pipeline. It has become one of Hilton's most significant growth engines.[16]

On Hilton, he said that the brand "continues to be the leading growth vehicle, with a pipeline of 160-plus hotels around the world." He added: "The brand remains a revered name around the world. And, it has made enormous progress in improving its service culture. We've also made a lot of progress converting Hiltons to DoubleTrees in some cases, which has benefited both brands. Going forward, given the scale, history, and global reach of the Hilton brand, we've needed to be deliberate about change in order to reach our goals. And I feel very confident in our longer-term plan to get us there."

The real sign of the success of the brand strategy was Hilton's return to the public markets. In 2013, Blackstone sold $2.7 billion of stock, valuing the company at $33 billion.[17] This was a 27 percent premium over the purchase price in 2007. It was the world's largest IPO for a hotel operator. When companies buy high, they are usually forced to sell low. But Blackstone defied the odds. It was able to buy at the peak of the market, suffer through the Great Recession, and come out with a higher value.

The price, though high, made sense. Hilton Worldwide has been the fastest-growing global hotel company since 2007. Today it has more than 4,300 hotels, spread across 12 brands. It has 715,000 rooms in 94 countries—a 37 percent increase since 2007, when Blackstone started the transformation.[18]

Nassetta forecasts considerable growth over the next 20 years. "The outlook for our industry is as good as I've ever seen," he said, in his letter to shareholders in 2014.[19] His optimism is founded on the growth of global tourism and the rise of the middle class in underserved markets. Hilton is well positioned to capitalize on these trends. It has 230,000 rooms in the pipeline—the largest number in the hospitality industry and a 68 percent increase since 2007. Also, it has more than 120,000 rooms under construction—a 144 percent increase since 2007. This places it in the number one spot in rooms that are in supply, under construction, and in the development pipeline.

"Our goal is simple," said Nassetta. "To serve any customer, anywhere in the world, for any lodging need they have. By doing so, we drive customer loyalty, higher market share premiums, and better returns for our hotel owners, which in turn drives faster net unit growth and premium returns for our stockholders."[20]

Hilton Worldwide's success so far is testimony to the power of a strategy that puts customer choice at the heart of the business.

Headline: Lessons from Hilton

There are three lessons to take away from the Hilton story. One is that you should trust the data from research about what really drives consumer choice. If you do this, you can expect to find large, or at least appropriately sized, demand spaces. As Hilton found, there was no point targeting the "cool and hip" space when its large corps of road warriors were searching for a place to "recharge."

The second lesson is that the technical cues, the little details, matter. Personal connection was the home run space for DoubleTree; it was the "what." But you've got to focus on the "how" as well. You can't hit the ball out of the park if you don't execute the details. Offering a cookie in the right way and at the right time was one of those details. Yet not every hotel did this. It was intended as an act of kindness, a show of hospitality. But some hotels treated it as just another thing to do. In other words, it lost its meaning and its connection with the guest. You have to deliver on the "right" technical cues to make the connection and win the space.

The third lesson is that every key element of your business can be a brand, with the potential to develop an emotional connection with your consumer. Who'd have thought that a loyalty program would thrive as a distinct brand, as important as a hotel brand? Hilton's loyalty program, HHonors, became a brand in its own right. Hilton listened to its consumers and turned the program into a real source of competitive advantage. It realized that the more connections it has with its consumers, the stronger it will be as a business.

*****

One Conclusion

If you have more than one brand, you need to make sure the brands are distinctive and distinct from one another. Hilton and Frito-Lay found that they had overlapping brands that were cannibalizing one another.

Once they stepped back and realized what really drove consumer choice, they were able to target clearly delineated demand spaces.

In the case of Frito-Lay, it was able to target the major macro snacks market rather than just the narrower salty snacks market. In the case of Hilton, it was able to separate the Hilton and DoubleTree brands and allow them to create valuable businesses in quite different markets.

Three Takeaways

1. **Know your demand spaces.** There's no such thing as a mature business. There *is* such a thing as a management team that has run out of energy and ideas. If you think you're losing momentum, invest in the demand-space tool. It allows you to breathe new life into your business. Frito-Lay and Hilton used the tool and achieved fantastic results. It allowed them to find new consumers. It allowed them to target new consumer needs. It was the difference between having no ideas and having dozens of ideas.

2. **Implement, implement, implement.** The demand-space tool itself does not give you growth. Growth requires creativity, experimentation, investment, and years of diligence. Frito-Lay and Hilton believe that the tool sparked their imagination, and they are on a path of growth. It's about recognizing the power of responding to distinct consumer needs. It's about marketing with precision and conviction. It's about creating a bundle of benefits that deliver to the demand space. And it is about separating your various offerings so that you do not doom your new efforts by sourcing volume from yourself.

3. **Make choices and prioritize.** The demand-space tool helps you prioritize your opportunities and decide how you can best allocate your investment budget across your portfolio of businesses. Feed your high-return, high-growth businesses. Starve your low-return, low-growth businesses. Frito-Lay invested in Lay's, Doritos, and Tostitos as well as in new marketing channels. Hilton invested in its flagship brand and DoubleTree. Decisive portfolio allocation leads to greater overall returns. Combine market insight with the power of incremental returns on incremental volume.

SOME KEY ACTION POINTS

1. Create a comprehensive map of the demand spaces.
2. Tailor your offerings to the largest, fastest-growing occasions, emotions, and uses.
3. Use your portfolio as an advantage and have distinct, separate areas of difference.
4. Understand and chase growth. Know that this will revitalize you.
5. Use the knowledge from demand spaces to target competitors.
6. Imagine the product as specified precisely. Don't force consumers to compromise. Get—and stay—hot.
7. Look both up and down on price points. It is usually easier to find profit upmarket. Downmarket is the domain of scale and cost advantage for profit.
8. Use early knowledge as a platform. Make each cycle of demand spaces a chance for further, deeper learning.

Create your demand-space map. Understand where you sit on that map, and where your competition sits. Describe the 30 most important technical, functional, and emotional factors. Broadly discuss the findings in your organization. Use the demand-space map as the starting point for all development activities.

CHAPTER FOUR

Looks Do Count (Because People Really Do Judge a Book by Its Cover)

THE CHAPTER IN A BOX

The Main Point

Consumers shop with their eyes. So, be visually stunning. Emphasize the aesthetic. Target all the senses. Shame on you if you offer anything ugly. Shame on you if you offer anything dull. Shame on you if you offer anything conventional. Visual presentation drives consumer champions. They describe what they see. They proclaim everything that is beautiful. The Italians got there first. It is their vision of the world that has been handed down by generations of craftsmen.

Why These Stories for This Chapter

In this chapter, we describe the rise and fortunes of a sweater king and the evolution of a theme park from a mecca for children of all ages to a vacation mecca for adults, too. What the two stories have in common are the rules of breathtaking and memorable design.

Brunello Cucinelli took the sweater to a new level. He added stunning color and used the world's finest wool. He presented his works in stark, clean showrooms. He expanded from tops to bottoms, from first layer to outer layer, and from sportswear to tailored clothing. He established a way to live a lifestyle from the eye of the designer. He captured the returns from visual merchandising in the form of consumer loyalty and reference.

Walt Disney created the sight lines for his parks to deliver fantasy. He created worlds where reality would give way to make-believe. The Magic Kingdom really does deliver magic. His successors took it to new levels. Armies of "imagineers" have spent billions of dollars keeping it contemporary and earning the highest daily admission fee of any park in the world.

Chapter Overview

When your customers look at you, what do they see? It might be the product on the shelf. It might be the smile (or grimace) of the salesperson in the store. It might be the time it takes to receive an online delivery. It might be the fabric you use in your clothes or the ingredients you use in your foods. It might be the way you respond to congratulations or complaints.

In other words, when your customers look at you, they might see almost anything. You need to understand this, and you need to take it seriously. Because, as we all know, first impressions last. Every encounter with your customers is an opportunity for you to be seen in the best possible light.

Don't hide away. In this digital age, you will be found eventually. Be honest, open, and transparent. Be prepared to show your face, body, and soul.

Headline: Visual Appearance Matters—And So Do Core Values

What you look like really matters. But it's not just the surface, the cover, that your customers see when they look your way. With one glance, they can read you. Your visual appearance—your face to the world—should precisely match your vision and your values. If your façade is fake, then you are doomed.

In this chapter, we look at two companies that have developed a distinctive style and a set of matching core values. The first is Brunello Cucinelli, an upmarket Italian apparel retailer that produces elegant, casual, handcrafted clothing that is reassuringly expensive. In certain circles, people "know" if you're wearing a Cucinelli item. They don't need to see a logo. And the brand says something about you: wealthy, dignified, thoughtful, and desirable.

The second company is Disney. It did, of course, invent the modern animated cartoon film. It knows everything there is to know about the power of the image. Here, however, we tell the story of its theme parks. They have to have all the hallmarks of a Disney film: entertaining, magical, and filled with family fun. And they do.

As we'll show, this unity of the visuals and the values requires constant vigilance. It doesn't just happen. It takes imagination and hard work. Develop a humanist approach, one that cherishes emotional connection. Devise a "magnetized" supply chain that links your customers, employees, and suppliers. Display a perfectionist's attention to detail.

Brunello Cucinelli

When first-time visitors arrive at the headquarters of fashion house Brunello Cucinelli, they are met at the top of a meticulously renovated fourteenth-century castle. The castle is in Solomeo, in the province of Perugia, in central Italy's Umbria region. The view from the top is spectacular: on a clear summer day, you can see for miles. In the distance, there are fields of cypress trees, sunflowers, grapevines, and olive trees. The castle contains the founding offices of the company, new classrooms for interns, a 200-seat theater, an outdoor amphitheater, and a commercial shop that sells goods to the public. It feels as if a modern-day Medici has created a stunning and painstaking renovation to celebrate history, culture, and spirit.

From the very first view, Cucinelli comes across as a company with a different alignment of values and priorities.

Its founder, Brunello Cucinelli, is a philosopher, historian, and humanist. "What I do in life, I do for the dignity of humanity," he told us, sitting in his pure white, modern office. He calls his company a humanistic enterprise, "a web of human relations woven not exclusively for profit but for man."

He is a picture from central casting for a trendsetter. On the day of our visit, he was dressed in distinctive Cucinelli clothing: a white shirt with a skinny gray tie; short, hip-hugging cargo pants; and half boots. He had a perfectly grown two-day stubble on his face. He presented a living image of casual sartorial precision. For three hours, he gestured and smiled, laughed and held court, while talking about his favorite topic: his "dream for man—ethics, morality, dignity, the role of business in creating a better world."

His office is decorated like the set of a movie. Light pours in through the massive floor-to-ceiling windows. The temperature outside is in the high eighties, but the office is cool, and a pin could drop and be heard in the quiet. You can see his books, the pictures of his heroes, and his affinity for soccer. You can see the central importance of cashmere. There is colored cashmere in vases on his walls—reds, yellows, purples, and greens. It is an office that speaks; the books and the cashmere are the source materials that inspire him.

At age 17, Cucinelli met his wife, Federica, a beauty from Solomeo, a short distance from his home in Perugia. She worked at a clothing shop that sold sweaters. While they were dating, he read an article by Ted Levitt, a Harvard professor and marketing whiz. He took from Levitt four principles:[1]

1. Focus on the customer.
2. Deliver quality, craftsmanship, creativity, and flair.
3. Concentrate and focus on category expertise.
4. Globalize.

He started his company when he was 25 years old. He was penniless. But he had 20 kilos of borrowed cashmere, friends and skilled artisans in his hometown, and a drive to create a humanistic enterprise. Following the lessons from Levitt, he focused on the consumer, targeting the most affluent and least price-sensitive customers. He gravitated toward Austrian and German customers who paid promptly, enabling him to grow quickly without taking on any debt. Also, he came to realize that goods sold on Italian high streets were often purchased by American and other tourists on holiday. At the same time, he imagined perfect-quality products based on better materials, better fabrication, and better display. He chose cashmere sweaters as his "best-at" category.

The late 1970s and early 1980s were the glory years for Benetton, the much larger Italian clothing company known for its vibrant wool sweaters. Cucinelli applied the same color principles to cashmere sweaters, dying the finished goods wild and vivid reds, oranges, purples, and many other shades. At the time, cashmere was in short supply and a very exclusive material.

Cucinelli converted the 20 kilos of cashmere into 70 sweaters and sold them for $180 each. Since then, the company has been on a roll. Its exclusive, casual-chic merchandise has appealed to wealthy customers in New York, Milan, Rome, Tokyo, Paris, London, and Munich. Repeat customers will sweep into one of the luxury boutiques and buy a single complete look, from head to toe, for up to $10,000 per outfit.

Sales through the company's approximately 100 monobrand stores are humming, with like-for-like sales growing more than 5 percent per year. Also, the goods are sold in major high-end department stores, including Neiman Marcus, Saks, Barneys, Bergdorf, and Harrods. In 2015, the company will sell more than $450 million in merchandise, with almost equal amounts being sold in North America and Europe (not including Italy), followed by Italy and a smaller amount in Asia.

The goods are styled for everyday elegance. They are sporty and high-tech. Cardigan sweaters go for $1,785. Crewnecks are $1,215. Linen suits are $3,345. A simple dress is $1,350. The products are designed to be worn in layers—the fabrics are lightweight, and the colors are soft, with a fashion feel. For the man or woman with resources, it is a style of dress that provides appropriate attire in all circumstances. The products are two-thirds women's and one-third men's; 85 percent is apparel.

Cucinelli cashmere is very fine fiber—14 to 15 microns. It is obtained from goats at a rate of 250 grams of "under-down" per year per goat. The Mongolian shepherds remove the fiber by combing the goat. There are no razor cuts, and no harm is done to the animals. The fiber is processed in nearby independently owned workshops.

The cashmere thread is central to the look and the values of Cucinelli's brand. The secrets of this brand consist of (1) better raw material, (2) exclusive design, (3) color coordination and outfit selection, (4) comfort, (5) a defined look and feel, (6) exclusivity, (7) authenticity, and (8) the backstory about the founder and the company's origin.

Headline: Branding Doesn't Mean a Logo on Every Item, but Rather a Distinctive Look

Cucinelli clothing has a definite look. It is identifiable without a logo. It has a distinctive slim, contemporary silhouette. It has a distinctive fabric.

It is created by Italy's finest artisan craftsmen. Cucinelli's hometown of Perugia is a hotbed of craft apparel, with thousands of small enterprises supporting elements of apparel production—fabric, cutting, fabrication, and quality control. From the start, Cucinelli took advantage of the natural supply chain and the skill of local craftsmen. By using them, he was capitalizing on 100 years of local know-how and design.

Designers merchandise the goods down to the last detail, laying out complete outfits—sweater, slacks, shoes, jacket, handbag, and display accessories. Visual merchandising is a prized skill at the company, and enormous amounts of resources are devoted to presentation. The result is more than a dressed mannequin; it is a lifestyle—aristocratic, casual, elegant Italian.

There is a long lead time for product development. The fall/winter collection is presented in January (men's) and February (women's), and work on the product begins a year earlier. Total elapsed time from "creation" to "sold to customer" is as much as six to eight months. The cashmere is sourced from Mongolia and China through Italian suppliers, notably Cariaggi Lanificio. Textiles come from Ermenegildo Zegna, Loro Piana, and other important Italian suppliers. Leather goods are provided exclusively by Italian tanners. Cucinelli uses 300 certified local artisanal laboratories, 80 percent of which are in Umbria, with the remainder being in the nearby Tuscany, Marche, and Veneto regions. The whole production process is subjected to a very intricate quality surveillance—from the yarn to the sewing, the finishing, the washing, the ironing, the final assembly, the delivery, and ultimately the "try-on."

The associated advertising, which amounted to 5.5 percent of revenues in 2013, is subtle and focuses on dramatic print ads. These have often included the handsome Cucinelli, his beautiful wife, Federica, and their now adult daughters. At the company's headquarters, there is a massive framed reproduction of an ad shot taken in a forest of cypress trees, with 100 tables set for 400 of the company workers. All the workers are dressed in Cucinelli clothing and accessories. It is a party that stretches far into the distance. It represents the infinity of the brand.

As well as through advertising, Cucinelli is careful to burnish his brand through newspapers and magazines. He is not media shy. In his office, there are reproductions of major articles that have appeared in the *New Yorker*, the *Wall Street Journal*, *Harper's Bazaar*, *Vogue*, *Le Monde*, and other major business and popular outlets.

But if traditional marketing is important, customer advocacy is more important. The brand has really grown by word of mouth. Consumers see high-quality fabric and contemporary design and say that it's a demonstration of their taste, affluence, and style.

We first became intrigued by the brand at a dinner party two years ago. A fellow guest leaned over and, with no real warning or introduction, commanded, "Touch my sleeve." We had just met the woman. Her sleeve was certainly soft. We learned that her name was Joy, and she was a Cucinelli apostle. "I discovered the brand on a trip to Italy 10 years ago. It was my secret until very recently. My Cucinelli sweaters are my pride and joy. I have 10 of them. They are soft luxury. I love the way they feel on my skin. But I have come to appreciate the skirts, the jackets, and the accessories. They are perfect for me."

Joy said that she had introduced her 10 best friends to the brand. She takes them to the Cucinelli boutique around the corner from Chicago's tony Oak Street shopping mecca or the store within a store in Saks on Michigan Avenue. "I prefer the boutique. I know the manager. He's a real Italian," she whispered.

"When I was married, my husband thought I was a nut to spend $1,500 on a sweater. He is no longer with me. But since we split, I took 'his' drawers in our dresser for my Cucinelli additions," she chuckled.

This 45-year-old marketing executive is not alone. Cucinelli says he receives letters and e-mails from many customers who want exclusivity and originality. Also, they don't want him to change a thing. "Don't grow, don't wear me out," they say.

The investors say this, too. In 2012, Cucinelli's IPO was oversubscribed more than 17 times, and its list of investors is a Who's Who, including Fidelity, Capital World Investors, BlackRock, and Zegna, an Italian luxury fashion house. The IPO was a source of capital for growth, but it did not signal a change in philosophy. Cucinelli says that his investors have told him "not to change anything about his strategy and to continue to seek a gracious growth in turnover and profit." After the IPO, Cucinelli retained 61.1 percent of the equity, which is now in a family trust and worth about $1 billion.[2]

Headline: Create a Humanistic Organization—Your "Look" Is About Your Values as Well as Your Visuals

"Economic value is nothing without human value," says Cucinelli. "I guide a humanistic enterprise."

As he talks, he draws on sheets of paper. He speaks some English, but he prefers to tell his story in Italian "to get the words right and precise." His face is animated, and he talks quickly. He fires off long phrases, and his interpreter can barely keep up. He pauses only between major thoughts and when he fumbles to put out a fresh sheet of paper to fully capture the story. It is like a fable, and he has certainly told it before.

In staccato, he tells his story of humanistic capitalism. It is built on an understanding of Marx, the socialist paralysis in Italy, and the harsh business world of the West. He likes to quote Marcus Aurelius, the last of the five "good" Roman emperors. In his meditations, Aurelius is the stoic philosopher who believes in service, duty, and everlasting trust. "We try to live by his words and acts every day," Cucinelli says. "We are helping to create a new form of ethical capitalism, a celebration of human dignity. We strive to produce without harming mankind. We would like to produce products that our customers never throw away. They pass them on to their children."

Cucinelli's approach to business was formed during his childhood. He grew up the son of a poor farmer and in a family of hard workers and sharecroppers. Yet he describes his early childhood as "heaven on earth." As he explains: "We had nothing, and yet we were so happy. I lived with 12 immediate family members, and with 14 other family members in nearby homes. There was no mechanization, no running water, and no electricity. But we had fresh food and love. You could smell the fruit of the earth. There was never a harsh word at home."

He does not consider himself the owner of his company. "I feel like the guardian. I aim to leave the company in a strong position. My job is to safeguard and embellish this small part of the world. We built the theater at the top of the mountain, for example, to be usable in 300 years." In financial terms, he is targeting "gracious," predictable, steady growth at 10 percent per year, as well as a fair profit.

Cucinelli applied his "humanistic capital" principles to his operation from the very beginning. He says, "Treat workers with dignity; provide craftsmen with a work environment of light, beauty, and safety; pay a living wage; encourage creativity and inspiration." Today, several people from the village (which has 500 inhabitants) work in the company and enjoy his €3.20 daily lunch, focused workday, investment in community art and sports projects, and investment in local renovation.

For employees, he is a dream employer, paying an estimated 20 percent higher wages and giving each craft worker a light-filled work space in which to design. His office complex, which has now expanded beyond the castle, has wall-sized windows, fountains, sculpted gardens, and visually stunning architecture. Also, he has established an Ethics Committee to "ensure that human values take first place in the life of the company."

This does not mean that he is a soft touch. "Like my great teacher Saint Benedict said: try to be rigorous and kind, a demanding teacher and a loving father." He is nicknamed "the German" because of his very structured, disciplined approach to work. The work schedule is the same for everyone: from 8 a.m. to 5:30 p.m. No one works past this hour. The employee cafeteria is a bright, modern room, with long tables that comfortably seat 12 to 16 people family style. On each table is a bowl of fruit and flowers. Waiters and waitresses bring out an appetizer course—risotto and vegetables on the day of our visit, with fresh bread and the limited-quantity Brunello-branded olive oil. A mixed salad with tomatoes is also provided. This is followed by veal and mushrooms. A light apricot pastry is served as dessert. To finish, there is rich Italian coffee. Many of the employees cluster outside after lunch before returning to work.

Cucinelli has around 1,300 employees. He also has 3,500 artisan partners. He has established a network of local suppliers—fabric houses, fabricators, designers—who are loyal to him on the basis of personal relationships and the longevity of their commercial relationships.

Today, the humanist enterprise, founded on secure relationships with both employees and suppliers, allows Cucinelli to deliver superior goods, to be a first mover in innovation, and to produce "Made in Italy" clothing for the United States, Europe, Japan, China, and Russia.

Headline: The Apostle Interview: The Customer Who Spends $100,000 a Year on Clothing

Faye is a very affluent 57-year-old who lives in Toronto and maintains a pied-à-terre on Park Avenue in Manhattan. Her husband is a private-equity investor who has done a dozen transactions over the past 20 years. Faye used to work full time on computer outsourcing projects for major companies. Today, she lives the high life: lots of travel, time spent on the family foundation, and entertaining friends at either of their homes—a beautifully landscaped mansion in Rosedale and her three-bedroom terraced apartment in New York.[3]

She can afford to spend—and really does spend—$100,000 a year on her personal apparel.

Her favorite brand is Brunello Cucinelli. "I discovered Brunello during a trip to Italy. The fabrics are soft, the styling is fashionable and modest, and the service in the stores is superb. I never have to think twice about what to wear and how I will feel when I put on one of my Brunello outfits," she says.

Faye has an extensive wardrobe in her 10-by-12-foot closet, where items are lined up by style, wearing occasion, and days of the week. The closet is not completely full, but the clothing is abundant. Her fall and winter wardrobe is 50 percent Cucinelli. No other retailer has more than two or three items in her closet. Her collection is split 30 percent casual, 30 percent wear-to-work, and 40 percent dressy evening clothing.

When we met her, her most recent purchases from Cucinelli were a dress, a coat, a pair of dressy slacks, and snow boots. The ticket was well over $5,000. "I love his clothing. I like the styling. It has a European edge. It is not matronly. And it lasts. I have things that I bought five years ago and still wear frequently," Faye told us. When items go stale for her, she gives them to friends or places them in charity used-clothing stores.

She doesn't just like the visuals. She likes the values, too. "I am very attracted to the story of how he takes care of his village, how he takes care of his workers. It is so different from the clothing companies that exploit workers in Bangladesh."

"I've never met him. But last year there was a lunch in the New York store where Cucinelli Skyped in to talk to his 'best customers,'" she enthused. "He was so impressive. He has such passion for what he does. It is not simply about making money. He is a community man, and so committed. It makes it easy to support him and them."

In her view, Cucinelli products have many technical advantages. "They use the finest-quality cashmere and silk. [There's] a feeling of luxury. [I like the] light fabrics. [They're] always appropriate." Also, she points to some emotional advantages. The clothing "gives a great deal of pleasure," she says. She "always [feels] well dressed without being indulgent."

She likes the fact that the clothing is exclusive. "Brunello is styled younger. But 28-year-olds can't afford it." But she's not altogether uncritical. "The colors are muted, which is both a positive and a negative. For anything beige, navy, even white, Brunello can't be beaten. But there is not enough bright, vibrant color."

However, the emphasis on browns, grays, and black is a conscious choice, reflecting the fact that Cucinelli products have been transformed since their inception. He used to favor vivid pastel colors. But not anymore.

Faye has recommended the brand to many friends. "I don't think the company does much advertising," she says. "So I am their advertisement. I tell my friends the salespeople are amazing, so wonderful to work with. They make you feel comfortable. They are not like other luxury stores. They are very friendly and down to earth."

Headline: Lessons from Brunello Cucinelli

Cucinelli started his company without capital and without a formal plan. For its first 12 years, the company was a specialist, concentrating on colored cashmere and creative products that were of top-notch quality. Now, the men's and women's collections offer a complete and total look. In 2013, to support the production of high-quality menswear garments, Cucinelli acquired the production assets of D'Avenza, the menswear business famous for tailored suits worn by Winston Churchill, Marcello Mastroianni, and Marlon Brando. Cucinelli considers tailored men's clothing a growth business, requiring specialized production skills and experience. He vows to innovate in this category and bring a new sensibility to the world of the office.

Today, Cucinelli's products are highly prized. The biannual collections, manufactured in limited quantities, are extremely sought after. A disproportionate percentage of the goods sells at the full retail markup. Cucinelli himself knows that he needs an increasingly global footprint in order to keep growing, as Ted Levitt's article made clear all those years ago. But he is not worried. After 35 years, he believes that his enterprise has a bright future. "We live in a world with opportunity," he says. "We are a specialist firm creating heritage products by craftsmen. Our customers appreciate the skill, the workmanship, the style, the innovation. No one has ever told me our products are too expensive. They have told me they wish they were less expensive so they could buy more. We offer the highest-quality creative product. We are a lifestyle Italian company. We make some of the world's most beautiful goods. We are entering a golden century. We are moving to a world where high quality, craftsmanship, exclusivity, and recognition are valued. We can do this in an environment of dignity, trust, and respect."

He sees his primary advantage as coming from brand identity, product quality, modern style, a "total look" product range, know-how on sourcing from Italian artisan firms, selective distribution, and geographical breadth. He vows to innovate on raw materials, sartorial skill, the expansion of sales, and the diversity of his products "as long as we remain who we are, inspire creativity, deliver luxury and elegance, satisfy the needs of our customer, and maintain exclusivity and elegance."

In what Cucinelli calls a $300 billion luxury-global-apparel industry, his company stands out as a young aristocrat with a conscience. He inspires with design, reduces the time it takes customers to look great by providing full outfits, and delivers magical in-store presentations. He has set his sights on providing all kinds of goods—from clothing to accessories to home items. He has built a company on rules of conduct and interaction that inspire loyalty and aspiration. He, personally, is the brand.

The Walt Disney Company

Walt Disney was a Missouri farm boy who moved to Hollywood in 1923 and founded Disney Studios with his brother. He was the first imagineer and the creative force behind the company until his death in 1966. Disney introduced the first synchronized cartoon short; the first licensing of the Mickey Mouse image for a pencil case; and the first full-color, full-length animated feature film, *Snow White and the Seven Dwarfs*. He developed the first amusement park that was "amusing, clean, and offered something even for Daddy." Today Disney is a company with a market capitalization of $154 billion.[4] His original business has been parlayed into a total entertainment-and-product company with a vast empire that includes television, movies, parks, consumer products, and services.

The house that Walt built was expanded by Michael Eisner, whose successor as chairman and CEO was Bob Iger, head of ABC. Iger added a new extension in the form of Pixar, Marvel, and Lucas films and brought about a global expansion, with billions of dollars invested around the world, particularly in Shanghai. We will not try to recount all the successes of this great company. What we want to focus on is how the core brand has maintained its vitality in the eyes of consumers. In a world that suffers from attention deficit disorder, Disney maintains its rank as a brand for youthfulness at all ages. It is a brand built around storytelling, smiles, shared experiences, and love. Walt planted the flag for Disneyland in 1955. Employees and investors viewed it as a bet-the-company move. Walt Disney believed that it was a sure bet. He knew it was the translation vehicle for immortality and high profitability.

Consumers are fanatical about the Disney brand. Disney does five things brilliantly. First, it pays extraordinary attention to detail—design, layout, cleanliness, training, and visual appeal. Second, it has multiple touchpoints through the media, parks, and merchandise. Third, it is engaging and has something for everyone, from toddler to grandmother. Fourth, it is a master storyteller—the narrative of fantasy helps consumers escape reality. Fifth, it is always at the forefront of experiential innovation. It polices the brand and defines the rules of behavior from the top.

No detail is left to chance. Workers at the parks are called *cast members.* They have extensive training and rehearsals. "The set," or the park, delivers the action, mood lighting, stimulating colors, and a cacophony of sound and feel. The operating teams at the Magic Kingdom are the directors and producers who measure, design, and reinvent. At the entrance to Disneyland, you see these words: "Here you leave today and enter the world of yesterday, tomorrow and fantasy." This Magic Kingdom is created around eight themed "lands": Main Street USA, Tomorrowland, Mickey's Toontown, Frontierland, Critter Country, New Orleans Square, Adventureland, and Fantasyland.[5] As we have observed, guests are excited, enraptured, and enthralled. Each themed land uses stage sets and lines of trees to keep guests in the fantasy, blocking out reality. The ubiquitous cast members are there to help guests and to answer any and all questions about the park and the characters.

Disney clones all the salient elements of a brand. It is distinctive, innovative, and emotionally compelling. It delivers a harmony of history and aspiration for consumers and "cast members." The company works as hard as any to achieve perfection at the moment of truth.

When you enter the park, you see the Magic Kingdom, with its wide streets and distinctive appearance. From the Main Street candy store, you smell the aroma of vanilla. From the popcorn vendors, you smell the popcorn. You hear the themed music from speakers hidden in the trees. And you can taste food customized for each of the eight themed lands.

For employees, learning the "Disney Way" takes three to five full days of training. That training has become so ubiquitous that the Disney Institute offers companies a training course. The "10 principles" emphasize warmth, teamwork, connections, and creativity. You can see all this in the results. Disney's theme parks in Florida, Japan, California, and France account for 92 percent of annual attendance for top parks in the world.[6] The company has eight "billion-dollar" consumer products franchises: Winnie the Pooh, Mickey Mouse, Monsters, Star Wars, Spiderman, Cars, Disney Junior, and Princess.[7]

Headline: Be an Imagineer: Create Your Corporate Narrative and Bring It to Life

There is nothing imaginary about the imagineers who bring all this to life. They are for real. They are gifted artists, engineers, designers, architects, and inventors. They think big. A full new addition to a Disney theme park starts at $1 billion. A major ride, with motion, sound, story, staging, and waiting area, can easily carry a $100 million to $200 million price tag. These installations take five years or more to invent, design, build, test, and refine.

"I am . . . awed by the tremendous creativity and commitment of the men and women who make up The Walt Disney Company. As always, our thousands of cast members and employees around the world continued to go beyond the expected to achieve the extraordinary for our consumer, our guests," wrote Iger in his 2014 letter to shareholders.[8]

Disney World is built on 25,000 acres. It contains the theme parks, 18 resort hotels with 24,000 rooms, and camping and recreational areas. The parks—Magic Kingdom, Epcot Center, Hollywood Studios, and Animal Kingdom—capture consumers. The Orlando property opened in 1971. Epcot was added in 1982. Hollywood Studios came in 1989, ESPN Wide World of Sports in 1997, and Animal Kingdom in 1998.

A Shanghai Disney resort on 1,000 prime acres is planned for 2016. Also, there is speculation that the Star Wars enterprise, bought from George Lucas for $4 billion, will result in a new major addition to the theme parks—and possibly a park of its own. Mickey Mouse and the other Disney characters will be joined by Darth Vader, Yoda, Luke Skywalker, R2-D2, Obi-Wan Kenobi, Chewbacca, and Han Solo.

This park will probably take its story line from the new Star Wars movie, *The Force Awakens*, and so will not evoke haunting memories in baby boomers. It will attempt to captivate millennial consumers with new characters like Rey. And it will certainly go beyond the simulator ride and Jedi Training Academy at the Disney parks today. Also, Disney is rumored to be planning a Star Wars–themed hotel.

The Star Wars venture is all part of the Disney approach to staying current and looking fresh. Disney makes older characters come alive in new venues and creates new characters with a multitude of licensing potential. And, of course, if the Star Wars concept does land at Disney World, it will lead to an incremental rise in the number of visitors paying for day admissions, lodging, food, and souvenirs. And that translates into an annuity valued in the billions of dollars. It makes the $4 billion price Disney paid Lucas look like a bargain.

Headline: How Consumers See the Disney Brand

In our brand-ranking survey, Disney is ranked highest on "wholesomeness," "family favorites," "always [having] something new," "clean," "exciting," "quality," and "tradition." Adult advocates say that Disney makes them happy—they feel like a great mom or dad. They feel that the experience is easy and worry-free, and fills them with a sense of youth, comfort, and calm. As one survey participant put it, Disney delivers "amazing customer service." This customer added: "They really do everything right. From the parks to the hotel rooms, from the vacation packages and other merchandise—Disney does it best."[9]

"I love everything the brand stands for and its rich history. It is everything that is good in the world," said another consumer. "It makes sure your every need is met to make your Disney experience as magical as can be. It brings back childhood memories and continues to create magical content."

"Disney means the world to me," yet another consumer said. "It is a huge part of my life. It represents love and family. Disney means family fun times that are memorable. Wholesome, rated-G entertainment that is good for the whole family with nothing embarrassing popping up. Families can bond over Disney."

The consumer Wordle for Disney consists of "family entertainment," "love," "magic," "quality," "everything childhood," "happy," and "happiness."

Headline: The Apostle Interview

When we met Hope, a beautiful, driven 23-year-old, she was about to have her life dream come true. She had grown up in what she calls a "Disney family" that would either drive or fly to Disneyland in Anaheim from their home in a San Francisco suburb every year. Now her dream come true is a Disney wedding: a marriage ceremony in the chapel, a reception at EPCOT, and a honeymoon at the theme park.[10]

Hope's home and her parents' family home each have a wall of Disney photos celebrating those trips when all of them were younger. "It's the good old days. Swimming on July 4 at the water parks, fireworks. A picture of my mom after she got the maximum 999,999 points at the Buzz Lightyear shooting range. Pictures from our first trip when I was three, eating ice cream with the Ferris wheels behind us." As a child, when Hope or her brother got a good report card, the family celebrated by going to Disneyland. She is the third generation of Disney apostles. "My mom's parents went to Disneyland when it opened in 1955," she said.

Hope said that she is "grown up now, but is still in love with Disney." She works in operations management and is on the fast track at a Chicago-based industrial-supply company that recruited Hope to that city. As part of her management training program, she has 20 people reporting to her.

She was preparing to marry Brian, her "true love and soul mate." He is two years older than she. At that point, they had dated for four years. They met at Boston College, where they took classes together, found friendship, and ultimately dated and fell in love. He is an IT consultant. They live in a one-bedroom apartment on the nineteenth floor of a Chicago high-rise with their dog, an Australian shepherd named Buzz after Buzz Lightyear, the astronaut toy character in the Disney movie *Toy Story*.

That's how central Disney is in Hope's life.

She loves Disney, and she loves her fiancé. "My fiancé is a good person—very caring and loyal. He's easy to talk to . . . a wonderful person. We have very similar personalities. Not overly social. We're good just hanging out with each other. Really good friends," she says. "And, of course, we both love Disney and Disneyland and Disney World."

Brian proposed without a hint, presenting her with "a beautiful one-carat flawless solitaire diamond from Tiffany." The proposal was made on a blustery Chicago morning in April on the waterfront with the dog as witness. Wedding plans were quickly in the works. Hope's father is a chef, and he wanted to prepare the meal himself at the family home in San Francisco. But, in unison, Hope and Brian said, "Disney World."

Hope and Brian are fitness fanatics. She weighs about 100 pounds and stands 5 feet 5 inches. She runs 5-k mini-marathons at seven-minute miles and has completed six marathons. Also, she and Brian swim and cycle. She says that Disney vacations are active—swimming, running, and 12 miles of walking around the park each day. She loves the variety of healthy, moderately priced restaurants at EPCOT. Hope and her fiancé hold annual passes for the Disney parks, which she says break even at 15 days' attendance.

She explained that a Disney wedding is easy to organize remotely. "On the company's website, you pick a venue, you name a party size, and then you get assigned a counselor." Hope and her fiancé ended up spending a day with their counselor on-site, budgeting, looking at venues, and taking a tour. She says there was no sales pressure. "He did give us buttons saying 'Just Engaged,' and we have a ton of pictures in front of the castles in the Magic Kingdom." They applied online for a Florida marriage license.

"We didn't have a set budget. We chose a relatively expensive venue, including the Wedding Pavilion for the ceremony and a reception at the Living Sea Salon in EPCOT. We will be in the Aquarium Room, which is all glass, and we will be surrounded by stingrays and turtles," Hope gushes. The tables will be named after Disney movies.

Hope and Brian invited 64 people, and they expect that 50 will come. The ceremony begins at 5 p.m. and will last a mere 30 minutes. It will be Christian themed but not religious. Then all the guests will go to the EPCOT facility in a bus. They will have cocktails at 6 p.m. and dinner from 7 to 11, with a DJ selecting their favorite music. Hope and Brian have booked three levels of hotels for the guests—all Disney properties at value, moderate, and deluxe prices. Some of the guests were quizzical about a Disney wedding. But Hope just said, "This is our dream."

Weddings are very lucrative for Disney. Hope and Brian expected the total cost of the wedding ceremony and reception to be about $30,000—including accommodations, the salon, the DJ, the minister, and all the food and drink. Then, those in the wedding group were likely to spend an additional $30,000 to $40,000 at Disney during their stay. Hope and her husband will stay at the Beach Club, their favorite hotel, which has a sand-bottom pool. The menu is beef filet, rosemary chicken, or black bean steak for vegetarians. There will be sliders, fries, and milk shakes at 10 p.m. so that the "heavy drinkers" don't leave inebriated. Hope, Brian, and her parents are going to split the costs.

"They make it really easy. It's personal, and we put our touches on everything. It's my dream come true," Hope says, not for the first time. "I'm looking forward to having children, so we can bring them to both Disney World and Disneyland. They will be the fourth generation."

Few companies have brand portfolios that look like Disney's. Few companies have nearly 100 years of heritage, history, memories, and power. But there are many lessons from Disney and many elements of the Disney magic that can be imitated.

Headline: Lessons from Disney Theme Parks: Map, Measure, Create, and Capture

Disney is now the owner of Marvel, Star Wars, ESPN, the Disney Channel, ABC, resorts around the world, and the Disney Cruise Line, and is one of the largest producers of consumer products through its extensive licensing division. Worldwide revenues were $45 billion in 2013, with net income at $6.6 billion. The theme parks provide 20 percent of operating profits. The rest of the profits are provided by the media networks, which account for two-thirds, the consumers, and the studios.[11]

We put Disney in the "experience your brand" category. For businesses of this type, *mapping* your consumers' experience is imperative. You need to fully understand their dissatisfactions, hopes, and dreams. Also, you need to understand your fulfillment record from order to delivery, your emotional touchpoints, and your failings.

Take a stopwatch, a calculator, and a blank sheet of paper to understand the underlying economics by *measuring* the impact of change. Then, you should *create* a fresh approach to provide a more flawless and seamless experience.

Finally, you should *capture* the new service approach. It sounds simple, but creating a consistent "theme park" experience in a store, restaurant, or service requires an enormous amount of clever, deep research, a real understanding of the consumer context, a ranking of alternatives, detailed design, the recruiting and training of the right people, and change management.

Is your company in the "experience your brand" category? Ask yourself these questions:

> ▶ Do you understand the entire experience from your consumer's point of view? Can you map each point of contact? Do you know the points of defection and why they occur? Do you manage each interaction for satisfaction, repurchase, and bonding?

▶ Can you identify the areas for improvement and specify the process, system, and training changes that are required?

▶ Have you quantified the financial impact of improving the experience? Can you quantify the first-, second-, and third-order impacts?

▶ Can you measure the performance consumer by consumer and segment by segment? Do you know how you stack up competitively?

▶ Does everyone in the company completely understand the vision of the consumer experience? Is success tied to hard measures, compensation, and status?

Talented, capable marketing teams often find it impossible to take a fresh approach. The level of detail and specificity surrounding the brand experience is cross-functional. There is no license to play. Operations, supply chain, HR—these functions are often stumbling blocks. The marketing function alone cannot tie the economics of change back to the core business. As a result, companies become stuck with the status quo.

Rigor across the entire organization, from the front line to the CEO, requires the broadest perspective. Nothing less than the net present value of your consumers' purchases and the purchases of all their friends and colleagues is at stake. Successful implementation transforms the organization.

Inside your customer file, are there many apostles like Hope? She will force 50 of her friends and family to experience the Disney brand. They will each have a fresh experience. At the theme park, cast members will be with them every step of the way to control and define the experience. You can be sure that in at least 25 homes in America, Hope's wedding-day photos at Disney World will be on display till death do us part.

*****

One Conclusion

When Walt Disney founded Disney Studios, he had no idea that he was creating what would become one of the most successful entertainment companies in the world. When Brunello Cucinelli acquired his first 20 kilos of cashmere, he had no idea that he would create a modern-day luxury success story. Inventors open the door. Their successors need to take the history of the brand and make it come alive every day. Great brands are a canvas that can stretch forever.

Three Takeaways

▶ **Be visually stunning in every way.** A Cucinelli store or a Disneyland set creates postcard effects in the memories of the company's core consumers. Consumers can describe in rich detail, and in color, the placement of products and their surroundings that create a fantasy. In the case of Cucinelli, it's about an aristocratic lifestyle. In the case of Disney, it's about a childhood fantasy of fun and security. If you can't create the postcard imagery that your core consumers will send to their friends, then you're not visually stunning.

2. **Your apostle consumers drive the economics.** Apostles for Cucinelli and Disney drive profits. They think about their favorite brands every day. They dream about their next experience and smile about their last one. How are you creating a lasting memory that entwines you into the lives of your apostle consumers?

3. **A good look doesn't come cheap.** Cucinelli and Disney spend more than their competitors on visual merchandising and presentation. You should, too, if you want to replicate their success. Visual merchandising becomes a core skill and a point of differentiation. Disney has its army of engineers, architects, and sound and lighting specialists—its imagineers. Cucinelli's live set at headquarters presents, for its stores and its customers, the full line as a lifestyle. How do you bring your brand to life? How do you tell your story in rich, complete detail?

SOME KEY ACTION POINTS

1. Design your presentation with an unlimited budget.
2. Create breathtaking visuals and carry them from the lowest product to the top end.
3. People will pay for art and memory.
4. Details matter.
5. Replicate around the world for amortization advantage.

CHAPTER FIVE

Transform Your Employees into Passionate Disciples (Because Love Is Truly Infectious)

THE CHAPTER IN A BOX

The Main Point

A really motivated front line engages customers and tells your brand story. Its members don't repeat the story in a monotone. They tell stories in Technicolor. They're energizing every day. And they are your greatest resource for generating new apostles. They create a cultural advantage. You can see it in the economics of the business: higher repeat purchases; higher realization every day; sales without promotion. Loyalty in the ranks creates loyalty in the user. It makes the competition easy pickings. Your rivals won't know what hit them, and they'll have no way to respond. Some companies think an inspired front line is the result of an accident, the best behavior by a few extreme natural "salesmen." They are wrong—and these two case studies show just how wrong they are.

Why These Stories for This Chapter

There may be a 40-year age gap between Zappos and Four Seasons, and they may target totally different consumers, but they have one thing in common: they represent best-in-class customer service.

Chapter Overview

You and your company may provide the best products or services in your industry. But if consumers are not spreading the word in a big way, your products or services are doomed to a mediocre reception at best.

Sure, advertising generally helps. But the return on advertising can be spotty; besides, advertisements portray every business in a positive way. And consumers know that, so they look upon advertising with a jaundiced eye.

So what's the key to building a brand that is a cut above *and* that consumers begin to hear about and then embrace?

Headline: Start with Your Employees

Your employees can, and *must*, become your true disciples. They spread your words; they make the all-important connection with consumers; their genuine belief in the "good" that you offer becomes your trademark and your trust mark.

Treat your employees with extreme care; help them come fully alive with your customers. Most important, listen carefully to their words every time they mention a concern or an issue. Their frontline feedback is essential to your brand. Suggestions from the selling floor can become a source of advantage and intelligence. If you are quick to respond to an issue, you eliminate a problem. If you are quick to respond to an opportunity, a request, or a need for additional product, you grow the top line.

What's your ultimate goal? To build a staff of employees who not only believe in your product as much as you do, but who are so ardent about it that their positive vibes and good acts will be noticed by your customers. Once they are empowered, your employees *and* your customers will take care of getting the word out.

In this chapter, we provide two case studies demonstrating the ability of passionate employees to stimulate loyalty, repurchase intent, advocacy, and profit. If you follow their lessons, you too can achieve a disproportionate share of your consumer's spending and drive higher profitability.

Best of all, your company will be seen by and will attract a growing and loyal customer fan base—customers who will adore your brand for life and who will go out and spread the word about how wonderful your company is to all their friends and colleagues.

The two companies profiled in this chapter are Four Seasons, the luxury hotel chain, and Zappos, the online shoe and clothing retailer. They both demonstrate the ability of passionate employees to connect with consumers on an emotional level. This doesn't happen by accident; it's all part of a deliberate and conscious plan by management to energize the company's employees to a higher level of commitment.

You will learn how the leadership drives staff recruitment, nurturing, engagement, enablement, and selfless service, and how this all pays off in tremendous branding. Yes, both companies do pay their employees significantly more than many of their competitors, but more money is not the driving force. In the end, their secret involves forging and fostering the right working environment. It's about belonging, tribal connection, and the nurturing of emotional ties. And when this is done correctly, the consummate prize is a workforce made up of employees who care deeply about the company, and customers who bit by bit come to be delighted by the brand—and, best of all, can't wait to tell others about it.

Zappos

Tony Hsieh was born on December 12, 1973, the son of Taiwanese immigrants. He grew up in the Bay Area of San

Francisco. His first real job was at Oracle (where he lasted just five months). He is a computer scientist with a Harvard degree. He is also the noted developer of the Las Vegas Downtown Project and the author of *Delivering Happiness*, which was ranked number one on the *New York Times* bestseller list for 27 weeks.[1]

His company is Zappos.com, Inc., an online retailer with a difference. Most online retailers try to minimize the amount of time that their sales staff spends talking to customers. They try to push all contact to e-mail and their website. That's because it's costly to have salespeople talk to consumers: the fully loaded cost of a U.S.-based call-center staff amounts to as much as 60 cents a minute on the phone. But Zappos—the name is a play on *zapatos*, the Spanish word for shoes—runs a phone-click-chat service that is the best in the online business. Its phone number is very prominent on its website and on every package. The sales staff is actively encouraged to talk for as long as the customer wants. In fact, the firm's 600-strong customer-service department tracks the length of phone calls with customers and celebrates the longest calls. The objective is to make an emotional connection on every call and thereby build loyalty and attachment.

Zappos makes its employees take pride in knowing how difficult it is to get a job there. This leads to commitment and to getting the job done right. There is no script, just natural conversation and engagement. This way, an emotional connection is created. The objective is that every customer is satisfied, feels that he has been listened to, and raves about Zappos later. It helps that each rep is empowered to do virtually anything necessary to satisfy the customer—not only to describe product benefits and suggest additional items based on prior purchase information, but also to warn about inappropriate products and offer substitutions, expedited shipment, and next-day replacement.

During our visit at lunch in the company cafeteria, a customer service rep who had joined Zappos five years ago told us about how she had given away $200 shoes to a customer who complained that the first pair was shipped worn. "I told her, 'That was a mistake.' I apologized three times. We talked about how to make it right. We agreed that she could keep the shoes or give them to charity, and that I would have a new pair in her hands tomorrow morning. Period. No obligation. Just an apology from us."

"We love our customers," the 28-year-old said over a lunch of BBQ chicken and corn salsa. "We aim to make a personal connection with everyone that calls. When someone calls, my job is for them to say 'Wow' afterwards."

This giving away "free product" to make something right is not an isolated story. It is programmatic. Another Zappos staffer, who used to work in customer service and now provides guided tours around the firm's newly refurbished headquarters in Las Vegas, said: "I once was on a call with a customer for four hours. The customer was from the same area of Pennsylvania as me. It creates conversation. We had not done a good job getting her a pair of riding boots for an event. I ended up telling her to keep the first pair of boots we sent. And then I sent her another pair overnight. And I told her it is all free. Four-hundred-dollar boots. Free. She is our customer for life. Periodically I check up on her orders. It's all about creating a PEC—a personal emotional connection."

Headline: Personal Emotional Connection

The PEC is a very powerful approach. Enthused by their one-on-one experience with a rep, customers commonly tell their friends why they too should shop at Zappos. The reps have created great names for themselves. They are called Customer Loyalty Ambassadors, and they think of themselves as Jedi Masters from *Star Wars*. By our calculation, each happy Zappos customer generates eight times the value of her own purchases through testimonials to friends.

The training in PEC takes two months. It is true on-the-job training. New recruits listen to and learn from experienced employees. After a few days, they are put into the "cockpit" with dual headsets. Their mentor is with them on every call, and they do a play-by-play review of the interaction. They learn the dos and don'ts, and they develop their own style. At the end of eight weeks of trial, they are offered either a full-time position or a one-time payment to quit.[2] It's not a job for everyone, but trainees have a successful graduation rate of 80 percent.

Headline: Happy Employees Create Happy Customers, and Fun at Work Makes the Difference in Attitude and Morale

People spend up to half their waking hours working and thinking about working. If you make their work fun, you will earn their loyalty. Laughter at work is good.

When we took the tour at the remodeled Zappos headquarters in Las Vegas, we experienced workplace vibrancy, harmony, and collaboration. The headquarters consist of the former City Hall and police station, located in the heart of a once-seedy part of downtown Las Vegas. The building is shaped like a round starship with a tower rising from one end. It has been given a painstaking 18-month renovation to build a totally open environment, with areas to play, eat, rest, work, and accidentally connect with coworkers and suppliers. As we walked into the center courtyard—the one and only entrance into the building—loud music from the score of the Broadway hit *Grease* came alive. It's like a college campus, with students aiming their big dorm speakers onto the college green. The energy is contagious, and the beat of the music sets the pace.

When you enter the main lobby, security guards dressed in neon yellow shirts and black pants hold the doors open for you. They smile as they let you in. The three receptionists— twentysomethings wearing tie-dyed T-shirts and sporting streaked hair—give you a very warm greeting and offer you a free drink: water, Mountain Dew, Red Bull, or Muscle Milk. You are then directed into a small room to watch a four-minute video on the company. After the movie, the lively, slightly wacky tour guides (they are called *culture guides*)—who are also dressed in bright neon T-shirts and colorful shoes—fire off questions to the audience. "What year did Amazon and Zappos get hitched, married?" they ask simultaneously in high-pitched excited voices. The first person to say "2009," when Amazon bought Zappos for $1.2 billion, gets a set of Zappos shot glasses.[3]

And then you are whisked off in small groups to tour the premises. You meet the customer loyalty reps who take thousands of calls every day. You see the brilliant, vibrant pop art—paintings of Marilyn Monroe, Lucille Ball, Leonardo DiCaprio, and George Clooney, plus imaginative fun sculpture, as well as casual seating areas with art. You see posters celebrating a diverse range of company benefits, including full free healthcare, free prescriptions, the fitness center, free healthy food options, the library, mothers' nursing rooms, employee discounts, and a program where every month, each associate can nominate a different coworker to receive a $50 gift certificate. There is an in-house concierge, a mobile beauty shop, and a car wash service. There is a Ping-Pong room, a wall of hammocks for rest, and a conference room filled with rolling balls for fun.

As you enter the office areas, you see that off to the left is a corridor with a row of chairs, desks, and PCs. Employees call this "Monkey Row." These are the open-air offices for the CEO, the vice president of finance, and the vice president of merchandising, as well as their assistants. The only people with closed-door offices are the on-staff company life coach and Zappos lawyers.

Everyone seems to be smiling.

Our guide on the tour is a 5-foot 5-inch former Las Vegas hotel worker. He's been at Zappos for five years and, like many employees, started on the customer service line. He is friendly, joking, and warm. He's about 50 years old and has had many jobs before Zappos. "None have been the total delight that I have here," he says. "I love working here. I can't wait to get here. I love what I do."

His comments are echoed in the firm's Culture Book, which is published every year. It looks a lot like a college yearbook, with signed commentary from nearly all the staff members on what they love about Zappos. It has 244 pages with photos, inspiring comments, and connecting words.

Here are a few excerpts:

- ▶ "Friends, family, and fun. The three Fs that make my life awesome."
- ▶ "Zappos means having an extended family that always has your back. Doing for others while expecting nothing in return."

- ▶ "For the first time in my life, I can honestly say I love my job!"
- ▶ "Oh Zappos, how I heart thee! Let me count the ways: 1. You treasure my uniqueness; 2. You are interested in my talents; 3. You want to make a difference; 4. You help me grow as a person and an employee; 5. Most important, you legitimately care about me."[4]

Headline: Creating a Corporate Utopia with Family Core Values

Zappos is a bubbly place like no other we have ever visited. It can be zany and amazing. Given this happy culture, it is not surprising that many employees hounded the company for employment. It has become a millennial refuge: most workers are in their twenties and thirties. The workforce is roughly 60 percent female.[5] Team spirit is downright bouncy. Typical language in the office is alliterative, hip, and offbeat.

But, for all this, Zappos is a serious business, selling shoes, accessories, and clothing with daily sales as high as $28 million. It contributes more than $1 billion a year to Amazon revenues. For consumers, its value proposition starts with the enormous range of products, the depth of the inventory, next-day delivery, free returns within 365 days of purchase, and a phone call service that is the best in the business by far.

The 1,600 Las Vegas employees are essential to its success. This is why Zappos treats them so well, and why getting a job at Zappos is harder than getting into Harvard. Zappos looks for people with the right fit, the right personality, and the right value compass. Each recruit goes through a painstaking interview process. They say that one in a hundred gets hired. It's like The Container Store's principle of one worker equals three—but with a twist. The recruits have to fit in socially, intellectually, and emotionally. They have to be ready for their new family. Cultural fit is the key hurdle.

Zappos says it is all about people. The company's recruiting materials state: "You're not just a number—you're a real person with a real personality and real skills." Zappos promises not to let anyone fall into a recruiting black hole and to give each applicant a chance to interact, ask questions, and understand what roles are available. It asks potential employees to join up as Zappos Insiders. Insiders hear about openings, can chat with Zappos "ambassadors" (current employees), and have access to online events.

Recruits are asked to send a video cover letter and to write something to the company along the lines of, "Be adventurous, creative, and open-minded." This is an actual assignment, aimed at identifying applicants who conduct themselves in the desired way and who are independent thinkers. Recruiters use social media, including Twitter, Facebook, Instagram, and Pinterest. Zappos will be one of the early users of Google Handouts, where potential employees can interact with recruiters and employees. Access to named specific individuals in specific job functions is offered; recruits are given details of that person's interests and hobbies.

For recruits who make it to campus, the ultimate decision to offer someone a job is a group decision. Almost all recruits are picked up at the Las Vegas airport by the company van. The driver is often asked, "Yes or no?" on the recruits. Zappos wants employees who treat all coworkers with respect. If the van driver says, "Not for us," the recruit will not receive an offer.

The reasons to join Zappos are many. As the firm's recruiting literature puts it: "Fun, extreme perks, flextime, inclusion, career development, Green DNA, corporate responsibility, and the good jobs." According to Zappos, one day 30 percent of all retail transactions in the United States will be online, people will buy from the company with the best service and the best selection, and "Zappos.com will be that online store."[6]

The motto inside Zappos is, "Where culture thrives, passion follows." The driving force behind this approach, and its success, is Tony Hsieh, the chief executive. He is a former whiz kid with drive, energy, charisma, and deeply held principles about corporate culture as the foundation for the brand. He is soft-spoken, but when he speaks, everyone hangs on his every word. This is because he is widely recognized as the person who created the core values, the sense of empowerment, the sense of community, and—frankly—the weirdness. An intense intellectual, he has gobbled up most of what has been written on psychology, worker joy, and consumer connection. He has devised his own unique company cocktail.

He became a computer programmer in his early teens and majored in computer science at Harvard. Upon graduation, he took a job with Oracle, which lasted just five months. He then started an imaginative, original online advertising company; he ran it until he was "not happy" and was able to sell it to Microsoft for $265 million.[7] Still only 24 years old at the time, he started to dabble in his own venture fund.

That's when he was introduced to Zappos.

Founded in 1999, at the top of the original dot-com bubble, Zappos was a struggling e-retailer when Hsieh joined the company as an investor and advisor (he became CEO in 2000). He set about rebuilding the company from the outside in, solving problems for the consumer and then engineering the company to break all the compromises in shoe purchases and satisfaction. He aimed to deliver any shoe for any occasion in every size the next day, with free returns.

He is renowned for his focus on creating happy employees to create happy consumers. He rattles off the things that customers really value—and he drills them into his employees:

- ▶ Customers value convenience and saving time, even over saving a few dollars.
- ▶ Customers value "curation," even above overwhelming selection (a paradox of choice).
- ▶ Customers value customer experience and customer service, even over saving a few dollars.
- ▶ Customers value simplicity over too many choices.
- ▶ Customers value ease of use and fewer steps over complicated customization.
- ▶ Customers value a box-opening *wow* experience over saving a few dollars.

Zappos goes through all this extensive screening of employees because, deep down, what the company is really looking for is employees who will become passionate cheerleaders for the Zappos brand. It is not interested in just finding smart workers. It wants to find only those individuals who will answer customer calls cheerfully and actively spread the good word about the company. This is the key to how Zappos builds its brand.

After establishing a real blueprint for what kind of employees Zappos wanted to hire, Hsieh put some very smart programs into place. First, he moved the Zappos distribution facility to Kentucky—a place with lower labor costs—and created a centralized inventory, a modern inventory-control system, and a proprietary system for distribution; the facility was also in close proximity to UPS, the global logistics firm. The idea was that this would ensure that Zappos could deliver on the promise of fast delivery. Second, he moved the corporate headquarters from San Francisco, with its high-cost labor and high expense, to Las Vegas, which was more affordable. Third, he invented a place where employees could be happy every day, where they could work with people whom they liked and who shared a similar passion for Zappos.

The heart of Hsieh's approach is something that he calls the *Zappos Family Core Values*. This makes him unusual. Years ago, he worked for a conventional "big" company and witnessed the CEO telling a 1,000-person sales force, "We are not a family. We are a team. You need to earn your place on the team every season." He warned, "If you do not perform, you will be cut." "Back then," Hsieh says, "we thought, 'Does this threatening message really resonate, or does it cause the sales team members with options to go to another company?'"

Hsieh's use of the word *family* is intentional. He is hiring people for the long term and taking responsibility for their mental and physical health, well-being, care, and future. "When we started, we didn't know what we were doing. We had never sold shoes. We never ran a call center. We never managed a warehouse. But not knowing how other people did things was an advantage," Hsieh said. "We did what we thought was the right thing. It evolved over time. We were committed first to employee happiness. We were committed to the Golden Rule."

Hsieh believes in a very supportive model of employee engagement. In his words, there are 10 key values:[8]

1. Deliver *wow* through service.
2. Embrace and drive change.
3. Create fun and a little weirdness.

4. Be adventurous, creative, and open-minded.
5. Pursue growth and learning.
6. Build open and honest relationships with communication.
7. Build a positive team and family spirit.
8. Do more with less.
9. Be passionate and determined.
10. Be humble.

These 10 values are quoted every day in conversations around the office. At the end of their training, employees need to know the values by heart and be able to explain them to colleagues. They can add their own words, explanations, and interpretation—but they must be able to repeat the core messages.

By drilling these values into its employees, Zappos knows that those employees are now better positioned and prepared to "spread the gospel" about the company and about how employees come first, and also that customers are to be treated so well that they will feel only goodwill toward the company's name and brand.

In short, the attitude is one of "Hey, I can buy shoes anywhere, but when I go and shop at Zappos, I know I'm going to be treated in a very special way." That's the key to the company's branding.

Headline: Transparency Is Not Always Risky for Your Business

Competitors can gain full access to the Zappos way of doing business. While we were touring the headquarters in Las Vegas, there were 10 businesspeople from a competitor in Australia who were also taking the tour. Hsieh believes that culture is the big strategic competitive advantage that cannot be easily copied. That's the real secret, and Hsieh and his management team have worked relentlessly to develop that culture, which pays off in his brand.

He tries to lead the way in transparency.

As if to prove the point, he let us peruse his personal e-mail over a period of several months. It's clear that he gets by on very little sleep—as little as three hours each night. His e-mails are about strategy, customer service, and details on improving the business, including inventory investment. In one e-mail, he asks for greater focus on the 20 percent of customers who create 80 percent of orders and the 20 percent of the 1,000 vendors who create 80 percent of the volume. He is never satisfied with what he has achieved. This is the company's trademark. Deliver as promised. Package perfectly. Make good on the promise. Be better than any other shoe retailer. Build the brand constantly.

Headline: Why a Call with a Customer Can Lead to Repeat Business and Long-Term Growth

"Speak to customers in a way that resonates with their mind-set, values, and language." Hsieh's injunction to his staff is clear. He knows that only 4 to 5 percent of customers will actually call. But he firmly believes that a successful call will lead to recommendations and more business—and the vast bulk of the business comes from repeat customers.

Shoes are a pathology for some shoppers. Our research suggests that consumers either love them and amass a collection or just buy them as a necessity. A real shoe lover can buy as many as two pairs a month—and keeps on accumulating them. So a call to Zappos is a real chance to connect and to learn from an expert in the shoe and apparel business about the latest trends, the most up-to-date fashion news, products the company has started to carry, fit, form, and function.

One repeat customer is Lauren, a 26-year-old Zappos apostle. She is a lawyer in a midsize firm, makes more than $100,000 per year, and lives in a very affluent part of Chicago. She is a striking woman—5 feet 11 inches tall, fit, and clean-cut, with all-American good looks. She played basketball, volleyball, and tennis in high school. She still plays sports most days. No one would know that in her closet are more than 200 pairs of shoes—sandals, wedges, flats, sneakers, gym shoes, running shoes, boots, flip-flops, work shoes, going-out casual shoes, going-out dancing shoes, and expensive shoes for that big night on the town. When she shops on Zappos, she uses all the online shopping filters for size, width, occasion, color, heel height, platform height, brand, price, materials, patterns, and product accents. The site lets her look only at products that the company has in stock and that are ready to ship. It makes decision making fast and focused. For a time-squeezed professional, it provides an economy of effort that she craves.

"Zappos is an integral part of my weekday evenings spent on the couch, with my laptop in front of me and the TV in the background," Lauren explains. "That's my way to laze around and recover from a tiring day." Although she is in a committed serious relationship, she does her shoe shopping "in the closet," away from her boyfriend's eyes.

She says Zappos is "stylish, cool, yet practical with a sense of humor." She continues: "If I have to personify Zappos, I would imagine a guy. Mr. Zappos is stylish yet practical, wearing dark denim jeans, slim fit but not suctioning his legs; brown loafers, not suede; a button-down shirt; and a blazer. He has a sense of style and a kind personality."

This does not fully describe Hsieh. In fact, he himself is not very interested in shoes. For him, shoes are the vehicle to create a business where people can work happily and earn good incomes.

Lauren estimates that the total value of her Zappos collection is $7,500. Although she is a multichannel buyer—department stores, specialty shoe stores, monobrand shoe stores, and fashion-brand shoe departments—Zappos has a 40 percent share of her shoe budget. And this share is growing.

But Lauren's value to Zappos isn't just in what she spends. It's also in what she does to influence others to spend at Zappos. "I taught my friends that Zappos exists, since not too many people my age know of it," she says. "Their shoe collections have expanded after spending time with me."

And this is exactly the payoff that Zappos is looking for. Not only does Lauren represent a hooked customer for life, but she also tells her friends about Zappos. You can't do better than that. She's become a disciple thanks to Zappos employees. She has become a walking endorsement for the Zappos brand.[9]

Headline: The Economics of the Business Have to Work

Engaging customers like Lauren is critical to the success of Zappos. It is dependent for new online visitors on the "shoe" conversations that take place. It does not spend very much on advertising. Instead, it relies on word-of-mouth messaging to generate referrals and testimonials, and that happens only as a result of the total emphasis not only on finding the right employees, but also on making sure that they are well trained in how to connect with their customers. This is no accident.

Zappos call staffers are important for another reason, too. Selling shoes is normally a skinny-margin business. The original markup is 100 percent, but most products are sold at sale prices, with a net margin of 20 percent and an operating margin in the low single digits. Zappos, however, sells most of its products at the full retail price. It doesn't play the sale game. Even on Cyber Monday during the Christmas holiday season, when most online retailers drop their prices, Zappos resists the pressure to put up "sale" signs. This is a very risky strategy in the shoe category. However, receiving the full margin allows the firm to pay for massive central inventory, high-touch service, overnight delivery, and free returns. In effect, Zappos is asking, "Can we earn a price premium for premium service?" This strategy sets Zappos apart from most online retailers, with their flash sales, almost daily promotions, and buy-one-get-one-free programs. So far, the signs are that while growth has slowed, profits have increased.

Headline: The Lessons of Zappos

Hsieh is a deep thinker. When asked where Zappos will be in five years, he leaned back in his chair and visibly sighed. We guessed that this was a sigh combining pride, anxiety, and a continuous search for a better way. There were at least 30 seconds of silence in the room. "I can tell you where we will be in a year. I can tell you what we will aim to be in 10 years. In a year, we will have many more passionate customers. In 10 years, we will have expanded dramatically—more categories driven where our customers want us to go," he said, keeping the mystery of the medium-term future to himself.

Going forward, Hsieh says that his number one priority is company culture. "A company's brand and a company's culture are two sides of one coin." He has created a customer service orientation that is extendable into a wide variety of businesses. This includes extensions as broad and as far as airlines and hotels. "Our brand is a platform that makes everything possible. Whatever we do, we will bring innovation from outside the industry."

He recognizes the importance of organizational tension to propel the company forward. Such tension comes from contrasting the way things are today with the way they could be. He is intent on creating what he calls "a complex adaptive system" that resolves organizational tension and creates the freedom to recognize each person's individual gifts.

If there is a mystery about the medium term, there is no mystery about Zappos' past success. It ranks employees first, customers next, and profits last. Even its owner, Amazon—which is a very different company, one that ranks growth first, category position second, and competitive advantage third—is starting to learn from Zappos.

Hsieh knows that unhappy employees can be a destabilizing force. Amazon now offers the same $2,000 posttraining resignation bonus as Zappos. This is all part of Zappos' search for totally committed and passionate employees who buy into the brand.

Hsieh's deal with Amazon, made at the bottom of the Great Recession, has left Zappos ring-fenced and largely independent from Amazon. The deal was shrewd from Hsieh's perspective, because Amazon's shares have appreciated enormously during the five-year period. In the last year, some elements of integration have occurred. Zappos has migrated distribution to Amazon-managed facilities and is now transitioning the Zappos website to Amazon technology. It is a much larger and more sophisticated system and permits a greater analytical capability, including suggested sales, product adjacencies, easier navigation, detailed product information, and customer references.

Four Seasons

Isadore Sharp was born on October 8, 1931, to Polish immigrants.[10] His first job was as a construction worker for his father. He is an architect by training. He is married to his high school sweetheart. He is an author, a noted philanthropist, and the founder of Four Seasons.[11]

On the day after Christmas 2004, the Four Seasons Resort in the Maldives was quiet. Around 6 a.m., tremors were felt from an earthquake nearly 1,000 miles away. The Sumatra quake was the longest quake ever recorded and released energy equal to that of a 100-gigaton bomb. It was measured at 9.1 on the Richter scale, high enough to cause total destruction and violent, permanent changes in the topography. Three hours later, a tsunami with a series of 14-foot waves began to ravage the island.[12]

According to one guest: "As wave after wave smashed against the resort, we watched, helpless, as in the distance we could see many of the 50 water bungalows that faced the reef disintegrating, instantly turning to matchwood as the waves pounded them, dumping guests, four-poster beds, TVs, and air conditioning into water so rough it was like a washing machine gone mad."

Another said, "I got outside and saw a wall of water, boiling, frothing, angry as hell, bearing straight down at us. There was a strange mist that looked like thick fog that blocked out the sun. I stopped breathing and tried to decide where to run. But where could I run, when there were no double-story buildings and we were just one meter above sea level, and there was deep water on all sides?"[13]

This terror continued for two hours. One guest stated, "It looked like *Titanic, Lost, Lord of the Flies*, and *Survivor* all rolled into one." Miraculously, no one at the resort died—but the devastation was widespread. The full force of the tsunami crushed palm trees, destroyed hotel rooms, and swept guests into the sea. During the day that followed, all 400 staff members at the hotel put their lives on the line for the 200 guests. They brought them to safety, gave them scarce supplies, and provided emergency medical care to guests who had been cut or had suffered broken bones and other injuries. That evening, all the guests were helped to what was left of the restaurant, where they huddled together until sunrise. The Four Seasons staff went above and beyond to ensure the safety and comfort of guests. Witnesses say that not a single staff member left the property for three days.[14]

Jet Li, the Chinese-born Hollywood actor, was staying at the resort. He was fulsome in his praise. In his blog, he wrote: "Throughout the initial chaos and the entire disaster, the Four Seasons staff demonstrated selfless bravery and compassion, the finest human qualities, in assisting us and the other hotel guests, even though their own family members were likely endangered."[15]

We first heard the story from the hotel manager of the Maldives resort. "This is what we do," she said simply. "We serve our guests." Isadore Sharp expanded on this point. "When the tsunami hit our hotel in the Maldives, our employees risked their lives for the guests. No one told them to do it. They each did it on their own. No amount of money can generate that response. There was an outpouring of gratitude from many, many guests. One wrote, and I quote, 'Let me stress that your group's strength rests on rock, made up of the local employees who, while having been selected for doing their job well, have shown in a time of utmost crisis a level of dedication that no training and no amount of money can ever generate.'"

Headline: Automatic Response in a Crisis Does Not Happen by Accident

Just how do you create a company where the employees are so passionate that they will go the extra mile and, in the process, convert customers into loyal advocates? How do you create a company where the line between self-interest and company interest is blurred? How do you motivate from the front line back?

As the word about the dedicated Four Seasons employees began to spread, one could see how the Four Seasons brand continues to shine and stand out. Loyal customers were not surprised, and potential hotel guests were amazed, asking, "Wow, can you imagine a hotel staff that would put their guests first, even in the face of a dangerous tsunami?"

Headline: Invent a New Segment—Four Seasons Created Luxury That Was Aspirational, Inviting, and Centered on Service

Isadore Sharp did not open his hotel with a grand master plan. He did not forecast that he would go from one hotel to nearly 100 and create billions of dollars in value. He was a humble home builder when he opened the Four Seasons Motor Inn in Toronto in 1961. In fact, he came very close to calling the property the Thunderbird Inn.[16] At the last minute, he agreed with a coworker that Four Seasons would be a better name. But what did Sharp know at the time? He was working for his father's construction company, Max Sharp & Son, digging ditches, laying bricks, and building walls. He had every intention of building more homes, apartments, and office structures. But he was also a dreamer. And he dreamed of a hotel that took care of its guests' every wish.

"When you are young, you have the courage to try things," he said, sitting in the living room of his palatial modern home overlooking a golf course in Toronto. "You can think of all the possibilities. When you get older, you think more rationally and temper the possibilities with the probabilities. But it was my night job. I was a builder by day."

Now 83 years old, Sharp is still handsome and witty. He speaks with force and passionate memory. The hotel he dreamed of was "not for dukes or duchesses but for people who wanted to be treated with respect, kindness, genuine hospitality." To achieve this, he realized that he needed hotel workers who were committed to delivering the very highest-quality service and hotel managers who would recruit and nurture the very best talent.

Today, some customers remember the grandeur of the hotels themselves. Oprah Winfrey once said, "The Four Seasons bed is the only bed better than my own." It is certainly a hallmark of Four Seasons hotels that they have architectural imagination and beauty, wonderful floral arrangements, distinctive and beautiful touches, clever room design, elaborate bathrooms, spas, restaurants, and reception areas.

But from the beginning, Sharp knew that the most important thing is a hotel's staff—including the doormen, maids, waiters, and dishwashers. Ultimately, he believed, "They are the real product. They are the differentiator."

What he discovered along the way was that a major result of having superb and loyal employees was that his customers noticed. Not only did they become repeat customers, but they also began to become apostles for the hotel chain. In short, they told their friends.

The service culture of Four Seasons has become the model for other companies. According to Sharp, in the book *The Apple Experience*, "Steve Jobs has acknowledged that the Apple Store was inspired by the Four Seasons." Its executives modeled its now-famous Genius Bar on the hotel group's concierge desks, where no guest question is inappropriate, and where no request for help is met with anything other than earnest attention. Also, many luxury competitors have modeled themselves on Four Seasons—for instance, Ritz-Carlton, St. Regis, Peninsula, and others.

Again, it's all about building the brand.

Headline: Use a Common Phrase as the Point of Engagement and the Decision Point on What the Right Answer Is—The Golden Rule

From the beginning, Sharp had big ambitions, although he had no idea that his vague premise concerning the highest-quality hotel would translate into a global institution, a synonym for luxury. "We wanted to be the best in midsize hotels up to 250 rooms," he explained. "We had it in our mission statement to be the best. We still have it written down. But we did not have a master plan. What we had was a passion to take care of people and to apply the Golden Rule."

He continued: "The Golden Rule is, 'Do unto others as you would have them do unto you.' That very simple statement is the foundation upon which the company built its core values. It is a universal belief system. It is the first line of human rights. It is reproduced in every religion. It is a way of life. My parents were immigrants. They spoke Polish and Yiddish. But it was the way they lived their lives."

But what did this mean in practice? As Sharp said: "How should our people behave?" His answer was simple. "They should be polite, thoughtful, and caring. It's not what you say—it's what you do."

Headline: Screen, Train, and Enable Your Team

Sharp set the bar high for workers at a Four Seasons hotel. But he had no doubt that he could find the right people. "The world is filled with people who are good in their hearts. We believed there was an unlimited supply of people who are genuine, caring, and service oriented." His confidence was well founded. In 1992, when the Four Seasons New York opened, there were 30,000 applicants for 400 jobs.[17] This distinctive hotel—designed largely by I. M. Pei, a Chinese-born American architect—is 46 stories high, has 400 rooms, and boasts a penthouse suite with a rack rate of $40,000 per night.[18]

But to get a job at the Four Seasons, applicants need to make it through five interviews. It is a rigorous, highly selective procedure, Sharp said. Each interviewer is looking at a specific angle. The HR director assesses willingness to work. The division head tests specific skills. The department head is looking for cultural fit. The resort manager assesses growth potential. The general manager, who meets with every prospective employee, is charged with looking for the potential to perform at another property. The company states that it receives 20 applications for every job.

Sharp says that the company is looking for recruits who are all of the following:

▶ Intuitive
▶ Dedicated

- ▶ Considerate
- ▶ Attentive to detail
- ▶ Creative
- ▶ High communicators
- ▶ Possessed with the ability to see situations from the guest's point of view

"It's all about the guest experience," he said. "We want people who care, people who will go the extra mile."

Recruits are asked to describe themselves, their experience, and their sense of the role at the Four Seasons, and to problem-solve potential guest service situations. They are also asked to provide examples of past experiences in which their true personalities can be demonstrated. Typical questions include: "Would you serve a guest a burned croissant?" "How do you stay healthy?" "What are your top weaknesses?"

The ones who make it to hiring receive extensive training and enculturation.

The result is an annual turnover rate of 11 percent, substantially below the hotel industry norm of 27 percent.[19] In the case of the New York hotel, the result is a property that holds a perennial spot on the AAA Five Diamond Award and Condé Nast Traveler Gold List.

Employees at the Four Seasons are not scripted. They are trained to be friendly and conversational and to share things about themselves. As Sharp explained: "We aim to nurture the full potential of every employee." All employees go through a three-month on-the-job training program. At a Four Seasons hotel, the service culture requires a groomed appearance; a welcoming approach, with smiles, eye contact, and an attentive voice; and a deep knowledge of the hotel. The goal is demonstrable care for the most discriminating guests. This code applies to everyone, from the general manager to the dishwasher. "When people believe they have a role to play, they play it. For a dishwasher, it is important that every piece of cutlery is perfectly clean and that no glass has cracks. They need to see that they prevent the guests from cutting their lips." Each employee has a mentor on-site. Employees start by shadowing an employee who is in their target job. They learn by doing.

At daily department meetings, they hear about issues, opportunities, and action plans. Guests are identified for special needs and treatment. You learn through imitation.

At one Asian Four Seasons property, a 30-year-old worker named Tam told us that Four Seasons changed his life. "I had nothing when I came to work here," said the slender, charming waiter. "Four Seasons transformed my life. I am married now. Next month, my wife and I are going to Hawaii. I was employee of the month, and my reward is an all-expenses-paid week as a guest on the Big Island. I will get to enjoy what you enjoy. I never dreamed that would be possible in my life."

Sharp said that hotel managers play a key role in the development of the staff. They are meant to be "communicators, not commanders; coaches, not cops." He extols the virtues of an approach called *proximity management.* With this approach, the general manager meets with every employee group on a regular and informal basis. The purpose is to fix any problems immediately. The company defines a problem as a recurrent area of guest complaint (for example, speed of check-in, quality of room-service delivered food, beverage needs, or services). "Senior managers who can't walk the talk are winnowed out," said Sharp.

But all hotel workers who deliver at the high standard are amply rewarded with a generous benefits package. Four Seasons pays in the top quartile. It's "a magic ratio that attracts the right people," revealed Sharp. Also, employees get pensions and dental and health insurance, as well as the privilege of being able to stay with their immediate family at any Four Seasons hotel worldwide for free, as Tam discovered. There's another bonus too: cash rewards for years of service. This is something that is paid out frequently, a reflection of the loyalty that Four Seasons engenders among its employees.

In 2014, Sharp attended the thirty-fifth anniversary of the Four Seasons hotel in Washington, DC. Its fortunes were transformed when Ronald and Nancy Reagan adopted it as their favorite in-town location, and prosperity was born.

Sharp revealed that this came about because Reagan, when he was a candidate for the presidency, was planning a major Washington fund-raiser. Reagan's chief fund-raiser asked the

Four Seasons for a donation. Instead of a contribution, Four Seasons graciously offered the former governor a complimentary suite whenever he was staying in Washington. And more important, he was treated to a full dose of Four Seasons hospitality from the hotel's staff.

Within a couple of weeks, Reagan had held a three-night fund-raiser at the hotel. Then business leaders and other contributors filled the hotel and got their first taste of the Washington Four Seasons. They were all hooked. From that day onward, the hotel was Nancy Reagan's favorite Washington property, and the hotel brand continued to spread.

The hotel attracted great loyalty from its staff. "There were people who had been at the hotel since it opened and . . . 241 people who have been with us from 5 to 35 years," said Sharp. "There was a lot of history at that meeting. It is those employees that have made that hotel great. We have a work environment where people are treated with respect. We embrace it in a manner that is sincere and appreciative. People are attracted to that."

Headline: Get Inside the Moment-by-Moment Emotions of Your Consumers

Sharp is understandably proud of his achievement. But what do the customers think? To find out, we conducted a major quantitative survey. A typical respondent was Mary, a 47-year-old HR professional with an investment firm in San Francisco. She's upper middle-class, with a family income of about $400,000.

She checked Four Seasons as her favorite brand in the world. "I love the Four Seasons. I love the way it makes me feel to enter one of their lobbies. I love the way they treat me, and the way they treat my children," she says. She and her family have been to 10 of the hotels. She aspires to go to all 93 of them. "They are not pretentious. They are genuine. It's a lot more expensive [than other hotels]—but it's good value. Remember, I buy my groceries at Costco and Trader Joe's. I don't like to spend $900 a night. But for $900 a night, I feel good. I am served by people who are happy to take care of me. They make you feel welcome. They are pampering."[20]

Sharp always says that the job of the Four Seasons staff is to create memories. And Mary has one particularly fond memory. "They made my son feel like a rock star. He's a finicky eater. But the server allowed him to create his own menu. My son specified what he wanted, how he wanted it prepared, and they allowed him to go back into the kitchen to make sure it was exactly what he wanted!"

Summing up, she said: "It is like an oasis. They don't skimp on anything. Other hotels are places to sleep. The Four Seasons are to enjoy and savor. I've told all my friends, Four Seasons is the hotel for you."

Headline: The Lessons of Four Seasons

The success of Sharp's approach to luxury hotels is defined by brand strength and differentiation. New properties live on the endowment of prior properties and guest loyalty. In 2007, Sharp sold Four Seasons to Microsoft founder Bill Gates and Saudi Prince Al-Waleed bin Talal in a $4 billion deal.[21] He kept 5 percent. Despite the global economic slowdown, there is no plan to scale back the company's ambitious growth plans. Today, there are 93 hotels. Within the next eight to ten years, Sharp expects Four Seasons will design and operate 150 hotels around the world. In China, there are already 9 hotels, with another 13 under development. He thinks that eventually there could be 250 hotels in the 194 cities that he believes are capable of hosting the Four Seasons brand.

Sharp is under no illusions about the challenges that lie ahead. Since the 1960s, when he invented the high-service model of luxury hotels, there have been a slew of imitators, including Marriott's Ritz-Carlton, the Peninsula, St. Regis, Shangri-La, and Mandarin Oriental. This has increased the competition for luxury customers and obliged the Four Seasons to move with the times and do some things that it has historically resisted—for instance, launch a loyalty program. Sharp says that the average hotel loyalty program is a giveaway, effectively a discount. He expects the new Four Seasons recognition program to be different, gathering guest information in a positive way and driving improved service delivery through an even greater understanding of guests' needs. Sharp's traditional approach to service, and the development of people who can deliver it, is arguably more valuable than ever in the fast-moving digital age. "For us, 99 percent customer satisfaction is not good enough. That 1 percent with poor experiences can tell thousands of people. What counts is what you do when something goes wrong. Do you make a sincere attempt to try to help them? Do you explain? Do you work to solve the problem? It used to be that one person will tell 10 if you have a problem. *Today he will tell 10,000 online.*"

"When we look at what Four Seasons really stands for, it's really the people behind it. It's all about the team effort. It's not about 'me,' it's about 'we,' and that's the way Four Seasons has got to where we are. It's the participation of many playing their part when needed and standing up and taking a solo when required," Sharp explains.

Amid the growing competition, this strong service culture should help Four Seasons continue to grow. "We have 40,000 employees now, and 90 percent are culture carriers. They understand the core values. It will continue to perpetuate. They will make sure it carries on.

"My approach is to see things through the customers' eyes," he says proudly. "Our objective is to retain the culture, to build the brand, and to never compromise. The first priority of the Four Seasons is the sanctity of the brand."

This special brand has made its way into the honeymoons, weddings, anniversaries, vacations, annual meetings, and business trips of millions of the most affluent people in the world. Consumers such as Mary count on Four Seasons for memories and stories that last a lifetime.

Ask Mary, and she is happy to tell you where to go on vacation for that special touch. More than that, she has been so thrilled by her experiences that she happily tells her friends and family. That's the key: convert your employees, and they will convert your customers, who will convert their friends—who will become your future customers.

*****

One Conclusion

Zappos and Four Seasons are very different companies. Zappos serves mostly younger consumers with younger service people. It is low touch, but high service. Few customers ever come on campus. It invented a new way for consumers to access an almost unlimited inventory of shoes. Tony Hsieh is messianic in his desire to provide happy employees with a satisfied work life. The central service site in an isolated part of Las Vegas allows total control of the work environment and the delivery interface with consumers. A lot of this is electronic—but the pizzazz is voice to voice.

By contrast, Isadore Sharp's Four Seasons is all about high-touch, in-person service, exceeding expectations every day and all around the world. He has created a brand model that can be comfortably re-created in his hotels, whether they are in Prague, Moscow, Bangkok, or New York.

Yet, despite their differences, the Zappos creed and the Four Seasons mission are very similar. *Their culture drives their brand.* Happy employees will take a bullet for their company. Little things make a big difference, and there is a particular emphasis on physical nourishment, encouragement, and safety. Transparency makes people feel safe. Every day on the job can be a celebration.

Both leaders take the view that if you can transform a job into a calling, and if you can enable those on the front line to make decisions on the spot, you can and will win the hearts and minds of the consumers for life. Both companies are dependent on these consumers becoming repeat customers and, most of all, spreading the good word to their friends.

In their different ways, Four Seasons and Zappos have found employee-based models that work to turn consumers into converts and thereby deliver brand apostles. The front line of contact with the consumer is so well trained, so memorable, and so service-oriented that it is impossible to not say, "Wow."

Four Takeaways

1. **Your recruits are your future.** When hiring, always remember that an individual's attitude will not change. What you see

in a recruit will continue when he becomes a veteran. A great attitude, humility, and engagement should be visible immediately in every recruit you meet. Set high bars. Never settle for the bottom of the barrel. Pay attention to detail. Ask all who interact with her: "Does this person fit?" If your workers have the power to make decisions, they become much more confident in their role and in dealing with clients and consumers.

Great employees are like wine. If you are making wine for long-term consumption and savoring over the next three decades or more, what you recruit today is the raw material for your future. If you start with bad grapes, you will create bad wine. If you start with the finest grapes, and then add skill, care, attention, and investment, you can create inspiration. Great employees are infectious, hypnotic without being creepy, and self-deprecating without exaggeration, and they beat the drum in a genuine celebration of associates' success. Spirits lift, and work becomes a calling.

2. **Successful new businesses redefine the world.** The inventor sees what is already there and does not imitate, but rather creates something new—something that is distinctly different and distinctly better, with a clear target consumer. Four Seasons redefined luxury to provide leverage for the user (a consistent experience where dependable provision of all daily needs allows busy executives to concentrate on the work at hand) and created delightful touches that energize the recreational guest. Zappos combined a superextensive shoe selection—which was available the next day with no worry about returns—with service that is memorable, entertaining, and distinctive.

3. **Promote the culture carriers.** The limit to your growth is your ability to bring on people who can become culture carriers. These people do the right thing every day on the basis of their experience with you and your direct reports. They also do the right thing according to their internal compass. Create employees who have your mission in their hearts and regard it as their own.

4. **Follow the Golden Rule.** The Golden Rule ("Do unto others as you would have them do unto you") is a universal touchpoint— so easy to say; so tough to do every day everywhere. If you really, really do it, magic happens.

SOME KEY ACTION POINTS

1. Invest in the front line; make it deep and clear.
2. Help the front line personalize and integrate your goals and aspirations for customer contact and relationship development.
3. You get what you pay for.
4. A personal emotional connection (PEC) requires skill, role modeling, apprenticeship, experience, and leadership.
5. A PEC is not on the balance sheet, but it is a primary asset.
6. How you recruit determines whom you get. Be distinctive in your approach, use the working team to screen potential employees, and have an exit plan at 30 days, 90 days, and one year.
7. Look for a culture fit; be detailed and specific in your criteria.
8. Expand your footprint beyond your local market: build a reputation, and provide incentives to expand outside of that market.
9. Adopt and believe in an inviting, high-energy title: use "partner" for your employees at every level.

CHAPTER SIX

Better Ramp Up Your Virtual Relationships (Because That's What Your Customers Are Doing)

THE CHAPTER IN A BOX

The Main Point

It's no secret that the digital age is transforming all our lives. Yet many companies are surprisingly behind the times. If they know that they need to be online, they have a peculiar way of showing it. If you lead one of those companies, you'd better act fast. There's nothing virtual about the relationships that you forge with your customers online. They are for real.

Chapter Overview

Your customers don't just shop online. They exist online. The dot-com world is where they dream, where they talk, and where they get information. It's a very functional world. They learn about products, and they pounce on those products. They extract information about technical performance characteristics. They read the views of other users. They read the complaints. No one falls in love online. But be warned: people can fall out of love. Online assassinations can annihilate your brand.

So you need to be there—forcefully, actively, proudly, and with great care.

Just having a website or an app is not enough. You have to ensure that your brand really lives online. On the face of it, the task is a beguilingly easy one. Who can't write a short blog? Who can't jot down a series of insightful messages in 140 characters?

In reality, however, the task of building an emotional connection with your customers in a digital environment is hard. But, as we'll see in this chapter, some companies have figured out the secret.

Headline: The Digital World Is Real, Not Virtual

By 2016, some 3 billion people—almost half the world's population—will be connected to the Internet. According to BCG estimates, the Internet economy in the richest 20 countries, the G-20, will be worth $4.2 trillion. It's still the fastest-growing channel of the consumer economy.[1]

The Internet has become an integral part of your customers' lives. In a survey of American consumers conducted by BCG in 2012, 83 percent said that they would give up fast food for a year rather than lose their Internet connection. Other lifestyle habits that some consumers were willing to forgo for one year rather than give up the Internet included alcohol (73 percent of consumers), coffee (69 percent), and even sex (21 percent).[2]

Why do they rate the Internet so highly? It's about immediate gratification. It's about the rapid conversion to purchase. It's about today. Tomorrow's too late. Some companies get this. Most don't. But everyone should. In almost every category, 20 to 40 percent of the volume is up for grabs.

You need to understand these new economics. Specifically, you need to understand what it takes to deliver precise value-added pricing, excellent service and reliability, and an unlimited inventory. You need to experiment, experiment, experiment—and learn deeply and completely with every experiment. In the digital world, you must test every day, everywhere. If you stand still, you're going backward.

In this chapter, we tell the stories of two companies. We start with Amazon, the start-up that has become the world's biggest online retailer. Originally a bookstore, it is now, as Brad Stone, a senior writer with *Bloomberg Businessweek*, explained—drawing on the words of its founder, Jeff Bezos—an "everything store."[3] Its success has come from putting the customer front and center in everything it does—and never ceasing to do this.

We also tell the story of a newcomer that has shot to prominence without serving a long apprenticeship. At the start of 2008, there was no Airbnb, the online private lodgings business. Today, it's valued as a $13 billion business.[4] It is among the 25 most-beloved emerging brands in BCG's Consumer Sentiment Index.[5] It has struck a chord with customers. It has forged powerful emotional connections by addressing some significant unmet customer needs. It has found ways to alleviate some pain points in its customers' lives.

Time will tell whether Airbnb can build an empire the way Amazon has done. Aggression, an expansionist approach, and a disregard for short-term profitability and the demands of Wall Street are the characteristics that have helped Jeff Bezos lead Amazon to unimagined success.

Amazon.com

Cadabra, a shortened version of the magical incantation *abracadabra*, was, according to the *Wall Street Journal*, the name that Jeff Bezos initially wanted to give his Seattle-based start-up after he left a secure job at a New York hedge fund in 1994.[6] It hinted at the seemingly impossible task that he had set for himself: to deliver any book to the customer's door at the click of a button on a computer. In the end, he decided on Amazon, after the world's longest river, because *cadabra* sounded too much like *cadaver*.

But the company's purpose didn't change. Bezos knew that there was a huge demand for online shopping. Just before leaving New York, he calculated that Internet usage had increased by 230,000 percent in the space of one year. The challenge was to solve the practical problem of sourcing the books and shipping them to customers in a timely fashion. For the Princeton graduate, whose expertise was in computer science and electrical engineering, this was a problem he thought he could solve.

History tells us that Bezos was right. Amazon is the world's largest retailer, generating revenues of $74 billion in 2013. It topped $90 million in 2014. No longer just a bookstore, it is the "everything store"; but more than this, it is the most beloved e-commerce brand on the planet. According to our research, it attracted more than six times as many "favorite" votes as its nearest competitor, eBay.[7]

But two decades ago, this popularity was not a foregone conclusion. When Amazon.com was launched on July 16, 1995, proclaiming itself "Earth's Biggest Bookstore," there was no one who predicted that Bezos would be named *Time*'s Person of the Year by the end of the decade.[8]

Bezos brought to the venture overwhelming ambition and a determination to achieve with persistence and aggression. Another success factor was a commitment to both innovation and trial-and-error experimentation. Above all, Bezos had a narrow focus on the consumer—delivering what he wanted and how he wanted it, and then making sure that he was happy with his purchases.

Headline: Be Ambitious and Aggressive in Pursuit of Your Goals, and Treat Every Day Like Day One

When Bezos launched his company, he was operating out of his garage, so the label "Earth's Biggest Bookstore" was clearly a statement of his ambition. For some, it was laughable. "I just met the world's biggest snake-oil salesman," said one book-seller after bumping into Bezos at a publishers' event in the mid-1990s.[9]

But Bezos has proved the skeptics wrong. He has never lost his ambition, even when Amazon did become the world's biggest bookstore. Every year, he has added new product lines to his shelves. Today, on Amazon, you can get movies, computers, TVs, toys, apparel, jewelry, sports gear, air conditioners, cars and motorbikes, cosmetics, and even fresh food.

More than this, Bezos has branched out far beyond retailing. With the Kindle, which he launched in 2007, Amazon became a rival to Apple as a digital-device manufacturer. With Amazon's powerful data-storage capability, it became a rival to IBM in cloud computing. It can count the secretive Central Intelligence Agency among its customers. There are some who think that the Big Data business and cloud technology could become Amazon's mainstay in the years ahead.[10]

More recently, he has started to encroach on the world of Hollywood. Amazon has a video-streaming service and has started to commission its own content, just like Netflix, its rival in this market. In January 2015, Amazon was awarded two Golden Globe Awards for *Transparent*, its series about a trans-gender father.[11] Soon after this, it unveiled plans to acquire, produce, and release dozens of films each year. It has signed up Woody Allen to develop a comedy series for its video-streaming service.[12]

Such relentless expansion has been possible because Bezos has fostered an unusually competitive culture. Ex-Amazonians talk of the company's confrontational, almost gladiatorial, atmosphere.[13] One of Bezos's foundational principles is, "Have a Backbone: Disagree and Commit."[14]

According to this principle, Bezos says, "Leaders are obligated to respectfully challenge decisions when they disagree, even when doing so is uncomfortable or exhausting. Leaders have conviction and are tenacious. They do not compromise for the sake of social cohesion. Once a decision is determined, they commit wholly."[15]

As we saw in Chapter Five, Bezos bought Zappos, which was winning a name for itself in the online shoe business. Then he bought Quidsi, another online retailer specializing in diapers and other mother-and-baby products. *Quidsi* is Latin for "what if?" But Bezos didn't wait to find out whether Quidsi would become another Amazon, expanding beyond its original product line. He went eyeball to eyeball with Walmart, which had put in an offer for Quidsi. As Brad Stone reported in *The Everything Store*, Bezos warned the founders that he would reduce Amazon's pricing of baby products to zero if they signed with Walmart. This would have inflicted a mortal blow on Quidsi, so they didn't dare call his bluff. With steely conviction, he won the day.[16]

Headline: Constantly Experiment, Constantly Innovate, and Accept That Some Failures Will Happen

Bezos does things differently. He has always defied convention. When he started Amazon, he quickly discovered that online retail is a Darwinian petri dish—it's cheap to experiment and you can see results fast.

In an early experiment that was controversial, he began allowing customers to post their own book reviews—good or bad. As Bezos recalled: "I started receiving letters from well-meaning folks, saying that perhaps you don't understand your business. You make money when you sell things. Why are you allowing negative reviews on your website? But our point of view is [that] we sell things if we help people make purchasing decisions."[17]

As we've seen, Bezos is no respecter of reputation or title. He says that the "decentralized distribution of invention throughout the company—not limited to the company's senior leaders—is the only way to get robust, high-throughput innovation."[18]

Some innovations are hidden from plain view. They are mechanical. They deal with the infrastructure of the business. And they are arguably the most significant innovations. For instance, at the heart of Amazon's success are its fulfillment centers. These make it possible for the company to commit to next-day delivery. "Nineteen years ago, I drove the Amazon packages to the post office every evening in the back of my Chevy Blazer. My vision extended so far that I dreamed that we might one day get a forklift," Bezos told shareowners in 2014. "Fast-forward to today, and we have 96 fulfillment centers and are on our seventh generation of fulfillment center design."[19]

These are large, industrial warehouses with up to 1 million square feet of space. Workers are said to fast-walk as much as 11 miles on a shift. They abide by the "just-in-time" and "continuous improvement" rules of *kaizen*. There are critics. According to the *New Yorker*: "Accounts from inside the centers describe the work of picking, boxing, and shipping books and dog food and beard trimmers as a high-tech version of the dehumanized factory floor satirized in Chaplin's *Modern Times*."[20]

Bezos sings the praises of his operations team. They are "methodical and ingenious." And they are committed to more innovation. In 2013, Amazon rolled out 280 major software improvements across the fulfillment center network. "Our goal is to continue to iterate and improve on the design, layout, technology, and operations in these buildings, ensuring that each new facility we build is better than the last," said Bezos.[21]

Amid all this success, there have been inevitable setbacks. For instance, the Fire smartphone has suffered some bleak sales figures. Amazon was required to take a $170 million charge on production costs and unsold inventory in 2014. It also had to cut the phone's price from $199 to 99 cents.[22]

Headline: Don't Just Be Customer-Centric, Be Customer-Obsessed

Bezos talks of having a "customer-obsessed culture."[23] He resists the pleas of Wall Street, which complains about his apparently "profits-last" strategy. He plows most of Amazon's profits back into the business for the benefit of current and future customers.

When he launched Amazon, Bezos personally answered customer e-mails. Customer service, he said, was "the cornerstone of Amazon.com." By 1999, he had a team of 500 people answering e-mails. Customers can personally write to jeff@amazon.com. He reads many of these and forwards complaints to the relevant executives, asking for an explanation and a solution. These forwarded e-mails, known as *escalations* inside Amazon, keep executives focused on the customer. As a senior executive once said: "Every anecdote from a customer matters. We research each of them because they tell us something about our processes. It's an audit that is done for us by our customers. We treat them as precious sources of information."[24]

But if Amazon takes note of what its customers *say*, it really takes note of what they *do*. Often, people say one thing and do another. It's human nature. Amazon understands this. It therefore makes sure that it truly understands what customers really want. It has built one of the world's great data-storage capabilities so that it can capture and compute every click a customer makes. Then, when the data are subjected to deep analysis, it can tell a thousand stories about what really moves customers.

In many ways, Amazon is a cold, calculating, hyperrational organization. But with the information from its Big Data systems, it has managed to forge an emotional connection with customers so that it has become the world's second-most-beloved brand, after Apple. In particular, it has wooed its most powerful advocates. As Bezos told shareowners: "Amazonians around the world are polishing products and services to a degree that is beyond what's expected or required, taking the long view, reinventing normal, and getting customers to say 'Wow.'"[25]

The classic product for these customers is Prime. Fundamentally, this is "all-you-can-eat, two-day shipping for a flat annual fee." But since its launch in 2005, Prime has expanded to include other benefits, such as Prime Instant Video, its video-streaming service.

The reason Amazon has chosen to focus on these special customers is simple. As our research shows, they are worth much more than casual customers. On average, an apostle customer spends $2,873 per year on Amazon.com. These customers typically make eight recommendations, mostly through word-of-mouth advocacy (60 percent), gifts (16 percent), and social media sites (13 percent). We have conservatively estimated the expenditures of a convert at $867. This means that an average apostle is worth at least 2.3 times her actual spending on Amazon.com.[26]

What customers love about Amazon.com is its convenience. This is the number one factor driving people to the site. Other factors are "trust," suggesting that it is a reliable service, and "good value for the money." One of the customers we interviewed is Julia. She grew up in a small Mississippi town, got married as a teen, and had two children with her first husband. Now she lives in an even smaller, more remote town. With a population of 1,500, it has few retail options. She has to drive 15 minutes to get to the nearest Walmart. And Dillard's, the nearest department store, is in Hattiesburg, a 30-minute drive away.[27]

About five years ago, Julia discovered Amazon.com. A friend told her about it. Today it is her largest single retail provider. She buys shoes, shirts, pants, home goods, kitchen appliances, tools, office supplies, and even an item as obscure as a marine-quality music player from it. "Every month, I spend at least $100," she tells us. "My partner jokes, 'What kind of a relationship do you have with that UPS man? He pulls up almost every day I go to work.' But I tell him the driver is just bringing me my Amazon delivery."

For Julia, Amazon is "convenient," "easy," "dependable," "good value," and "geared to my timeline." She says, "I shop when I want to, not when the 'store is open.' Amazon is always open. I go online and comparison shop. They have very good prices and very broad variety. It makes me happy."

For her holiday shopping list, Amazon will get the lion's share of her purchases, including gifts for her mother, children, stepdaughter, partner, and friends. "There's something for everyone, and I don't have to fight the mall traffic or waste my time. When I order from Amazon, I know it will be here when they say it will be—or earlier."

Julia does explore other websites. But time and time again, she returns to Amazon. "It's my go-to source," she said. "I look at the other sites, but Amazon is generally the cheapest, offering the broadest assortment."

Headline: The Lessons of Amazon

Ever since Bezos launched Amazon.com, he has stressed the importance of price. Early on, he offered discounts of 10 to 30 percent. No one could match his prices. Also, he has stressed selection and inventory. Amazon offers almost any book—new or old. In the first year, he arranged for mobile billboards to appear near Barnes & Noble stores, emblazoned with, "Can't find that book you wanted?" and promoting Amazon's website address.[28]

To keep this commitment to prices and inventory, Bezos has needed to stay firm on costs. One of his principles is frugality: "We try not to spend money on things that don't matter to customers."[29]

Ultimately, Amazon is a utility. It provides exceptional value and service. It gives the upper middle classes comprehensive access to products. It has benefited for years from an exceptional cost benefit in the form of no sales tax; however, this advantage is slowly eroding as Amazon adds facilities in various states and as state legislatures require tax collection. The company operates on razor-thin margins. As a result, it has gained an enormous share of the market in many categories of goods. This, in turn, has meant that it has enjoyed an immediate potential improvement in profits and cash flow. It competes against focused competitors with a deeper offering and competitive delivery charges.

Will Amazon attain $200 billion in revenues? Will it learn to translate ubiquity and habit into enduring emotional connections with its consumers?

Time will tell.

Airbnb

On New Year's Eve 2009, 2,000 guests and hosts were using Airbnb. Five years later, 550,000 rang in the New Year on Airbnb, staying in 20,000 cities in nearly 200 countries around the world.[30] This online community marketplace, where users can rent private homes or list their own home for use as a place to stay for a short period, is one of a handful of digital companies that broke through the $10 billion valuation barrier in 2014. The others were Uber and Snapchat—which, along with Airbnb, appear in BCG's list of the world's top 25 most-beloved emerging brands—and Dropbox, SpaceX, and Xiaomi.[31] All of them have come, seemingly, from nowhere. They have grown fast. Their founders have struck it rich in record time.

Brian Chesky, Airbnb's chief executive, was in his midtwenties when he and his roommate, Joe Gebbia, cooked up the idea of renting out air beds in their apartment in San Francisco to cover the rent. The city was hosting an industrial design conference, and many of the hotels were full. So the two of them hastily constructed the website Airbed & Breakfast, offering an air bed and a hot breakfast for $80 per night.[32] Three people booked, including a 38-year-old from Razorfish, a digital marketing agency, and an industrial designer who was "even older." As Gebbia, now Airbnb's chief product officer, told *Fast Company*: "They broke every assumption we ever made about who would stay on an air bed at a stranger's house."[33]

As Chesky recalls, people thought the idea of renting to strangers was a "weird thing, a crazy idea."[34] But there were two people who thought it was brilliant: Justin Kan and Michael Seibel, cofounders of Twitch, the video-gaming community that has since been sold to Amazon for $1 billion.

They introduced Chesky to the movers and shakers in Silicon Valley. The result was an investment by Y Combinator, the incubator that financed Twitch and Dropbox. Then Sequoia Capital invested $600,000. This was a big boost to Airbnb—and turned heads. Founded by Don Valentine, who is sometimes dubbed the grandfather of Silicon Valley, Sequoia was an early investor in Apple, Google, and YouTube.[35]

Airbnb searched for other major events to promote the service, including the Democratic National Convention in Denver, Barack Obama's inauguration in Washington, DC, and the London Olympics. These spurred growth, and further rounds of investment followed as Airbnb attracted more bookings: 100,000 in 2009, 750,000 in 2010, and more than 2 million in 2011. When Airbnb raised almost $500 million in April 2014 from TPG, T. Rowe Price, and Dragoneer Investment Group, it took its total investment to around $800 million.[36] This accelerated growth makes one ask why Airbnb is so successful. It is not, after all, the only company to offer private lodgings online. Others preceded it, including HomeAway and Vacation Rentals By Owner, which is now part of HomeAway.

The answer lies in Airbnb's ability to drive real business-model innovation. It did this by tackling both the value proposition and the operating model at the same time. First, Chesky and his colleagues attacked two distinct and unmet emotional customer needs, improving the value proposition of the lodging business. Second, they developed new operating models to facilitate the delivery of the technical and functional features that could satisfy those needs.

Headline: Offer Your Customers Unique and Authentic Experiences, and Make Things Easy for Them

Airbnb has come a long way since 2008. Then, the only creature comfort was an air bed on the kitchen floor in San Francisco. Now, customers can choose from more than 1 million properties. Thus, Airbnb is bigger than either Marriott or InterContinental Hotels. Its top cities are Madrid, New York, London, Chicago, Brooklyn, Washington, DC, Amsterdam,

Paris, Boston, and Vienna. Affordability remains a significant part of the portfolio. More than 50 percent of the rooms on the Airbnb website are priced at less than $100 per night. But there is a growing list of luxury properties, too. For instance, there is a Las Vegas penthouse for $1,900 per night. Alternatively, you can choose an eighteenth-century hilltop villa in Umbria for $1,669 per night. Or how about a six-bedroom farmhouse set in 1,000 acres in Brazil for $3,778 per night?[37]

What Airbnb has worked out is that customers are looking for unique and authentic experiences. Many of them are tired of the generic experience provided by the big chain hotels. Consumers from the millennial generation especially praise Airbnb. They like the social experience, the affordability, and the unpredictability. Also, as Chesky told the *New York Times*, they are naturally inclined to borrow, rent, or share. "I think now, for the younger generation, ownership is viewed as a burden. Young people will only want to own what they want responsibility for. And a lot of people my age don't want responsibility for a car and a house and to have a lot of stuff everywhere."[38]

But older consumers are taking to Airbnb, too. Right from the first time they rented air beds, Chesky and Gebbia were taken aback by the enthusiasm of older travelers. We spoke to one seasoned traveler named Britt, a 57-year-old logistics professional from Nashville, Tennessee. He lives with his wife and daughter, and they have a household income of $150,000.[39]

"I only heard about Airbnb a few months ago, and I've already stayed four times," he told us. One of these stays was in a beautiful loft in Quebec. "It turned out to be on the main street you want to be on," he recalled. "It was about $100 a night, and the hotel I had booked was by the airport for $250 a night."

The experience has transformed his vacations. "I stay at a lot of hotels, and they are always right next to the airport. Half the time it's a Sheraton, half the time it's a Hilton, and half the time [when] I get there, I don't even know which one I'm at—they're so generic."

Airbnb's secret has been to figure out what some customers really want and give it to them. Too often, customers struggle with the basics when looking for private lodgings. Finding desirable properties is the first problem. Completing rudimentary tasks that they take for granted when they stay at the big chain hotels, such as reserving a room or checking in and out, is another problem. Then there is the question of trust. Can you, as a customer, trust the people you're renting from? Can you, as a host, trust the people you're inviting into your home?

Airbnb has addressed these pain points. It is for this reason that it has been hailed as the pioneer of the "share economy," which *Forbes* magazine estimated was generating revenues of $3.5 billion in January 2013 and growing at more than 25 percent per year.[40] If you go to Airbnb's website, it is easy to find and book a property. Payments are facilitated by Airbnb, which gives reassurance to both customers and hosts. Now, hosts can also approve bookings via the mobile app, which speeds up the transactions during booking and checking out. Other features include a $1 million insurance policy and a 24/7 customer-service hotline. (These were hastily introduced after an episode dubbed *ransackgate*, when a guest trashed a host's apartment in 2011, generating unfavorable publicity.[41])

Perhaps most important, Airbnb has fostered a two-way conversation between hosts and guests. There are bios of participants. Identities can be verified through Facebook and other social media. No one is anonymous. And everyone can converse online. The thousands of user-generated reviews that exist are widely trusted by the Airbnb community.

Two people that Airbnb brought together are Dom, a casting director from Paris, and Peter, an automated-engineering technologist from Ontario. In 2012, Dom decided to list his plush two-bedroom apartment on Airbnb. He charges $186 per night for a minimum stay of three nights. It's situated in Le Marais, literally "the marsh," in the fourth arrondissement, a sought-after neighborhood on the right bank of the Seine. On Airbnb's website, you can see Dom's photo, his wonderful apartment, and some personal details. He was educated at the Lycée Charlemagne, one of the top high schools, before entering the movie business. He welcomes browsers with, "Hey, I'm Dom!"[42]

Dom has attracted 70 reviews. The reviewers have verified identities. Peter is one of these. He lives with his wife in Fergus,

Ontario, Canada. He says his daughters are "the heart of my life." He has a verified e-mail address, phone number, LinkedIn profile, and driver's license. In January 2015, after his stay at Dom's apartment, he wrote: "Dom was a very helpful host throughout our stay in Paris. He gave us excellent directions to get to his apartment and inquired as to our comfort. The flat was perfectly situated for lots of different adventures in Paris. It is in a little courtyard slightly off the beaten path. Wonderful restaurants and shops right in his backyard! It was about a five-minute walk to Notre Dame and a charming bookshop, Shakespeare and Company. It was only about 15 minutes to the Louvre. However, everything was so easily accessible from the metro just minutes away. The apartment was equipped with everything we needed for the stay. Although paint was peeling from the ceiling, the eclectic vibe was charming. We had a very comfortable and enjoyable stay!"[43]

Often, virtual relationships become real relationships that endure long after an Airbnb stay. As *Wired* magazine reported: "We are entering a new era of Internet-enabled intimacy."[44] Our research has found that in many cases, hosts actually offer their properties for less than the market price just to make sure they maximize the number of personal connections they make. As Lori, a 58-year-old retired professional from Bethesda, Maryland, told us: "I live in a four-bedroom house with a 21-year-old son who is not there. I have the space. It didn't have anything to do with the money." She had become a host after enjoying a stay with Airbnb. "I came back and I thought, 'Wow, that was really cool!' I met all these wonderful people, and I had a fabulous time—I'll sign up to be a host."[45]

But for many hosts, the money is an important incentive. More than 50 percent of them depend on it to pay their rent or their mortgage, just as Chesky and Gebbia did when they started out. This is, of course, part of Airbnb's value proposition: "Airbnb is the easiest way for people to monetize their extra space and showcase it to an audience of millions."[46]

For this service, Airbnb has devised a new operating model that seems to satisfy everyone—the hosts, the customers, and the company. This is how it works. For a three-night stay at a property in Chicago charging $100 per night, the customer would pay \$100 plus a \$12 service charge per night—a total of \$336 for the entire stay. Of this, the host would keep \$291—the \$100 per night charge minus a \$3 service charge per night. Airbnb would receive \$45: \$12 each night from the customer and \$3 each night from the host.

As the New Year celebrations got under way at the start of 2015, Airbnb could reflect on the fact that millions of people had used its services since 2008. As of this writing, some 25 million travelers had stayed at an Airbnb accommodation. In a short space of time, it has become trusted, beloved—and profitable.

Headline: Help Your Customers Dream, and Then Fulfill Their Dreams

There is a pathway to every purchase, whether it's a chocolate bar, a gold watch, or a brand-new SUV. In the hospitality business, there's a very structured pathway. There are four distinct phases: dream, plan, book, and share. We've done some detailed analysis on how much time aspirant travelers spend on each of these phases.

We found that the dream phase is the most time-intensive. For a typical four-day stay, a customer will spend more than 42 hours on the logistics. Of this, some 18 hours will be spent on the dream phase. This is not expended in one single chunk of time. Customers may spend several weeks on the dream phase—and with the growth of mobile, they can dream anywhere and everywhere. Think of all the people thumbing their smartphones in the grocery store checkout line or while sitting at a restaurant eating lunch. Almost certainly, their minds are elsewhere.[47]

Airbnb understood this behavior. The company realized that travelers love to dream. People love to imagine themselves in different places, different countries, far away from their everyday experience. For our research, we spoke to lots of customers. One told us: "I just fantasize, compare, think about where I am going to stay, and I just get lost." Another said, "It is part of the pleasure . . . getting lost online and looking at all of the possibilities. It's an obsession. I have a travel porn addiction."[48]

To help customers dream, Airbnb has created a beautiful mobile app that has great design and photography. Of course, other hotel groups have an online presence intended to tempt prospective customers, but this is an area where Airbnb has overinvested. Chesky and Gebbia know a thing or two about design. They met while studying at the Rhode Island School of Design, one of the top art academies in the United States.

Where other hotel groups have one graphic designer, Airbnb has dozens. Where others have a few photographers—or, worse, instruct local general managers to take a picture on their smartphone—it has thousands of professional snappers around the world on staff or on retainer. Airbnb effectively changed the operating model, diverting resources to create a new activity that is hard for traditional hoteliers to replicate.

So when a new host signs up, a photographer is dispatched to take a photograph that is dreamworthy. Once a customer falls in love, the emotional connection is made, and the move to the "book" phase becomes an inevitability.

The success with which Airbnb has managed to help customers dream has prompted Chesky to go beyond the company's original purpose of helping customers find a place to stay. Now, he wants to participate in the "entire trip" of the $6 trillion global travel industry. As he told *Fast Company*: "People went to Dell for the computers. But they go to Apple for everything. That's the difference between a transactional company and a transformational one."[49]

Airbnb wants to be a transformational company. Chesky, like his customers, is building his own dreams. But for these to be realized, he must continue to fulfill the dreams of others.

*****

One Conclusion

Amazon and Airbnb come from two different eras of the digital age. However, they are both about speed, power in the hands of the consumer, and convenience. There is a common lesson: you have to move quickly or you'll be left behind. Be the first to identify an unmet consumer need. Be the first to attack it aggressively with every digital weapon at your disposal.

Your customers are online, and they are quick learners. They flit from one new digital product to another. Amazon has been masterful in the way it has jumped from books to general retail to cloud computing and now to Hollywood-style video production. Airbnb has deftly moved from air beds to castles, all the while responding to the customer's demand for a system that can truly be trusted. According to Thomas Friedman, the *New York Times* columnist: "That was Airbnb's real innovation—a platform of 'trust'—where everyone could not only see everyone else's identity but also rate them as good, bad, or indifferent hosts or guests."[50]

If you are a nascent company, then Amazon and Airbnb provide textbook case studies on how to disrupt your competitors. If you are a traditional company, with little digital heritage, then they show you what you are up against and what you need to do to counter them.

You have to create trust. There should be no distinction between your online and offline reputation. Above all, you have to make digital a priority. You have to overinvest in digital technology. Don't marginalize it. Too often, we have seen that the digital business is the responsibility of the marketing or IT division. But when that happens, it gets starved of cash and blocked by politics. If you're the CEO, you need to make it *your* business. Have the digital officer report directly to you.

Three Takeaways

1. **Digital is here to stay and part of the core.** It's not some nice-to-have option. It's real, not virtual. An app or a website won't get you to where you need to be. You must fully embrace the digital age. You must change the way you do business. Appoint a chief digital officer. Make her one of your top eight executives. Invite her to every important discussion about the future of the business. If you bury digital, it will bury you.

2. **Digital is real. It's also magical.** At last, you can deliver your customer's wildest dreams: next-day delivery of an out-of-print book, or an affordable apartment near the Eiffel Tower in Paris.

Use digital technology to stay close to your customers and anticipate their unmet needs. Then use it to satisfy those needs.

3. **Digital is relentless.** You can't coast. You can't take it easy. There's always something new. There's always a new competitor. So treat every day as if it's your first. Be as energetic and enthusiastic as you were at the beginning, when you started your company or your job.

SOME KEY ACTION POINTS

1. Merge your online and offline capabilities.
2. Do it to yourself before it gets done to you.
3. Nothing but experience counts—you need to deliver as promised and stated.
4. The world today is one without limits.
5. Remember James Monroe and the Monroe Doctrine: view any encroachment by rivals as an act of aggression that must be repulsed.
6. Focus everywhere, on everyone.
7. Profits are a residual part of the endgame. They will come in the end. But until then, it is a land grab.

CHAPTER SEVEN

Take Giant Leaps (Because You're Not Going to Win with Timid Steps)

THE CHAPTER IN A BOX

The Main Point

There are those who advocate continuous improvement, incremental advances, and consolidation. But no one ever changed the world that way. No one ever built a great company that way. To do these things, you must show foresight, fearlessness, and fortitude. Take long strides. Anything less will never get noticed. Be clear and vibrant in your claims. With giant leaps, you get where you want to go quickly.

Why These Stories for This Chapter

Natura Cosmeticos and Mercadona, the two companies featured in this chapter, are led by executives with big personalities and big ambitions for their businesses. Natura started as a small shop and laboratory and quickly realized the enormous potential of the Amazon rain forest as a source of health-giving ingredients for its health and beauty products. Mercadona started as a butcher shop in Spain and quickly realized the enormous potential of private-label products. They have each forged ahead by leaps and bounds, guided by some core principles.

Chapter Overview

You need to be demonstrably different and better in all the ways that matter to your consumers. No one has ever dramatically changed a market by offering timid, incremental improvements. Dramatic market-share shifts can happen only when consumers are surprised and excited. It is about glorious differences. You need to be bold.

You won't get there in one cycle of improvement. Realizing your dream takes persistence and patience. It takes daring and determination. When you think you've gone as far as you can go, you have most likely gone only half as far as you need to go.

Headline: Dare to Dream and Dare to Act

Every successful company starts with a dream. This is what drives its founders. This is what connects them with their original customers. But there are far more dreamers than there are successful companies. Why? Because successful companies are led by people who have not only dared to dream but also dared to act. The entrepreneurs do not know all the answers, but they are not inhibited by fear or a desire to protect the status quo. They are prepared to lose everything for a chance at the big win. When confronted with risk, they bet boldly.

In this chapter, we look at two companies that started with next to nothing but their founders' dreams. After a series of giant leaps—redefining their markets, deeply understanding the latent needs of their consumers, and providing highly differentiated products—they have grown into leaders in their markets and created fortunes for their founders and early investors. The founders were not motivated solely by profit or wealth. They were guided by a deep commitment to other people—their customers, of course, but also their employees and suppliers—as they took a series of leaps toward their destination.

The first is Natura Cosmeticos, a Brazilian company that now ranks as one of the world's most profitable cosmetics companies. It has turned the Amazon rain forest into a mystical source of ingredients for beauty, transforming the lives of 100 million Brazilian women and driving up the standard of living for 1.6 million female sales consultants.

The second is Mercadona, a Spanish company that began as a butcher shop and now ranks among Europe's largest, most profitable, and fastest-growing grocery retailers. It has created an extended family of employees and suppliers, as well as their friends and families, all of whom have collaborated to serve the "boss"—the customer.[1]

Natura Cosmeticos

The Amazon rain forest is one of the world's most miraculous and globally important natural resources. Scientists call it the *lungs of the planet* because its rich, diverse vegetation recycles carbon dioxide into oxygen. A full 20 percent of the earth's oxygen is produced by the Amazon's plant life.[2] Under the canopy of Amazonia live half of the world's species. At the floor of the Amazon forests, only 2 percent of the sunlight penetrates. Yet you can find 175 types of lizards, 300 types of other reptiles, some 500 different species of mammals, and 1,600 species of birds. Scientists also count 40,000 species of insects, 5,600 different fish in the massive Amazon River, and 16,000 varieties of trees. In the Amazon, it is always warm and humid—86 percent humidity during the rainy season and 77 percent humidity during the "dry" season. The mean temperature is about 80 degrees, with highs of over 100 degrees common during the dry months.[3]

This tropical environment is home to an amazing collection of plants and vegetation. Using modern science and "medicine-man" know-how, they can be combined to create products that perfume, moisturize skin, clean hair, protect skin from the sun, speed healing from cuts and bruises, and provide antidotes to age and disease. The environment is also fearsome—dark, moist, isolated, and home to electric eels, red-bellied piranha, the air-breathing fish pirarucu, poison dart frogs, parasitic candiru, anaconda, jaguars, payara (vampire fish), giant reptiles, and many other dangerous predators. In the forest, trees with 16-foot trunks and massive roots reach 200 feet into the sky. Below them are the canopy trees. They have dense leaves that filter out the light. They create a hospitable environment for flowers and fruit trees. In the shadows under them are low flowers and fruits and enormous concentrations of insects. In the bottom layer, the vegetation is decomposed by leaf insects, scorpions, earthworms, and millipedes.

This is a fragile ecosystem that is susceptible to the ravages and intrusions of man. The Amazon rain forest encompasses 2.124 million square miles—twice the size of India. Scientists believe that it has played a critical role in slowing global warming and stabilizing our climate. But the rain forest is under threat. It has been shrinking at 1.5 percent per year. And as it is burned off to make room for industry and farming, large quantities of carbon are released into the atmosphere.

Anthropologists say that 500 years ago, 10 million Indians lived in this vast jungle. The European conquistadors either annihilated them or spread diseases that killed most of them. Ambitious logging, farming, and road-building efforts have choked off the Amazon's abundant food supply, killed wildlife, and altered the balance of nature. Only 200,000 indigenous people remain in Amazonia. These 350 different ethnic groups live in dire poverty, surrounded by resources of almost infinite value.[4]

From generation to generation, native medicine men have passed down formulas for dried potions from various plants to promote health and wellness and cure disease. Their secrets have been the source of many drugs now marketed by global pharmaceutical companies. Approximately one-third of the drugs prescribed today by our modern medicine contain ingredients from Amazon plants. Treatments for cancer, childhood leukemia, malaria, schizophrenia, dysentery, and many other diseases contain active ingredients from these plants. Most of the Amazon medicine men are elderly, and they hold the secrets of the forest in their heads and in undocumented regimens. Scientists are now discovering that many of the plants are sources of new drugs for conditions including AIDS, Alzheimer's, arthritis, cancer, diabetes, and heart disease.

One company has decided to make a difference in the future of the Amazon, the people of the Amazon, and women worldwide. It is not a pharmaceutical company; it is a cosmetics firm.

In 1969, Antonio Luiz Seabra founded Natura Cosmeticos as a small laboratory and cosmetics shop in São Paulo. He was 27 years old and full of ambition.[5] He was the company's first door-to-door salesman. His start-up capital was around $7,500. Today the company delivers revenues in excess of $3.1 billion and earns $637 million in EBITDA (earnings before interest, taxes, depreciation, and amortization).

Some 85 percent of the company's revenues come from Brazil, and it is Brazilian women, as both customers and consultants, who have grown this beauty business. Brazilians are proud of Natura; it is a national hero in its home country.

Natura's secret has been to take a series of five giant leaps. First, use native Amazonian sourcing for the active ingredients in its products. Second, create a people-focused multilevel selling organization. Third, recruit, train, and enable 1.6 million sales reps who are willing to sell their heart out for the company. Fourth, use a philosophy of doing good to drive goodwill and a positive image. And fifth, stay focused geographically on Latin America, where the company understands consumers and exports Brazilian beauty.

Headline: "The Future We Dream Of": Build a Business on a Philosophy

From the beginning, Natura was a values-driven company.

During its first three decades, it was managed by a founding triumvirate. Seabra was the company icon who pledged to avoid manipulative advertising and help the customers develop their inner beauty; Guilherme Peirão Leal was "the head," in charge of process and organization; and Pedro Luiz Barreiros Passos was "the body," in charge of practical, operational arenas. They shared power and a vision.

The three founders refer continuously to cultural drivers: commitment to the truth, caring for relationships, continuous improvement, doing things well (simply, in a disciplined way, and with honor), innovation, sustainable development, and pleasure and joy (conveying meaning in everything they do). Their mission is "to contribute in an innovative and exemplary way to the improvement of society, causing changes in attitudes and values that materialize the ideal of a fair society."

More specifically, as Seabra says: "Natura's reason for being is to create and sell products and services that promote 'well-being' and 'being well.'" It's a train of thought that he got from Plato. "At age 16, I was given this quote from Plato: 'The one is in the whole; the whole is in the one.' That was a revelation to me. This notion of being part of a whole has never left me."

He goes on to explain the idea of "well-being, being well" (or *"bem, estar, bem"* in Portuguese): "Well-being equals the harmonious, pleasant relationship of a person with oneself, with one's body. Being well equals the emphatic, successful, and gratifying relationship of a person with others, with nature, and with the world."[6]

To carry out this mission, Natura implements a triple bottom line: (1) economic: cash, growth, and profitability; (2) social: wealth creation for consultants, corporate social responsibility investment, and benefits to the supplier community; and (3) environmental: carbon neutrality, refillable packaging, sustainable extraction, and extensive use of recycled materials, focused on economic, social, and sustainable performance.

The Amazon is central to everything Natura does. Its Amazon roots work for Brazilian women, too.

One of the myths of the Amazon is the story of the Amazonian woman. She was described by Dominican monks as "fierce, fiery, and deadly." According to legend, she could fire arrows at a rate ten times faster than men, and had the accuracy to pierce the break in the armor between the shoulder and head of the heavily armored conquistadors. The fierce resistance of these women is said to have saved the Amazon from full conquest for decades. In 1542, Gaspar de Carvajal, a Spanish Dominican missionary to the Amazon, wrote: "These women are very white and tall, and have hair very long and braided and wound about the head, and they are very robust, with their bows and arrows in their hands, doing as much fighting as ten Indian men. . . ."[7]

Natura is dedicated to the preservation of the Amazon and the prosperity and well-being of women worldwide. It carries the legend forward.

Headline: Innovate Products, Selling Channels, Positioning, Source Material, and New Age

"Pitanga means red in the language of the Tupi Indians of Brazil." So says the label on one of Natura's hand soaps. It continues: "Red is the color of the fruit from the Pitanga bush native to the Atlantic Rain Forest. Tart and very Brazilian, the Pitanga fruit is an expression of Brazil's tropical nature. This gentle hand soap, with Pitanga oil, has a pleasant fragrance inspired by the wild freshness of the Pitanga fruit. It cleans and perfumes your hands, leaving them silky and soft."[8]

Natura has more than 700 natural products: perfumes and face and body care products. They include mother-and-baby goods and everyday items such as shampoos and shower gels. Its major brands are Ekos, Tododia, and Mamãe e Bebê. Although Natura uses precious ingredients, it is not a luxury company. It targets the premium mass-market and midtier price points. The Ekos product line, launched in 2000, is based on ingredients extracted from the rain forest: essential oils, seeds and nuts, and leaves. It is created through a combination of "science," traditional medicine, and biodiversity. It has captured the hearts and souls of 100 million Brazilian women.

Iguatemi Costa, who is in charge of sourcing for Natura, says that the company continues to use the Amazon as a source of advantage. It is a world of discovery where new ingredients can deliver leaps in innovation. "We have a new factory, a center of innovation, in Amazonia," he says. "We aim to have 30 percent of the value of raw materials come from this special land."

Natura has innovated not only in products but also in ingredient sourcing, packaging, sales distribution, imagery, and philosophy. There is a day-and-night difference between Natura and not only the high-end global cosmetics companies, but also other multilevel-selling companies. Natura has created a streamlined hierarchy, from company to manager to sales consultant, so that there are fewer people taking profits from the frontline reps.

Natura's products are directly inspired by ancestral Brazilian traditions, with ingredients sourced from 36 local Brazilian communities. The company uses 36 native species, 38 exotics, and 56 raw materials from the Amazon, including acai berry, Brazil nuts and Brazil nut oils, cacao seeds, cupuacu butter, cumaru, guarana, lemongrass, jambu, passion fruit, and piri piri roots. Its ingredients include *Aloe barbadensis* leaf extract, *Chamomilla recutita* flower extract, *Malva sylvestris* extract, allantoin, carica, and papaya fruit extract.

It is not easy to get these ingredients. To do so, Natura's scientists must fly to Brazil's northern Atlantic Coast. Then they drive four hours on mud roads and travel by boat for several more hours to the interior rain forest. The journey from São Paulo is a 55-hour trip. When they arrive, they find indigenous Indian families harvesting nuts, flowers, and roots from the rain forest to make ingredients for the company's perfumes, soaps, and lotions. This crop delivers as much as $2,400 per acre in cash income—money that is desperately needed by the native Amazonians.

The products are sold as part of the Brazilian heritage of beauty, sensuality, and raw energy. On the company website, consumers are asked: "Do you know the tradition of the Brazilian *banho*? At all times, different cultures attributed to the waters a mysterious power. Bathing is more than body wash. [It has] magical powers associated with beauty, pleasure, happiness." Natura continues: "The bath has always been something sacred and magical, especially when it is associated with power plants. Herbal baths wash, treat, fortify, repel dangers, and bring good luck. Magical powers are also present in the tradition of the scented bath. It also has a protective function, and good luck. Patchouli, wood angola, Cumaru seeds, roots priprioca, jasmine, sandalwood, cedar, vanilla are some of the Amazonian plants that go into the recipe scented bath, 'fragrant scent' of Pará, which has the power to ward off bad luck and the evil eye and bring happiness. It is recommended to take a bath at midnight and not to dry the body with a towel."[9]

Headline: Customers as Sales Consultants— Give Them the Opportunity to Break Out of Poverty and They Will Reward You

Natura took its first great leap when it launched the company, originating an advanced set of values and opting to use the Amazon rain forest as its product laboratory. In 1974, it took its next giant leap by beginning to develop its direct-sales capability. Natura sales consultants sell the company's products to their friends and family. With more than 1.6 million consultants—formerly stay-at-home moms—Natura ensures that it can successfully pitch a health, beauty, and wellness line of 1,600 items to more than 60 percent of Brazilian households.

The consultants are extremely effective representatives of the company. They forge deep, close relationships with their customers. They know the products intimately, and they know their customers' hopes and dreams. They understand what it is to have economic limits and a desire to be beautiful. They can speak about all the technical, functional, and emotional benefits of the product as well as its authenticity. They can describe the product's origins, why it's so beneficial, and how it works.

When these consultants encounter skeptics, they use their deep product knowledge and their understanding of the customer. As one told us: "Many customers complain that the product is expensive. When this happens, I do not speak as a seller. I speak as a consumer. I say it is more worthwhile to buy a product that costs more and is good than a cheap brand you cannot trust."[10]

Given the importance of its part-time sales force, Natura is careful to nurture the individuals. It is committed to training. "Natura consultants have the opportunity to develop skills and capacities to improve their relationship with themselves and their communities," says Alessandro Carlucci, a former CEO.[11]

For full-time staff members, Natura pays well. On average, women get higher salaries than men. The company pays 1.4 times the minimum wage as well as benefits for nursery care, healthcare, life insurance, and fitness. The average consultant makes $1,100 per year—a 25 percent boost in household income and a massive difference in her family's standard of living. Many consultants use Natura as a stepping-stone out of poverty.

Natura benefits from the accumulated "friend lists" and the sweat energy of the individual sales consultants. It has come to be the fourth-largest direct seller in the world. More than 15 percent of its sales are outside Brazil, largely in Argentina, Colombia, Mexico, Chile, and Peru. It now beats Avon, the global titan, in Brazil and other Latin markets.

Headline: Commit to Sustainability, Well-Being, and Relationships

Natura has high ideals. It is a New Age company that talks about a "chain of relationships, commitment to the truth, greater diversity leading to greater wealth and vitality, a search for beauty."

It has committed its resources and its corporate power to the perpetuation of the Amazon. One way it is doing this is by helping the native Amazonians earn higher incomes, receive education, and progress in their lives. It sources the ingredients for its products from 3,000 local Amazonian families. Natura's goal is to source 30 percent of its raw materials from 10,000 families in the Amazon.[12] The company states: "We want to increase their profits, so we continue to use them. We contact them and ask for authorization to study the ingredients where they live in the forest. Then, when we develop products, we buy from them, pay a fair rate for the ingredients, and share some of the profits from the products."[13]

Apart from its commitment to Amazonian families and other stakeholders, Natura has demonstrated a profound interest in developing Brazil with its education initiative. Since 1995, the revenues from its Crer para Ver ("seeing is believing") product line have been donated entirely to education. The proceeds have been used to educate teachers and to improve educational programs and tools. To date, the program has affected 3 million people through 180 projects. It supports 350 municipalities and 5,700 schools. Some 15,000 consultants participate in the Crer para Ver program, forgoing their commissions to improve education. One consultant, Maria, says, "I only attended primary school, and I could not afford many things. I would like to see every child in school, and the Crer para Ver program is very important to support education. If I could, I would help more."

Beyond these steps, Natura is investing millions of dollars to improve logistics, reduce its environmental impact, and invest in social infrastructure, helping the local people see sustainability as being in their interest. This is essential because the company processes 12.8 million orders per year to 1 million delivery points and targets 100 million consumers.[14]

Natura's commitment to sustainable development has proved successful with both investors and customers. Since it went public in 2004, Natura's stock has grown 916 percent—four times the BM&FBOVESPA index.[15] "Our responsibility is not only to shareholders," says Carlucci. "We take our economic results into consideration, but also the socioeconomic results. We try to align all of them. It's in the DNA of the company."

Natura's management constantly measures and reevaluates what it calls the *materiality matrix*, a cross-reference of social and environmental topics that stakeholders regard as important. This matrix has seven priorities: education, sustainable entrepreneurship, relationship quality, biodiversity, reducing solid waste, saving water, and contributing to climate stability.

For a midsize company that is still largely based in one market, sustainable development is a bold aspiration. But Natura believes that it can be achieved. Luciana Hashiba, an executive in the innovation team, says that Natura "does not have to make trade-offs between doing good and doing well."

"We have high financial return to shareholders, employees, and other stakeholders through sustainable development," she says. "We provide consumers with cosmetics that enhance their well-being and sense of themselves. We support local economies and the areas around them. Our programs generate funds that are invested in projects that foster social reinforcement, the creation of alternative sources of income, food security, and leadership."[16]

Headline: An Apostle Speaks—Brazil's 100 Million Women Remain Fiercely Loyal to Natura

Vanya is a 38-year-old receptionist from São Paulo. She has a high school education, is married, and has three children.

More than a decade ago, a friend visited her home and made the initial sale of Natura products. Vanya became a convert. "Natura products are good for the environment and natural," she says. "I like the Natura company because it is worried about the environment. It makes me happy when I buy things from Natura—I feel like I am helping others."

She buys 15 products per year, including Mamãe e Bebê shampoo because "it smells good on the baby's head." She also likes the "hard soap—it lasts forever," the lipstick because "other lipsticks irritate my face," and the moisturizer because it "makes my hands nice and soft."

She has given products to foreigners as presents. "I have gifted them to a lot of people abroad—five people in the United States this year," she said. "These people already know and like Natura. When I go to the United States, I take Natura products as a gift because I think that it represents Brazil in a good way." She talks about the "good smell, good product, good packaging."[17]

Headline: Always Look for the Next Great Leap

In our conversations with Natura, the leadership team was proud of the company's growth.

The company has already established strong positions throughout Latin America. Also, it has launched in France and acquired in Australia. And it obviously has its eye on the United States. In 2012, it established a small office in Manhattan's SoHo neighborhood.

Natura's leaders desperately want not to become a conventional corporation. They have tried to avoid bureaucracy, layers of decision making, and decisions made solely on bottom-line criteria. They view their strength in the market as an opportunity to reinvest in their core values: saving the Amazon and its indigenous people, contributing to a more sustainable planet, giving their sales consultants a chance to break out of poverty, and educating poor Brazilians.

Any strategic decisions that they take will involve answering the following questions. This is the internal checklist that they use to evaluate every decision:

1. Are the company's investments building the brand?
2. Is the company objectively connected to outcomes for the greater good? Is the company's social purpose fully aligned with its business mission and strategies?
3. Is the investment tangible and real and does the market see it: Regard, Loyalty, Price Premiums, Brand?
4. Is the company focused on a key area of social investment and impact—for example, health, education, or nutrition?
5. Are there complete and full measures of activity, outcomes, learning?
6. Is the CEO personally involved and active in the orchestration?
7. Is the level of spending high enough to make a difference?
8. Is there internal congruence connecting the future world, the lives of employees, and the communities in which the company operates?

Headline: Natura Fits the "Consumer to Convert" Model Squarely

Natura is a company that delivers on our six brand principles, listed here:

Inspire. Put into effect singular inspiration and obsessive leadership that are authentic and original and that "break the frame."

- ▶ *Well-being, being well* is the company mantra to which all decisions are linked.
- ▶ The focus is on sustainability and innovation, and how they connect.

Empathize. Be inside the head of the consumer. Understand what she considers to be trade-offs and compromises, and what her hopes, dreams, and fears are, as well as her vision for a better life.

- ▶ A network of 1.6 million independent consultants allows the company to have a direct conversation with the local community (where the consultants live) and provides a robust channel for product development and feedback.

> ▶ Natura takes a flexible approach in order to serve different customer segments. As the *Economist* reported: "Lower-income customers are being enticed with a new range in lighter, cheaper packaging that gives up every drop of its contents, prompted by the firm's discovery that cost-conscious consumers were using a spoon to scrape out its containers."[18]

Dazzle through design. Innovate ingredients, manufacturing, and packaging to reflect Natura's concept of beauty and desire. Natura's package designs are intentionally modest. They use single-color corrugated packaging. The secret is in the sauce.

Innovate and refine. Never stop. Never rest on your laurels. Always seek what's next.

> ▶ Natura was ranked number 11 in the 2013 Forbes World's Most Innovative Companies list. It was number one in Latin America.
> ▶ Natura's core focus is on promoting products that represent and foster well-being.
> ▶ Natura is targeting international expansion to the United States through an innovation hub that it opened in New York two years ago.

Engage and evangelize. Early users set the tone, drive referrals, and recruit more users. Personal endorsements drive trial and enthusiasm and provide an opportunity to listen to what customers have to say.

> ▶ The first consumers of Natura became its first salespeople. They literally carried the bag to their friends.
> ▶ Engagement was around product, the routine of beauty, and a celebration of femininity.

Treat people well. Employees and suppliers should be treated with respect and dignity, as Natura does with its suppliers and the broader community of the Amazon basin. The company is very aware of the issues surrounding sustainability and its own impact on the environment. For example, it assesses how much water it uses.

Headline: Lessons from Natura

There are four lessons.

First, one company can make a difference. Natura does it every day for its 1.6 million sales reps. It gives them training, income, and a position from which to engage in a commercial dialogue. It pays its full-time employees wages that are 40 percent higher than required, provides on average a higher wage for women than for men, and continuously focuses on opportunities for improvement. For the native Indian families in the Amazon, it furnishes employment, cash wages, education, and links to the modern world. To consumers, Natura offers natural products that make the customers feel more beautiful, pampered, and cared for.

Second, share the benefits. Natura treats its sales reps with respect and honor. It takes care of its suppliers. It pays its workforce above-market wages. It aims to deliver above consumer expectations. Everyone connected to Natura benefits.

Third, develop a philosophy and follow it. Natura stands out for its "well-being, being well" philosophy and its triple-bottom-line approach that takes into consideration society and the environment as well as its own financials. Its product innovation has the twist of being based on Brazilian Amazon secret ingredients, with their myths, science, and medicine-man mystique. The sales force is the customer. Consultants receive training about the products, but also training in self-discovery, self-esteem, and empowerment. The company has invested significantly in logistics to provide 24-hour delivery to 4,800 cities in Brazil. This is beyond the availability of traditional retail products. There is a huge emotional benefit for consumers and consultants, who garner respect, inclusion in the larger world, a sense of belonging, pride, and "real" beauty. Long before Dove soap's celebrated campaign for real women, Natura was showing the full range of Brazilian women in natural surroundings. Other brands that compete in the space are more transactional and are perceived to be of lower quality. Natura reps stretch hard for the company and deliver up to three times the productivity of the competition.

Fourth, don't stop taking great leaps. The Natura leadership team talks about the beginning of a new growth cycle. It has the resources for worldwide acquisitions. It has momentum in its home market. It has an army of sales consultants calling on 100 million consumers. It has the imagery of its innovation and production facilities in Manaus, deep in the Amazon. It takes innovation seriously and seeks consistency with Natura's objectives—sourcing of ingredients from the Amazon; a sustainable, limited carbon and water footprint; and truth in its claims. It sees an opportunity to be innovative in broad categories, connect better to its consumers' needs, and take its value-driven business forward.

Mercadona

Thirty years ago, Mercadona was a little-known laggard in the ancient Mediterranean port of Valencia, Spain's third-largest city. Today, it's the country's number one retailer. Not only that, but it's Europe's most admired grocer, topping better-known retailers—such as Carrefour, Ahold, Delhaize, Tesco, and Walmart—by far in BCG's proprietary Brand Advocacy Index, which rates companies according to consumers' recommendations.[19] Mercadona has added about €15 billion of market cap value in just two decades. It has defied the worst global economic crisis in 75 years. Above all, it has reinvented the supermarket segment in a global context. In its own market, it is considered to have a price offering similar to that of the lowest discounters *and* a quality and home-brand attractiveness that matches and even exceeds that of the best leading consumer brands. The Mercadona story is as significant an innovation and as powerful an industry influence as Walmart, IKEA, and Amazon.

It has achieved all this by doing the following:

▶ Using its intimate knowledge of its customers to produce a heavily curated assortment of high-quality home-brand products. Customers go out of their way to buy Mercadona's products rather than world-renowned brands.

▶ Consistently delivering outstanding value. Through smart innovation in the way it works with suppliers, as well as in manufacturing, packaging and supply chain automation, the home-brand products are on average 40 percent cheaper than their rivals.

▶ Constantly taking giant leaps with new products and business models. Every fourth year, we have seen Mercadona introduce business model innovation. For example, how it distills customer insight, or creates real customer advocacy, or empowers its employees.

The result is that it has left its competitors trailing in its wake. Around the world, the battle lines are drawn between retailers and suppliers/manufacturers. Big-brand manufacturers are retreating as home-brand or private-label products surge in value. In Spain, private-label products command 45 percent of the market value—well above the European average of 37 percent.

Who's going to win the battle? Mercadona has found a unique way to integrate its preferred suppliers and beat its rival retailers. Cleverly, it has not needed to buy its way into manufacturing. It has stayed asset-light by pioneering a system of virtual integration. It has become both a retailer *and* a manufacturer—or, as it prefers to say, a "totaler": a company that develops products in close partnership with its customers and suppliers.

Above all, it has taken giant leaps, not timid steps, on its journey. At each crucial turning point, Juan Roig, the company's main shareholder and chief executive, has dared to be bold. Little did he know that by doing so, he would become a billionaire and Spain's fourth-richest man.[20]

One of his favorite phrases is, *"El cambio es lo único que no cambia en Mercadona."* Translated, this means, "Change is the only thing that never changes at Mercadona." It sums up his philosophy. It explains Mercadona's restless quest to be better. The world never stands still, and neither should you. If you do, you will get overtaken by events—and by your competitors.

Headline: Giant Leap Number 1: Offer Your Customers the Lowest Prices—Every Day of the Week

Juan Roig and his wife, Hortensia, took control of Mercadona in 1990. He bought a majority stake from his brother and sisters. Ten years earlier, the siblings had bought the company from their parents, who had started the business as a butcher shop.[21]

The business was small. There were just eight grocery stores across Valencia. But it had prospered in its first four years as Spain enjoyed a period of rejuvenation after the restoration of the monarchy in the mid-1970s.

Over the next 10 years, Roig and his siblings steered Mercadona toward sustained growth. By 1991, it boasted 150 stores. But then it encountered its first real problems. It faced stiff competition from international rivals who were breaking into the Spanish market. One of these was Carrefour, from neighboring France. This supermarket giant was at the forefront of the new trends sweeping through the retail industry: investing in larger stores, economies of scale, automation, a wide selection of global grocery brands, and often hypermarkets on the periphery of towns and cities.

Mercadona looked old-fashioned. It was a classic "high-low" supermarket, with lots of promotions to tempt the customer. It was clear to Roig that his business was in urgent need of reinvention. With bankruptcy staring him in the face, he studied successful retailers abroad, including Walmart.

He vowed to offer what he called "everyday low (low, low) prices." This was a major strategic shift. Until then, Mercadona had pushed products using periodic promotions with reduced prices.

Headline: Giant Leap Number 2: Keep Prices Low, but Don't Compromise on Quality—and Surprise Your Customers

Mercadona is not merely a discounter. Roig deeply understands the power of the equation *price times quality equals value*. Soon after launching his low-prices strategy, he looked for a way to keep prices low without compromising the quality of his products. He also wanted to be different. After 15 years at the helm of Mercadona, he knew very well that he needed to "surprise" his customers. Otherwise, why would anyone choose to shop at his stores?

His solution was to work with a select group of suppliers to produce home-brand or private-label products. This way, he could be sure that he was offering something that his rivals couldn't. This really was a giant leap—his second. He understood the enormousness of the decision. It would pit him against the big-name brands from around the world. He had to prepare for the battle of his career and do so from a position of disadvantage—a one-country footprint, and small scale. Only local market insight could fuel his success.

Roig turned to a few of Mercadona's 2,000 suppliers. These suppliers were midsize, often family-owned businesses. They often owned the brand that was ranked third or even fourth in their category. He asked them to manufacture Mercadona-branded goods. He asked them to deliver unique products of exceptional quality at an exceptional price. In return, he offered them special long-term relationships and a guaranteed market.

But the relationship is not simply transactional. It goes deeper. There is a real integrated partnership. Mercadona, like most of its suppliers, is a family-owned business. Roig is the president of the supervisory board. His wife and his four daughters all sit on the board as well. He understands how the suppliers work and how they think. What he has done is take a family ethic, in which people are connected by a common emotional bond, and extend it to encompass all the people whose working lives are devoted to making Mercadona a success. The principle is simple: look after your suppliers, and they will help you look after your customers.

The suppliers' fortunes have been transformed by their union with Mercadona. Their founding families have become rich. Their workers—more than 43,500 people—have earned good wages. For its part, Mercadona has achieved "virtual integration" without the cost of actually acquiring the supplier companies. They say that there is complete transparency and complete trust. Mercadona has an "open book" relationship, giving it access to the suppliers' financial data. Equally, the suppliers get exceptional access to the bank of customer insights that Mercadona has collected.

To see how this relationship works, take the case of Siro Group. Until 2005, Siro was a secondary player in its core activity as a cookie manufacturer. Then, influenced by Mercadona, it entered the lucrative sliced-bread business under the supermarket's Hacendado brand. At the time, this market was dominated by two companies: Bimbo and Panrico. Mercadona was keen to break this duopoly because these companies did not give it preferred access to their products, and, as a result, it could not respond to consumers' demands for better-priced, better-quality, fresher bread.

Allied with Siro, Mercadona coinvested in new manufacturing equipment. Together they spent €250 million—and guaranteed the market for Siro's sliced bread. The results were immediate. In 2005, Siro's net sales were €105 million. The following year, they rose to €158 million. By 2014, they had risen to €600 million, boosted by sales of other new product lines created specifically for Mercadona: fresh and frozen pastries, savory snacks, and dried pasta.[22]

Today, there are 120 integrated suppliers known as *interproveedores*.[23] They manufacture some 2,000 Mercadona products that account for more than 55 percent of the supermarket's sales. As well as Hacendado, there is Deliplus (cosmetics), Bosque Verde (drugstore items), and Compy (pet care). The great strength of these products is that they are not just cheaper than their branded rivals, but also distinctive. They are designed to "surprise and delight" the customer.

Look at the products created by RNB Cosmetics under the Deliplus label. This family-owned business, founded in 1990 by two pharmacists in Valencia, produces skin care products. It has been a Mercadona supplier since 1994 and an integrated supplier since 1999. Its chief executive, Vicente Ruiz, sees eye to eye with Roig. "We are true partners, and our partnership is based on a win-win," he says. "We believe that people need surprises. They need to be delighted."

In 2009, RNB launched Oliva, a body cream that uses olive oil, which is greatly favored by Spanish consumers. Although other creams also use olive oil, RNB developed its product and packaging around this distinctive ingredient. It went the extra mile by partnering with Lavernia & Cienfuegos, a design boutique, to create the perfect container. Then it set the price at a third that of its branded rival. The result was stunning. Oliva soon started selling 1 million units every month. As one customer told us: "One of my finds of the summer is Mercadona's Deliplus olive oil body cream. If you can save a few euros on a product that you know is going to work, why wouldn't you?"

With these products, Mercadona has sealed its place in the hearts of Spaniards. In a survey of 5,200 households by TNS, a market research firm, its products were ranked number one in value for the money.[24] Deliplus, which can be bought only in Mercadona stores, is now one of the leading health-and-beauty brands in Spain, with a market share of nearly 20 percent. It is striking that its stellar growth has occurred during the depths of the global economic crisis. In 2008, it controlled just 8.2 percent of the market, as opposed to L'Oréal's 25.5 percent and P&G's 13.5 percent. Now, it has overtaken P&G and is just 2.6 percentage points behind L'Oréal.

Why has it been successful? Its products are well priced, and they can't be found anywhere else. Another product that has wowed consumers is Deliplus Chica Fashion for Girls, a deodorant. "I used to use Rexona Girl because I was crazy about the smell," one consumer told us. "But since I discovered this deodorant from Mercadona, I'm never going back."

Headline: Giant Leap Number 3: The Power of Reciprocity—Look After Your Customers and Employees

Like many of the leaders in this book, Roig is driven by a greater purpose. It's not only about making a profit. One of his most important principles is "reciprocity," the idea that if you are to be satisfied, you must first satisfy others. "When I finished my studies, I had only one dream," he once said, "to create a company whose objective was not only to generate profits, but also to take care of customers and employees."[25] Throughout his career, he has sought to fulfill this dream. The various measures he has taken together constitute his third great leap.

Customers

Roig's core belief is that the customer must be at the center of everything. Of course, many companies say this. But Mercadona's story shows just how it should be done: by creating an emotional bond with the customer that will survive the most trying times. It means listening to customers. It means reacting to or anticipating their needs. It means delivering not once, not twice, but time after time.

For Mercadona, the customer is *el jefe*—"the boss." This is not just another way of saying that the customer is king. From Mercadona's perspective, the king is a distant figure, whereas the boss is an immediate and commanding presence, with powerful emotions that need to be listened and responded to. Many of the bosses, as conceived by Mercadona, are female. The name of the business stems from the words for *market* and *woman* in the local Spanish dialect of Valencia: *merca* and *dona*.

You ignore the boss at your peril. As Roig explained recently: "Our 'bosses' . . . have been the guiding light of the decisions we have taken, because every step has fulfilled our commitment to prescribing the best solution for them to put together their total shopping with the highest quality at the lowest possible price."[26]

This "prescribing" role—what we call *advocacy*—is critical. Ultimately, Mercadona aspires to be the shopper's trusted advisor. Its stores are smaller than many hypermarkets. But it has refined the art of retailing so that it is renowned for its assortment or selection.

Typically, a conventional supermarket carries 15,000 to 25,000 items. Walmart, always the exception when it comes to size, stocks 140,000 items. Mercadona, by contrast, stocks just 8,000 items.[27] But it takes great care to pick those products—from among more than 1 million available in Spain—that offer the best quality-to-price ratio without sacrificing quality or safety. For instance, according to our analysis, the typical Carrefour hypermarket carries 120 SKUs (stock-keeping units) of detergents, as opposed to 45 at the typical Mercadona. If you look closely, Mercadona's 45 SKUs actually cover more specific customer needs than Carrefour's 120 SKUs. In other words, Mercadona helps its customers get what they really want—and more quickly.

To understand how Mercadona can do this, it is necessary to look at how it interacts with its customers. Most retailers use advanced analytics to track the spending habits of their customers and to help serve them better. In this respect, Mercadona is no different from its rivals. It was the first Spanish company to use scanners to read bar codes at the point of sale. On a routine basis, its market analysis department analyzes cash register receipts to form a profile of the needs of the average customer, inspects published data on pricing and supply, and reviews the stores' product assortment data, including the total number of sales and the speed of inventory turns.

Where it does differ, however, is in its commitment to developing a face-to-face relationship with its customers. For a while, Mercadona conducted in-depth research groups. Regular customers, typically 12 to 14 people, were invited to the store for a 90-minute meeting with employees to discuss a new product or a new product category. Each session followed a prepared agenda: a welcome speech by the leading employee, then introductions by each of the customers (discussing what they like to buy), and then a deep-dive presentation on the new product (its key features, how it is manufactured, and advice on the best way to use it). At the end, customers were given a "goodie bag" with the product to take home and share with family and friends.

At the peak of this initiative, Mercadona held 180,000 meetings and attracted nearly 2 million customers. It created pride and ownership among store employees and strong emotional connections between Mercadona, its employees, and its customers. We talked to several customers who attended these groups. "In these sessions, you can try their products and they tell you who manufactures them and the quality controls they follow," one customer told us. "You learn so much and you feel safe when using their products."[28]

Employees

If Roig cares deeply about Mercadona's customers, he cares deeply about his workers, too. The company has become recognized as a national trendsetter when it comes to employment issues. In 1995, it launched its plan to offer permanent contracts for all employees, which it now does.[29] It also offers stable hours—and no Sunday work. "People have a family life," said one executive.

There is equal pay for men and women and a generous profit-sharing scheme for all levels of staff. Even a cashier or shelf stocker who has been with the company for more than four years can get the equivalent of two months' salary in bonuses. In 2014, Mercadona generated €543 million of net profit. Of this, some €263 million was given to employees. In many ways, Mercadona operates like a cooperative. Employees really feel that it is "their" company.

In another sign of his long-term commitment to his staff, Roig sanctioned the investment of €37 million in 1.4 million hours of training. He believes that, properly trained, "an employee has unlimited potential to satisfy our 'bosses.'"[30] Much of the training focuses on the skills that employees need in order to advise customers on the best products to choose for any particular household task. This could be a Mercadona product or, equally, a product manufactured by a big-name brand.

This investment is paying off. Mercadona's employee turnover is one of the lowest in the retail industry across Europe.

Headline: Giant Leap Number 4: Never Fall Asleep—There's Always a Crisis Waiting to Get You

The story of Mercadona might seem like one giant leap after another, without any missteps.

Until 2008, it looked that way. Then the financial crisis struck. Spain was one of the worst-hit countries. Unemployment among young people exceeded 50 percent. Mercadona was not immune to the savage impact on customers. The crisis exposed the fact that Mercadona had not kept its promise to deliver "everyday low prices." As Roig told his board of directors: "In times of plenty, we fell asleep."[31]

Later, he met the CEOs of the privileged group of *interproveedores*. He was livid. No one who was there has forgotten what Roig did. As one executive told us, toward the end of the meal, Roig left the room. A few minutes later he returned, wearing a tie but no shirt. There was a deathly silence. But no one dared question him. Eventually, he asked them why no one had wondered why he had taken off his shirt. "You can't remain silent," Roig said. "You have to be brave, make proposals and take decisions." He then pinched the fat on his waist. As he did so, he said: "This fat is not necessary. We must eliminate anything that does not add value and that the customer will not pay for."[32]

After this, Roig stood up and asked the CEOs to follow him. He led them to the car park. There, he pointed to all the grand cars parked next to each other—the executives' cars. He did not need to spell out the obvious: that the suppliers' executives, not the customers, had been the real beneficiaries.

His point made, Roig demanded major price cuts. This was his fourth giant leap. "We have to start pinching pennies," he said. He set them the task of cutting the cost of the average household grocery bill from €600 per month to €500 per month.

To do this, the *interproveedores* changed the packaging on hundreds of products. For example, they cut the amount of plastic used in water bottles and the amount of cardboard used for packaging milk. The changes were seemingly slight. For example, the amount of cardboard used to make each milk carton was reduced by only 1.3 grams. But the impact was significant: overall, 440 metric tons of cardboard were cut, resulting in reduced manufacturing costs and a transportation bill that was lowered by €2 million per year. Likewise, the amount of air in packets of cereal and nuts was reduced, cutting costs by nearly €1 million per year. In all, since the economic crisis struck, Mercadona has achieved €3 billion of annual savings from clever innovations in packaging.

Another significant cost element for any retailer is distribution. In 2007, Mercadona had started to pilot warehouse automation. Then, as the crisis broke out, it went against the current and decided to triple its investments in large, fully automated warehouses for all kinds of groceries—ambient, chilled, and frozen. As a result, the accuracy and frequency of delivery were further increased. Also, Mercadona started to codevelop supplier parks located next to their warehouses to reduce logistics costs. Today the company has four large, fully automated—or "intelligent"—warehouses across Spain and a level of overall supply chain automation that is unique in the supermarket segment worldwide.

IN HIS OWN WORDS

Mercadona's Boss on the Real Bosses: Juan Roig on the Customer

"Our results come from satisfying 'the boss,' as internally we call our customers. They are at the center of our decisions. In Mercadona, we firmly believe in the universal truth that first you have to give to receive. It is a law that is always fulfilled. It is based on the figure of the mother, who always is the first to give without initially wanting anything in return.

"The boss is the customer, because she has the power of life and death of the company when we lift the blinds at nine o'clock each morning. That is why we strive every day to fully meet the needs of our bosses. To achieve this, we need to know their expectations and understand what their real needs are.

"We are aware that we have to work in the digital area, and we are doing it little by little. In fact, we are conducting a Digital Transformation Plan 2012–2018, in which we aim to invest €126 million. We have begun putting in place a new Data Processing Center (DPC) that allows us to have computerized dry products and fresh products. That will allow us to streamline processes and manage the assortment in real time to further strengthen the efficiency and productivity of the company and suppliers.

"Our customers told us in late 2008 that they thought we were sleeping. So they forced us to react. We had to make decisions and review our assembly line. We anticipated: we reduced prices and reviewed the line. Along with our integrated suppliers, we reviewed all the processes to lower prices while maintaining quality. Since then, we have managed to save €3 billion for the bosses.

"Our daily challenge is to continue to strive to provide the highest quality at the lowest possible price and the best service to our customers—and try not to sleep, not to distance ourselves from our model because past successes do not ensure future successes.

"The most important thing is to be consistent between what you say and what you do. If the boss perceives that there is a difference between words and actions, she will lose confidence. Therefore, the results should be the result of, first, satisfy the boss; second, achieve sales targets; and third, obtain profits. The way to keep track of the daily activity of the company is to be in the field, constantly observing the environment and, of course, following the daily pulse of numbers."

Headline: Giant Leap Number 5: Innovate, Then Implement

Private-label products are often dismissed as cheap imitations of branded products, which are seen as the real thing. Roig always resisted this slur. But in the wake of the financial crisis, he renewed his commitment to give customers products that were not only cheaper than before, but also better than before. He achieved this with his fifth giant leap, radical innovation. As he reduced prices for customers, he invested in two new initiatives. In the middle of the economic storm, he opted to add cost to the business. He hired and developed a collection of experts who were skilled in interpreting and implementing what customers really want. He then launched a series of innovation centers.

The Monitors

Roig is on a constant mission to get even better intelligence on what customers really, really want. Mercadona's focus groups, which were attended by millions of people, had been an enormous success. But they were complicated and costly to run. As the economic crisis got worse, he had to find another way to collect and act on customer insight.

His solution was a fast-track system to establish what customers were thinking and to execute the best of their recommendations. The core rung of this ladder is the "monitor." There are 186 of them. They are stationed in stores and in innovation centers across the country. They are human listening posts. They are the people who gather customers' opinions from the stores, from social media, or from other sources.

Every year, Mercadona receives some 340,000 suggestions and inquiries from the bosses. This provides clear input for product development and innovation. The monitors also collect information from employees, who are encouraged to know their regular customers by name and to spot opportunities for new and better products.

Of course, it is one thing to listen to customers and quite another to act on their suggestions. The reason that Mercadona can make these innovations so quickly is that the crucial information is passed to the decision makers rapidly. Roig has been especially scrupulous in ensuring that the voice of the bosses is heard loud and clear by the top executives.

Mercadona learned this lesson the hard way. A few years ago, during a face-to-face meeting to taste one particular product, 19 customers expressed satisfaction. But one didn't. Disregarding this minority voice, Mercadona pressed ahead with the launch of the product, only to find that it was not popular: the one critic had been right after all. Since then, Mercadona has been careful to respect the views of individuals. One of the phrases commonly heard at the stores is, "A single complaint is just the tip of the iceberg."

Innovation Centers

From the mid-1990s, when Mercadona launched its first home-brand products, it has been committed to "surprising" customers with innovative products. But with the financial crisis, it committed to radical innovation. This required a different level of investment. So, in 2011, Mercadona launched its first innovation center. Here, regular customers were invited to spend up to four hours in "real-life" settings, where they could be observed trying out different new products.

Since launching its first innovation center, Mercadona has added another 11. The centers cover a broad product range, from cosmetics to chocolate. Hosting some 12,000 customers every year, they have allowed the company to launch new products that surprise customers on a regular basis. Mercadona is constantly introducing innovations and refinements. In 2014, it made changes in 450 of its SKUs—10 percent of its total number. For example, sticking a plastic lid on a large tin of tuna made it easier to open and increased its sales by 60 percent in 2010.[33]

One innovation center focuses on dairy, desserts, and ice cream. It was launched in October 2012, and it has been visited by more than 2,000 bosses. It adopted a "listen and observe" approach—and responded quickly to the wishes of customers. For instance, it introduced a sweet-and-sour ice cream called Caramel Popcorn. Also, it developed a liquefied rice ice cream for people who are lactose-intolerant and mini-bonbon double chocolate ice cream for people who are conscious of their weight. Some of its ice creams have been ranked in the top 10 innovative products by Kantar Worldpanel, a market research company.

Headline: Great Leap Number 6: Make Change Your Watchword and Your One Constant, and Don't Be Afraid to Go Back to Your Roots

Mercadona has been a startling success, one that's all the more remarkable in that its growth has not been stunted by the global economic recession. From being on the brink of bankruptcy in the early 1990s, Mercadona has grown to become a giant, with €31 billion in revenues. From 1999 to 2011, profits rose 23 percent. Market share nearly tripled from 8 percent to 23 percent. Today, Mercadona has 1,521 stores across Spain.[34]

Throughout the retail industry, supermarkets are cutting costs, shedding jobs, and removing old-style counters. Daring to be different, Mercadona is going in another direction. It is returning to its "shopkeeper" heritage with a focus on fresh food: fish, meat, fruits and vegetables, and bread.

Mercadona has trained a host of specialist shopkeepers— bakers, grocers, fishmongers, butchers, and charcutiers. Moreover, it has tested the best way to present the fresh products in six "laboratories" positioned in selected stores. This has allowed it to pursue its classic approach: questioning each strategy every day and applying only those that the customers, through their response, confirm that they want.

Just as it forged close relationships with selected suppliers of packaged goods, Mercadona is now building links with the suppliers of fresh food—the farmers and fishermen. Across Spain, this sector numbers some 22,000 people, including 12,000 fishermen, 6,000 crop producers, and 4,000 livestock producers. As Roig explained: "We have to get to know them and to work together, because they, through their effort and involvement, are the ones who are going to help us guarantee quality and service to win over our bosses."[35]

Mercadona's readiness to work closely with farmers and fishermen underscores the big point: every retailer must provide the consumer with a connection to the core products it puts on its shelves. This could be the ingredients in a detergent or face cream or the freshly caught fish in the market.

Already, as a result of its "fresh" initiative, Mercadona has opened fish, fruit and vegetable, and bakery sections in every supermarket, as well as fresh meat and deli meat sections in 252 stores.

Headline: The Power of Brand Advocacy: The Value of Listening to Your Customers

It intuitively makes sense to think that if you listen and respond to your customers, they will reward you with their loyalty.

Of course, there are the corporate numbers, which point to significant growth as a consequence of customer approval. But there is another proof point. BCG compiles an index based on a company's performance in a survey of 32,000 consumers in the United States, the United Kingdom, Germany, France, and Spain. It ranks companies on the basis of spontaneous and nonspontaneous or prompted recommendations and criticisms. Among grocers, Mercadona is the top-rated company, with an overall Brand Advocacy score of 54 percent, as opposed to the industry average of 24 percent. This places it above all the traditional "incumbent" supermarket chains in the different countries across Europe and the United States—that is, Carrefour and Leclerc in France, Aldi in Germany, Tesco and Sainsbury's in the United Kingdom, and Walmart in the United States.[36]

One consumer we spoke to is a 23-year-old medical student from Valencia, Mercadona's home city. She has known about Mercadona all her life. Her mother took her there as a child, and she would play in the aisles while her mother did the shopping. "When I was a child, I remember that going to other places with my mother was like an obligation, but going to Mercadona was fun."[37]

"I know that in Mercadona, I can find everything I need to make a nice dinner," she said. This is not to say that she is uncritical. As she pointed out, she has to go to Carrefour to get sushi. But she does the bulk of her shopping at Mercadona. "I can usually find something new to inspire me to create a new dish."

In our survey, some 66 percent of consumers said that Mercadona provides a "great" or "good" experience. This places it above Aldi and Lidl, Europe's leading discounters from Germany. Indeed, it puts it on a par with feted consumer brands such as Apple's iPhone. With this level of advocacy, Mercadona does not need to spend money on traditional marketing. It can instead allocate its resources to brand development, innovation, and word-of-mouth marketing.[38]

Mercadona is especially good at focusing not only on customers, but also on noncustomers. It drives customer advocacy. The company invited nearly 500,000 women to attend in-store sessions on its cosmetics brand, Deliplus. These demonstrations had professional trainers tell women about the products' benefits—give the technical advantages, explain the science, translate it into functional benefits, and show how it works.

It was an immediate success—and a major contributor to same-store sales growth of 5 percent annually during the intense Spanish recession.

*****

THE STORY OF COOP ITALIA: WHEN THE CONSUMER IS ALSO THE OWNER

Another European retailer echoes the lessons from Mercadona. Coop Italia traces its roots back to 1854.[39] It predates the foundation of the Kingdom of Italy. Today, its revenues approach €18 billion, and it is thriving. The Coop is the largest Italian retailer. It is directly owned by consumers, like the outdoor equipment retailer REI in the United States.

Its mandate is to defend its members' purchasing power by collectively acquiring goods at better terms than the members would achieve individually.

The Coop has been able to set itself apart from other companies by establishing strong links with the people and their communities.

"Consumers expect more from a cooperative than from another type of player," said Silvano Ambrosetti, former president of Coop Lombardia.

According to Turiddo Campaini, president of Unicoop Firenze, "The distinctive element of Coop is that the member is at the same time shareholder, client, and citizen. Responding to the needs and aspirations of members implies conditioning all our activities, forcing everyone in the cooperative to continuously verify the alignment of his or her activity to that mission."

Coop offers its members exclusive financial services (loans and credit cards) and a dedicated Coop organization. This includes 1,400 centers for health, wellness, culture, and sports, along with other services, including psychological and legal assistance, payment of utility bills, and free home delivery for the elderly and disabled.

Headline: Consumers Trust, Love, and Promote the Coop

"I am a member, and so is everyone in my family," says one 52-year-old female consumer who we talked to in Milan. "I have two children. For each one, I have opened a saving account with Coop. I've been shopping at Coop once a week for the past 30 years, and I often participate in my local Coop's cultural initiatives. Coop is the supermarket I shop most frequently; actually, I almost never go anywhere else. I have dedicated promotions there."

"When I think of Coop, I think of product safety, consistency, and confidence," she continues. "Coop is always available to me and is honest. Whenever there is an issue, or even when I purchase the wrong product, they are willing to exchange it or refund me. There is a great assortment, and Coop always carries excellent brands. Other supermarkets don't offer such a great variety, and there's great care about best-before dates; I never have to worry about that. As a member, you are treated with great care. I remember not more than a few months ago I was about to buy a new cellphone. The lady behind the electronics counter asked me if I was a member. After I said yes, she pointed out that in a week's time there was going to be a promotional sale on the same model that would save me 25 percent. This does not happen at ordinary supermarkets. This is a reason for coming back on a regular basis."

In the last few decades, Coop revenues have grown steadily: €2.6 billion in 1980 (valued in 2003 €), €6.2 billion in 1990, €9.3 billion in 2000, and about €14 billion in 2013. It has held a 15 percent share and has 8 million members. Private-label goods represent one of Coop's key strengths, strongly recognized by its consumers. Today Coop has the highest private-label penetration of all grocery retailers in Italy—about 27 percent, as opposed to its main competitors' average of 17 percent.[40]

Coop's private label is an extension of its core values through the product concept and the supply chain. Private-label products are meant to be healthy, convenient, environmentally friendly, ethically guaranteed, and of good quality and taste. Coop guarantees strict sourcing definitions and multiple product controls. Standards are set to meet external certifications, and the organization partners with 24 universities and research institutes. Private-label products cover a broad range of Italian delicacies, from cured ham made from free-range pigs to buffalo mozzarella and Tuscan extra-virgin olive oil.

According to Marco Pedroni, the current president of Coop Italia, "Cooperatives are organizations with a very long life. This is due to the fact that they have always capitalized on the results achieved in good times, and at times of crisis, before winding down the business and shedding jobs, they use the capital accumulated over the years. We have accumulated capital over 150 years through a variety of processes. This form of corporate enterprise is very resilient in the face of varying market circumstances."

One Conclusion

The stories of Natura and Mercadona are stories about founders who achieved ascendancy with customers. The core of Natura is its 1.6-million-person sales force. These people are consumers, advocates, and connectors. They speak about their experience with and the benefits of the products. They explain how the products are used and celebrate the beauty of expression. Mercadona's customers are the "bosses." These people look for innovation, experimentation, and value. Mercadona endeavors to provide this on a continuous basis—every day.

Three Takeaways

1. **Consumers hang on your every word.** They look for special, magical ingredients. They look at how you manufacture and package your products. They want to know all about the secrets inside those products. Natura learned to use Amazonian ingredients and to make them a point of differentiation. Mercadona found ways to make home-brand products that rivaled products from big-name brands.

2. **Make bold investments.** You need to distort your resources when you're in a crisis and when you're attempting to take advantage of an opportunity. You need to make decisions about parts of your business. Natura has invested in sales and manufacturing. Mercadona spent more than 50 percent of its R&D budget on a handful of high-visibility products. In your consumers' eyes, you win when you create spectacular offerings that deliver a vision for them. Do this every day. In 2014, Mercadona introduced 450 new SKUs—more than one for every day of the year.

3. **As leader, you make the first giant leap.** All eyes are on you when you are the leader. When you speak the truth, your organization listens and accepts it. You must use this power to move your company forward in decisive ways. Natura's Antonio Luiz Seabra and Mercadona's Juan Roig are powerful, positive spokesmen for their brands. They are front and center of everything that their companies do.

SOME KEY ACTION POINTS

1. "Me too" will not get you where you want to go.
2. Create a visual and communication touchpoint.
3. Richly describe your target consumer. Know your "bosses" intimately.
4. Build everything so that the consumer can see it in a snap—be able to integrate your concept and your advantages.
5. Never give up trying to evolve and improve. Paradoxically, giant leaps happen only when you're continuously looking to deliver the unmet and latent needs of your customers on a daily basis.

CHAPTER EIGHT

Find Out What Schismogenesis Means (Because It Will Save Your Relationships)

THE CHAPTER IN A BOX

The Main Point

Anthropologists have a word for human relationships: *schismogenesis*. They use the word to mean relationships are not stable—they are cycling up or down. Little things can turn into firestorms between people and can lead to war. The right eye contact or smile can lead to love. Here, we have applied this term to brands, because they rely on their emotional bonds with customers. At any moment, your brand could be lifted high or knocked down low by events. Take nothing for granted. You can drive a cycle up or you can yield to the winds of destruction.

Chapter Overview

The word *schismogenesis* does not trip easily off the tongue, but you should know what it means and how it applies to you. It is a term from anthropology that refers to relationships that are not stable. In the context of brands, it describes the fact that they are inherently unstable: strengths can become weaknesses, and weaknesses can be converted into strengths. Every brand has the potential to cycle up or cycle down. If it's not cycling up, then it's contracting.

When things are going well, it is easy to forget the laws of schismogenesis. Who can predict that a fall is lurking just around the corner? Equally, when things are going badly, it is easy to forget that sparks can fly and a turnaround is possible. When you're at the bottom of the "V," it almost always feels impossible to recover. But remember: there is almost always a way back from the brink.

Headline: Confront a Crisis

What happens when a crisis strikes a company? How do the company's leaders react? How do they treat customers and suppliers? What do they do when government agencies attack their reputations and their values? What do they do when the competition circles them, offering large rebates, incentives, and glorious promises if consumers switch brands?

In this chapter, we tell the postrecall story of Toyota in the United States. It is a case study in courage, conviction, and reliance on values. It is a story about leadership from the top and commitment to a dealer network that is the backbone of the consumer brand. Toyota is a textbook story of recovery and prosperity. We also tell the story of the National Football League. Right now, it is in the middle of a crisis. No matter how exciting any NFL championship game may be, there are deep wounds inside the league. These wounds have to do with values, value, and human weakness. The crisis is about the clash of characters and the clash of character. We offer these two contrasting stories as proof that schismogenesis is alive and well.

You are never stable as a brand. You are either moving up or moving down. When you move down, it is often with accelerating velocity. When that happens, many brand owners panic. That's the equivalent of buying high and selling low. When you are in a tailspin, don't panic. Take the time to do a holistic assessment. What are the roots of your original success? What do your original brand advocates think now? What is true in your core that can be your salvation? What was your original point of light and good? What is the truth about the competitiveness of your offering? Do you still win on technical and functional benefits? Do you have an emotional claim that is now covered with error and confusion?

Toyota

Toyota entered the U.S. market in 1956.[1] Back then, its cars sold for less than $2,000. Branding was primitive. The first model was called a Toyopet. It had a reputation for shaking, overheating, stalling, and guzzling gas. In those days, "Made in Japan" was often a term of scorn.

But over the next two decades, the company invested in world-class manufacturing, product improvements, and claims-based advertising. It continuously gained share against the Big Three in the United States—Ford, General Motors, and

Chrysler. In 1965, Toyota was awarded the prestigious Deming Prize for quality. The company's growth accelerated after 1968, when it introduced the Corona and Corolla models, cars that took volume from the high-selling Chevrolet, Pontiac, and Buick brands. In its original advertising, Toyota was positioned as 40 percent less expensive, delivering perfect reliability, and inviting conversation and engagement. "Invest $1,726 in a Toyota Corolla 2-door and see what happens," according to the print version of the advertisement. This hard value positioning allowed Toyota to take 15 percent of the market between 1965 and 2010. GM lost 31 share points during this period.

By the 1980s, U.S. consumers consistently rated Toyota cars as having better value, getting a better resale price, and being substantially more reliable than American cars. It was a heady time to run Toyota USA—dealerships were bigger and better financed than the competition's and had higher inventory turns. The company needed order takers, not skilled salespeople, on the dealership floor. Cars sold on a Toyota lot delivered a higher dealer margin per car than those made by GM, Ford, or Chrysler. In addition, we estimate that, at the peak, the cars had a $1,500 per car cost advantage over equivalent American models. They also packed in more features, had better reliability and safety, and had a much higher resale value. By the time of the first crisis, Toyota had 39,000 employees in North America. It had invested an estimated $24.5 billion in plants in Kentucky, Mississippi, Indiana, Ontario, Texas, and Mexico.[2] It was a leader in hybrids and electrics. In fact, Toyota worldwide sold more hybrids and electric vehicles than all others combined.

The combination of lower cost, higher price realization, and momentum made the U.S. auto business look like a chess game at checkmate—winner, Toyota.

Headline: Create Some Core Guiding Precepts That Can Endure Trying Times—The "Toyota Way" Led to Sustained Brand Leadership and Heritage

Toyoda, later renamed Toyota, was founded as a car company in 1935. The founders had sold the patents and equipment for their original family business, a textile loom operation, and decided, with encouragement from the Japanese government, to become a leader in the Japanese car industry. At the outset, the Toyoda company developed a very modern set of operating principles, written with foresight and gumption. Introduced during the company's first year, the Toyoda Precepts, according to the company archives, consisted of five tenets:

1. Be contributive to the development and welfare of the country by working together, regardless of position, in faithfully fulfilling your duties.
2. Be at the vanguard of the times through endless creativity, inquisitiveness, and pursuit of improvement.
3. Be practical and avoid frivolity.
4. Be kind and generous, strive to create a warm, homelike atmosphere.
5. Be reverent, and show gratitude for things great and small in thought and deed.[3]

These appear to be precepts that a modern humanistic enterprise would use, although with somewhat old-fashioned word choices: collaborate, innovate, deliver technical advantage, create a positive work environment, and be grateful.

There was no immediate impact. In its first year of business, the company sold only 21 cars. So its move into the United States was a bold decision. Imagine for a minute what it must have been like for Toyota in the year it launched in America. In 1956, GM's market cap was $104 billion in 2014 dollars. It was the largest market-cap company in the United States, and its influence, reputation, and power were great. By contrast, Toyota had a market value of well under $500 million. It produced 46,716 cars in 1956—all made in Japan.[4]

In just 54 years, this pecking order was reversed. By 2010, GM's market cap was zero and its largest shareholder was the U.S. government. The Obama administration inherited and accelerated a car bailout plan for GM, aiming to keep the company alive. Today, Toyota is the twelfth-largest company in the world by revenues. It has produced 200 million vehicles and has the highest market cap of any company in Japan. In 1968, it sold 1 million cars. In 2008, it sold 10 million units worldwide.

The root of Toyota's success was the Toyota Way[5]—the modern interpretation of the 1935 Precepts. The five updated principles are as follows:

1. Challenge
2. *Kaizen* (continuous improvement)
3. *Genchi genbutsu* (go and see)
4. Respect
5. Teamwork

The principles are aimed at affecting daily behavior on every level. *Genchi genbutsu* means "go find the facts needed to make correct decisions, to build consensus, and to develop achievable goals." *Kaizen* indicates that no process is perfect and that there is always room for improvement.

Together, these two principles, when applied to Toyota's modern crises, would prove to be pivotal.

Headline: What Went Wrong?

Beginning in 2008, three crises appeared, one after the other. At Toyota, it felt like three sucker punches in a row.

First, the Great Recession hit. Suddenly the U.S. new-car market fell by nearly half. This was Toyota's largest and most profitable market. The company had invested in six major production facilities in North America. When volume plummeted, profits disappeared.

Then, two years later, reports of "unintended acceleration" were tied to Toyota cars. And a year after that, the third crisis was the earthquake and tsunami in Japan, where most of the company's parts suppliers suffered devastation. Around the world, production ground to a halt. Profits in the U.S. market swung from a $2 billion positive to a $2 billion negative, according to the company's financial reports. This was the greatest crisis in the company's 75-year history.[6]

We can distinctly remember a conversation about Toyota with a lifetime customer at the time of the unintended acceleration problem. "I've never been so fearful," said Elizabeth a 63-year-old retiree. She drove a Lexus SUV. "I always believed in Toyota. I always thought their cars were the safest, most reliable. I drove Camrys for years, and then my husband traded me up to a Lexus. I love the car, but is it safe?" she asked. "Is it safe?" was the question on the minds of millions of Americans.[7]

In the 1980s, claims of sudden acceleration had struck the Audi brand, and it had taken more than a decade for the German automaker's reputation to recover. Toyota could not afford to take a decade to recover.

What made things worse was the government and media frenzy surrounding the problem. The U.S. National Highway Traffic Safety Administration said that the accelerator pedals on a wide variety of Toyota models caused sudden acceleration.[8] The words and phrasing were often misunderstood and misinterpreted. Toyota says that it disclosed the sticking pedals and that the condition did not cause high-speed acceleration. Nevertheless, the full force of the U.S. government shattered Toyota's image of safety and reliability. There were media reports on the nightly news. Many of these are now widely seen as having exaggerated the severity of the problem.

According to several automotive industry journals, competitors reacted to Toyota's throttle-pedal and floor-mat recalls by offering current Toyota owners incentives to purchase their cars. Chrysler offered a $1,000 cash trade-in offer. Ford offered a $1,000 rebate. GM offered $1,000 toward a down payment or lease termination. Hyundai offered $1,000 to Toyota owners. These were bounties aimed at breaking loyalty.

The definitive account on the problem was published by *Popular Mechanics*[9]:

> To judge by press accounts and statements from government officials, those innocuous-looking Toyota sedans and SUVs in millions of American driveways are somehow kin to the homicidal '58 Plymouth Fury in the Stephen King novel *Christine*—haunted by technological poltergeists and prone to fits of mechanical mayhem. In the midst of three major recalls, Toyota has been hammered by daily newspaper and TV pieces suggesting it has been slow to address safety problems. U.S. transportation secretary Ray LaHood announced that anyone who owns one of the recalled

vehicles should "stop driving it." (He quickly backpedaled on that pronouncement, but warned, "We're not finished with Toyota.")

Does Toyota—or any car company—deserve this? Well, if they are knowingly selling an unsafe car, yes. But is that what's going on here? Not so fast. . . . Every major carmaker receives occasional reports of sudden unintended acceleration (SUA). In the last decade, the National Highway Traffic Safety Administration logged some 24,000 SUA complaints. Less than 50 of these red flags were investigated. Why so few? The main reason is the nebulous nature of SUA. Often the problem occurs once, never to happen again. It's tough to fix a defect that can't be replicated.

Amid the turmoil, Toyota adhered to its enduring precepts. "We held our position and our values," says Bob Carter, senior vice president of automotive operations at Toyota. "We were looking up from the bottom of the valley and knew if we did the right things, we could recover. But it was a very frightening time. We were not sure if there would be another crisis that would flatten us."

Headline: Don't Panic—Develop a Clear-Cut Work Plan

Carter is a Toyota lifer—an American employee who started in sales and worked his way up through the company hierarchy. As the crises erupted, he decided that he needed a complete diagnostic and a total review of the options. This diagnostic concluded that Toyota's problems could not be attributed solely to the recall or the tsunami. Instead, competitive advances by Ford and Hyundai were the major cause of Toyota's share loss. It was a technology war, and Toyota was losing the battle. The big differentiators were miles per gallon and the costs of ownership and operation. Advantage was shifting to what the industry called *telematics*—telecommunication access and driver information in the vehicle—as well as to fashion interiors, colors, and trickle-down luxury.

Companies that were poised to succeed in the U.S. automotive market were delivering technical, functional, and emotional benefits to target consumer segments. They were highly focused on product development and the positioning of car models, zeroing in on age, income, gender, and demographics. Toyota could not take for granted the assumption that it would sustain its advantage in resale value, reliability, and durability. The domestic competition had caught up. The European luxury brands were siphoning off volume from the vast middle market that Toyota served. Toyota had a massive R&D and marketing budget, but it could not afford to play in every segment.

Headline: Your Loyal Consumers Can Show the Path to Recovery and Growth

We knew that Carter's plan was going to succeed when we met with a customer in her home in Arlington Heights, Illinois. Jenny was 48 years old at the time of our interview. She is the mother of two and a schoolteacher. Her husband is an accountant. Their children were ages 14 and 16. She and her husband, Bob, had owned six Toyota Camrys during their 20-year marriage.

"These cars last forever. They are cheap to repair, and when we trade them in, we always get more than we think they are worth," she explained. "When we think 100,000 miles is enough, we can get half of what we paid for it and the new owner thinks they can get another 100,000 miles. They are practical cars for practical people."[10]

Jenny took us outside into the windy, cold Chicago weather to admire her new Camry. "I bought it from my same dealer," she said. "I know Toyota is going through hard times. I know everyone says they are down and out. I got a phone call from the Chevrolet dealer asking if I wanted to trade in my Toyota for a Chevy. I told them, 'No way.' A Chevy is never going to deliver the reliability, safety, and economy of a Camry."

We discussed the recall, the accelerator problem, and all the bad press that Toyota was receiving at the time. "It's not fair," she said. "Why don't they talk to me? I'll set them straight. Toyota makes fine cars and sells them at reasonable prices. They make them here in America with American workers. You can't pile carpets and mats on top of each other and expect the pedals to work. Stupid and sad. Toyota is like onions—you like them and you want them, but you are hesitant to cut into one because you know it's going to make you cry."

Jenny says her next car should have even more miles per gallon, easier music access, a no-hassle dealer experience, and storage for her purse. "I have strong emotional ties to Toyota. They are really up there on my list. Now that the recall happened, I have a little broken heart." In the consumer research, we asked her to make a collage expressing her feelings about Toyota, her Camry, and the recall. She found a headline that she pasted above the Toyota logo: "How bad are your past sins really?"

She remains committed to giving Toyota a fair chance. "Camry people are practical, down-to-earth people that don't have to be showy," she said. "Toyota is not the biggest mansion you can buy, but it's comfortable. I'll give them the benefit of the doubt. But, of course, actions speak louder than words."

Headline: Take Responsibility, Stand Up and Be Counted, and Put Your Name on the Nameplate

The best defense is a strong statement by the leader. In the middle of the hailstorm, the new CEO of Toyota stood up bravely. Akio Toyoda is the grandson of the founder. He joined Toyota in 1984. He holds an MBA from Babson College.[11] He is widely described as a "car guy," deep into engineering and safety improvements. He was willing to step forward and go in front of the congressional committee investigating Toyota safety. This is how he began his opening testimony:

> I myself, as well as Toyota, am not perfect. At times, we do find defects. But in such situations, we always stop, strive to understand the problem, and make changes to improve further. In the name of the company, its long-standing tradition and pride, we never run away from our problems or pretend we don't notice them. By making continuous improvements, we aim to continue offering even better products for society. That is the core value we have kept closest to our hearts since the founding days of the company.
>
> Toyota has, for the past few years, been expanding its business rapidly. Quite frankly, I fear the pace at which we have grown may

have been too quick. I would like to point out here that Toyota's priority has traditionally been the following: first, safety; second, quality; and third, volume. These priorities became confused, and we were not able to stop, think, and make improvements as much as we were able to before, and our basic stance to listen to customers' voices to make better products has weakened somewhat. We pursued growth over quality.

I have personally placed the highest priority on improving quality over quantity, and I have shared that direction with our stakeholders. As you well know, I am the grandson of the founder, and all the Toyota vehicles bear my name. For me, when the cars are damaged, it is as though I am as well. My name is on every car. You have my personal commitment that Toyota will work vigorously and unceasingly to restore the trust of our customers.[12]

He echoed these comments in the *Washington Post.* They are worth repeating at length. In an essay published on February 9, 2010, he wrote:

Toyota has not lived up to the high standards we set for ourselves. We have not lived up to the high standards you have come to expect from us. I am deeply disappointed by that and apologize. As the president of Toyota, I take personal responsibility. That is why I am personally leading the effort to restore trust in our word and in our products.

For much of Toyota's history, we have ensured the quality and reliability of our vehicles by placing a device called an andon cord on every production line and empowering any team member to halt production if there's an assembly problem. Only when the problem is resolved does the line begin to move again.

Two weeks ago, I pulled the andon cord for our company. I ordered production of eight models in five plants across North America temporarily stopped so that we could focus on fixing our customers' vehicles. Today, Toyota team members and dealers across North America are working around the clock to repair all recalled vehicles.

But to regain the trust of American drivers and their families, more is needed. We are taking responsibility for our mistakes,

learning from them and acting immediately to address the con-
cerns of consumers and independent government regulators.

The issues that Toyota is addressing today are by far the most
serious we have ever faced.[13]

He went on to talk about a top-to-bottom review of global
operations. This involved investigating complaints and increasing outreach to government agencies. He promised to build the
"highest-quality, safest and most reliable automobiles in the
world." It was a clear statement of apology, a clear statement of
responsibility, and a clear vow to correct any problems. Within
the company, his message was unambiguous: "We will build safe,
reliable cars and return to our roots and there will be no excuses."

The Department of Transportation enlisted NASA engineers
to review the problem. Late in 2010, the department's report
concluded: "Driver error, not defect to blame in Toyota Sudden
Acceleration."

The worst was over.

Headline: Kick-Start Growth with an "Action Plan to Win"

The recall crisis had a significant impact on the core health of
the brand. In addition, competitors had significantly improved
their brand equity over time. The gap in opinion between
Toyota owners and nonowners posed a large challenge to future
"conquest growth," or the sale of Toyota vehicles to nonowners.
Bob Carter and his management team needed a holistic plan
to win—a truthful assessment of the state of the brand, a clear
set of target consumers, a defining message, a plan to execute
to those segments of consumers, and a way to bring along his
powerful brand network.

How do you do this?

It starts with data: a comprehensive baseline of the current
state of the Toyota brand and the opportunity. In car marketing,
this is called the *brand funnel*—awareness, interest, shopping,
inquiry, and sale. The team needed an independent assessment
of the competitive position of the brand, plus clarity concerning
the gaps in product, features, and delivery. To create the data,

you have to get a qualitative and quantitative understanding of the consumer view. We do shop-alongs and in-home in-depth consumer interviews to understand needs, dissatisfactions, and barriers.

For each high-priority consumer segment, the company had to craft a brand value position—the specific technical, functional, and emotional benefits that would turn homogeneous groups of consumers on. It needed to develop a creative brief for its agency and then work out an activation plan. For each segment, it needed a product and feature "change map," and it had to hit on the hard messages about the quality required. The efforts all needed to fit together into a multiyear, comprehensive plan to win. That meant segment-specific win plans across all segments and the rollout of timelines. This needed to be communicated succinctly across the organization. Toyota needed to develop clear accountabilities, and teams had to be launched to deliver the initiatives.

Carter and his head of marketing, Bill Fay, embraced the new strategy fully. He vowed to spend with conviction, focus, and target; build consumer-centric products; and improve the selling experience. He also vowed to spend his more than $2 billion marketing budget better.

Toyota was staged for recovery. But to succeed, it had to synchronize marketing, sales, and product development. It would subsequently unleash a product improvement program across its four primary series of cars that delivered an ownership and operation cost advantage, value, safety, color, fit, and task accomplishment. It was going to be the highest level of new product activity in Toyota's history. It was the end of complacency and a call to action for the dealers. The company would measure the consumer experience, improve engagement and time to a sale, and provide flawless delivery.

Carter and his team would reallocate current spending on low-effectiveness activity and invest more in Toyota's "Core 4" brands: Camry, Corolla, Prius, and RAV4. They would eliminate brand campaigns that did not provide clear technical, functional, and emotional benefits. They would reduce or reformulate spending on events with low return on investment. They would reduce spending on nonpriority series. The new Camry message would emphasize miles per gallon, hybrid technology, lowest ownership and operating costs, best navigation, best audio and communication, and so-called fit and fabrication improvements.

Consumers like Jenny were very clear about what they wanted. They wanted cars that held their value and were safe and worry-free. They did not care if the cars were cool or feature-laden. They cared about miles per gallon, driver comfort, convenient and clever storage, high-quality materials, and visibility from the driver's vantage point. They appreciated the quality of service—fast, low pressure, no gender discrimination, and fair or preagreed pricing. Toyota could achieve this with segmentation, targeting, focused advertising behind its most important products, and skillful use of PR and digital media.

A turnaround was possible if management could develop a very focused program. In this case, leadership vision was critical. The management team needed to avoid incremental improvement, force cross-functional alignment, and use the power of the Toyota dealer network to drive consumer trial and visits. Toyota dealers sell twice as many cars as most other brands' dealers. They are highly synchronized with the company and would be pivotal to the recovery.

Carter and the rest of the leadership team needed to provide a complete change agenda: product improvements, clarity around the safety message, and the targeting of women, Hispanics, and economically oriented baby boomers.

The team created a one-page strategy that could be shared throughout the organization. It answered the four key questions: Where do we want to go? How do we plan to get there? What actions will we take now? How will we measure success?

Toyota was once again focused on a sustainable win.

*****

Toyota in the United States is not a flawless case study in recovery. But it has resulted in a strong win: share gain, profit recovery, and image recovery.

When we caught up with Bob Carter at the end of 2014, he said that Toyota can't build any more trucks and SUVs. "We are producing at 110 percent of capacity."

He added: "At the bottom of the recall, we didn't understand the power of our brand. We have 25 million satisfied consumers. The most valuable conversations were the ones between neighbors talking about cars, where our customers would say, 'I've had seven Toyotas, and they are the best cars I've ever had.' That's what drove a spectacular recovery. We had one study that said it would take 10 years for us to get back. The consumer shortened that time."

Toyota took particular care to look after the car dealers. "Our direct customer is the dealer. They are the ones that sell and demonstrate confidence," says Carter. "Most of our dealers sell more than one brand. They tell us we are different. We are partners. During the crisis, we paid the dealers to invest in their consumers. They opened 24 hours for repairs. They gave extra terms and conditions on new sales. Today we are all benefiting. Our dealers have record profitability."[14]

Carter sent his dealers $30 million with no strings attached. He made a point of sending the money as checks rather than as electronic transfers. He wanted the dealers to physically receive the money. The arrangement was not contractual. It was a gift to support the dealers during a tough time. It worked. "We are still hearing about the check five years later," he says. "Dealers were very creative with that money. They added technicians, they sent flatbed trucks to pick up cars, and they provided consumers with lunch while they waited for their cars."

"We did have a design-problem issue with floor mats," he says. "We trimmed three-eighths of an inch from the mat. From a media perspective, dangerous floor mats are not a very sexy problem. But unintended acceleration is.

"Following the crisis, we went to more distinct North American autonomy. We are hitting the mark with new products. Current share is 14.5 percent. We are capacity restricted and could be at 15 percent. We had fallen to 11 percent in the crisis."

He continues: "There is a new energy with this company today. We had gotten arrogant. There is a fine line between confidence and arrogance. We want to stand on the line."

Compare GM and Toyota today. GM has global revenues of $156 billion and net income of $2.6 billion. Toyota has $219 billion in revenue and net income of $16.3 billion. Toyota's operating margin is 9.15 percent, whereas GM's is 1.17 percent.[15] The difference comes from price realization through brand strength and manufacturing cost advantage.

According to Jack Hollis, the head marketer at Toyota USA, it is a difference in philosophy.

"Toyota is successful because it is not driven by a sense of the profit margin," Hollis says. "Profit is only part of the business. I've been with the company for 23 years. We ask, how are we benefiting society? Are we making transportation safe and reliable? We respect the land. We safeguard the resources of the earth. We build cars for the benefit of society. One of the pillars of Toyota is *kaizen*—we can always be better." Hollis adds, "Our recovery outperformed most people's expectations. But we will never be finished. There is always a next element. This rapid recovery comes from looking in the mirror to challenge our processes and from the humility to say 'It's not as good as it could be and we must do better.' Our CEO said we must become a new Toyota. It was a turning point for the whole company."[16]

Hollis is aiming the company's advertising at more emotional elements. He says, "Our new tagline, 'Let's go places,' is aimed at inclusivity, bringing us into the transcultural mainstream that includes African Americans, Asian Americans, Hispanics, women, and progressive youth. We are moving faster now, [using] online video, targeted placements, and social media. It is a pretty significant shift. We will be 50-50 digital [and] conventional media soon. I want to bring enjoyment and inspiration to the brand, beyond quality, durability, and reliability."

Bob Carter says that 80 percent of all Toyotas sold in the United States over the past 20 years are still on the road today. The cars are still perceived to have the "QDR" advantage: quality, dependability, and reliability.

But Toyota isn't resting there. It is spending hundreds of millions of dollars to build a new U.S. headquarters in Plano, Texas. Before the crisis, sales and marketing were in Torrance, California; most product engineering was in Japan; and most of the manufacturing was in the various plants across the United States, notably Ann Arbor, Michigan. These will all come together in Plano and create "combinations" not seen before, aimed at generating the next 50 years of growth.

Headline: Lessons from Toyota

Toyota looked doomed, but now it's number one. (Volkswagen is number two.) This shows that no game is ever over. That's the nature of schismogenesis. That's the first lesson.

And, having rebounded, Toyota's prospects look good. Consider this: in the most recent year, Toyota delivered $17.7 billion in operating profit and had a $201 billion market cap.[17] Volkswagen—with its Audi, Porsche, and VW divisions—delivered only $12 billion in operating profit and had a market cap of $106 billion. Upstart Tesla had a speculatively high market cap of $29 billion—a price-to-sales ratio of 10. It is forecast to produce only 40,000 units in 2015. Toyota is set to introduce its hydrogen vehicle in 2015. This vehicle emits only water vapor— no CO_2. It has a top speed of 111 miles per hour and goes from zero to 60 in 9.6 seconds. It has a range of 300 miles. Reviewers describe it as the future brought forward. A small number of refueling stations are being built in California and Rhode Island. If this is successful, it has the potential to leave Tesla in the dust.

Another lesson is that great companies stay true to their core values. They will sacrifice a little bit of growth and share for products that do not cut corners. When you are confronted with health and safety issues, you must use both your heart and your head. You need to consider every single decision in the context of loyal consumers. You also need to recognize that 70 years of integrity do not go up in smoke in one incident. In most major recoveries, the top guy takes the rap. As Harry S. Truman said: "The buck stops here."

A third lesson is that you need to keep communicating during a crisis—to all constituents at all levels, with empathy, kindness, and an appropriate recognition of responsibility. You must personify the problem and explain many more times than you think is necessary. You can use the crisis to get to the root cause of the problem and correct the full range of elements that caused it. You can also use the crisis to speed change and get beyond the short-term problem to a range of advantages that include accelerated innovation and stronger, higher-return marketing investments. You must focus on the core customer and reinforce all the elements that create loyalty and advocacy.

National Football League

The National Football League is the world's richest sporting brand. Soccer, baseball, basketball—these pale in comparison to the value of NFL teams, franchise revenues, and television contracts. In 2014, the NFL generated revenues of approximately $10 billion—more than the GDP of 50 countries. More than 200 million people, or two-thirds of the U.S. population, watched any given game.[18]

Yet the NFL is facing enormous challenges and is a brand that can go farther up or drop like a football spiked into the ground.

Hardly a day goes by without some bad-news story about the NFL. At the heart of the problem is a cultural clash that divides the powerful owners of the 32 teams from the 2,000 or so athletically gifted players from diverse backgrounds. For 50 years, there has been an uneasy truce between them, as each has collaborated with the other to achieve their quite different dreams. The owners dream of Super Bowl glory and a substantive return on their investment. The players dream of money, fame, women, and freedom from their impoverished roots.

It's not all about themselves: they both also dream about changing the trajectories of others. For the owners, it's their cities. For the players, it's their families and their hometowns, the people who supported them on their way to the summit of the sport.

American football is gladiatorial. Fans watch because of the battle between two teams: the precision throwing and decision making of a quarterback; the explosive leaping and instinctive cutting of a running back; the pain-inflicting tackling of a 250-pound linebacker. No one is under any illusions about the violence of the collisions—not the players, not the proprietors, not the fans.

The helmet was made mandatory as far back as 1943.[19] But these days, helmet-to-helmet collisions have escalated, causing concussions on a massive scale. Nearly 30 percent of players, according to the NFL's own calculations, will ultimately suffer from "accelerated cognitive impairment." In protest against the spiraling incidence of head injuries, 5,000 players joined a class action lawsuit against the NFL. In 2013, it was settled out of court, with the NFL paying out hundreds of millions of dollars.[20] But there is continued evidence that American football—a sport that, according to the *New York Times*, "grooves on manliness"—shows blithe disregard for the safety of its players.[21]

The concussion issue has reached the White House. In 2014, President Barack Obama told the *New Yorker*, "I would not let my son play pro football."[22] Obama, of course, has no son. But some other parents who do have sons are taking the same view. A big tackle used to be shrugged off as another case of a player "getting dinged." But not anymore. Figures released in December 2014 showed that youth participation in tackle football at the junior and high school level has fallen over the past five years, dropping 27 percent since 2008.[23] In baseball, the drop was 19 percent; in basketball, it was 14 percent; and in soccer, it was 9 percent. Given that a 2012 report from the *Annals of Biomedical Engineering* showed that even a seven- or eight-year-old typically receives more than 100 head impacts in a season, this drop-off is not surprising.[24]

The crisis for football is deeper than just physical injuries, broken bones, and fractured lives. There is a moral issue, too. The NFL players seem to live in an environment in which anything goes. Most of them grew up dirt-poor and were the first in their families to attend college, albeit for their sporting ability rather than their academic ability. At young ages, they become celebrities. But there is no guidance counselor attached to them. Often, they get into trouble. Rape accusations, assaults, possession of weapons—these are not uncommon. Think Ray Rice or Michael Vick. When you consider that more than

40 percent of the fans are female,[25] this is a critical issue for the owners. But even the most die-hard fans do not give the players license to commit crimes.

Will the NFL come through the crisis? Or will football end up being a pantomime sport like wrestling? It could go either way. But there is reason for optimism. The owners who preside over the sport do have a genius for knowing how to create a powerful and enduring brand.

Back in the 1960s, American football was an underresourced sport that was struggling to thrive. People *liked* it, but they didn't really *love* it. Now, that's all changed. For 20 million Americans, mainly men, it is their life. They put it first, ahead of family and friends. As one fan of the Chicago Bears told us, if there were no NFL, "I wouldn't have anything to do."[26]

For the past 30 years, it has been the most popular sport in the United States. Some 35 percent of Americans say that it is their favorite sport, ahead of its nearest rival, baseball. "Football simply has an iron grip on our collective psyche," said J. R. Moehringer, a Pulitzer Prize–winning journalist. "We love it. God help us, we love it."[27]

The secret of the NFL's success has been the way the owners have created an emotional bond that connects rich and poor, north and south, moms and hard-nosed businessmen. They have found a way to keep the equilibrium between different stakeholders: owners, players, and fans. In many ways, American football has become emblematic of the United States. People from disparate communities come together with a shared passion, a shared dream: success in the NFL, victory at the Super Bowl, life-changing fame and fortune. It is a case study in branding excellence: tight emotional connections; unique benefits; increasing time exposure and content.

It starts with the proprietors and the players.

Headline: Harness a Dream: How to Build an Emotional Connection

Madison Avenue and Muck City, the nickname for a city in Florida—these two places reflect two very different sides of America. In so many ways, they are worlds apart. Yet during the winter months, they come together every weekend when the gladiators of the gridiron take to the field to play in the NFL, purveyor of the world's richest sport.

It is along Madison Avenue in New York that the NFL has its headquarters. Around the boardroom table are 33 chairs: 32 for the owners of the 32 teams in the NFL, and one for the commissioner. When they all gather together, they constitute the wealthiest corporate club in America.

Every owner is a billionaire. They have to be: the cumulative value of the clubs is more than $34 billion. The Dallas Cowboys, owned by Jerry Jones, is the most valuable, at $2.3 billion. In 2013 it generated revenues of more than $500 million.[28] Other famous owners include Paul Allen, the cofounder of Microsoft, who controls the Seattle Seahawks, and Martha Ford, of the automobile dynasty, who controls the Detroit Lions.

When the Buffalo Bills were put up for sale in 2014, there was a race for a coveted seat around the boardroom table on Madison Avenue. In the end, Terry Pegula and his wife, who made their fortune in the oil industry, beat Donald Trump, the real estate entrepreneur, and Jon Bon Jovi, the rock star. Their winning bid was $1.4 billion.

If the NFL is owned by billionaires, then it is played by millionaires. And the promise of riches beyond imagination is what connects Madison Avenue with Muck City.

Muck City isn't a real name. It's a nickname for Pahokee and three other towns in the sugarcane fields of the Everglades, roughly 1,200 miles south of New York. All told, these towns have just 40,000 people. Yet, over the years, they have sent 48 players to the NFL. If you live in one of these towns, you are more than a thousand times more likely to make it to the NFL than anyone in any other city in America.

Pahokee is hot, dry, dusty, and dirt-poor. When Bobby Bowden, the legendary head coach of Florida State University's football team, was asked to describe the place for an ESPN film, he thought for a moment and then chose his words carefully. "Blue collar," he said. But, as the narrator commented, "When Coach Bowden says 'blue collar,' he's being nice."[29]

For most people from Pahokee, there is nothing to do and not much hope. "It's in the middle of nowhere," said Santonio

Holmes, a former wide receiver for the Pittsburgh Steelers. "There are no shopping malls to go to. There really aren't any restaurants. There's not a lot to do, man."[30] No Walmart, no JCPenney. The nearest supermarket is a Publix, and that's 15 miles away.

What there is, however, is football. And for superfast athletes such as Holmes, there is a way out to fame and fortune. In 2009, Holmes was named Most Valuable Player of Super Bowl XLIII, after catching nine passes for 131 yards, including a game-winning six-yard touchdown pass from Ben Roethlisberger with 35 seconds left in regulation time.

Every kid from Pahokee dreams of making it to the NFL—and doing what Holmes did. Every mom there dreams that her son will star in the Super Bowl, the end-of-season game when the best teams compete to be champions. It is a dream that they share with the owners on Madison Avenue. To improve their chances of making the grade, the boys from Pahokee turn to an unusual pastime that has its roots in the grinding poverty of the region. For decades, the boys have chased rabbits—for food, for money, and for conditioning. Chasing a rabbit is tough. It requires speed, mobility, and agility. These days, a Muck rabbit goes for $2. The quicker, nimbler cottontail carries a premium—it goes for $3. But that's not why boys chase rabbits today.

When they chase rabbits, they are really chasing their NFL dream.

"We chased rabbits in order to get faster," said Holmes. "Rabbits are a lot faster than humans, and in order to catch them, you have to chase them." This strengthens the leg muscles and sharpens speed and agility. "You've got to be athletic because they are going to zigzag many times."[31]

The raw athletic ability of players from places such as Pahokee provides the foundation for the popularity of the sport. But the phenomenal success of the NFL as a business and as a brand is largely attributable to the entrepreneurial genius of the 32 billionaires. They know how to connect with consumers; that is, after all, how they built their own individual empires. We have analyzed their strategies, and we have found that they deliver on four customer emotional spaces: loyalty ("this is my team, no matter what"), hopefulness ("we can still win this game"), connection ("I know these players"), and anticipation ("I can't wait until the game on Sunday afternoon"). Go to a gym or a bar on game day. You hear comments that support each of these.

To cultivate and strengthen these emotions, the owners did five things, in particular: (1) they created a common mission and what they call *league think*; (2) they transformed the NFL into a property with a carefully controlled brand image; (3) they built an emotional connection through NFL Films; (4) they targeted the superfans; and (5) they took care of the needs of the next generation—the kids—and their moms.

Let's look at each of these strategies in turn.

Headline: A Common Mission

The NFL, launched nearly 100 years ago, started small. In its early days, it endured some rocky times. During the Great Depression, the number of teams fell to its lowest level: just eight. Such up-and-down fortunes prompted the owners to think differently about how they ran the league. There is no question but that they are fearsome rivals on the field. Off it, however, they come together for their greater good.

The NFL is not organized to make a profit—at least, that's what its constitution and bylaws say. On the other hand, its primary purpose is "to promote and foster the primary business of League members," with the members being the 32 owners. In recognition of this, they have signed up for a series of initiatives that have been dubbed *league think*. As the late Art Modell, owner of the Cleveland Browns and the Baltimore Ravens, once said, they are "32 Republicans who vote Socialist."[32]

For instance, they have agreed to a revenue-sharing system that means that the poorest teams, such as the Oakland Raiders and the Jacksonville Jaguars, can stay competitive with the richest teams, such as the Dallas Cowboys and the New England Patriots. Likewise, they have set a cap on the number of active players each team can have: 53. Also, during the annual draft, when teams select players from the college leagues, the worst-performing team has first choice of the best players.

There is still a gulf in the financial power of the teams. In 2013, the Cowboys, the richest team, with a valuation of $2.3 billion, was three times as valuable as the Raiders, the poorest team, with a valuation of $825 million. Revenue for the Cowboys was twice as much as that for the Raiders ($539 million as opposed to $229 million), and operating income was 13 times as much ($251 million as opposed to $19 million).[33]

But the sense of common purpose means that there is every chance that the Raiders can defeat the Cowboys whenever they meet. The NFL treasures the hope that teams can go from "worst to first" in a season.

Headline: A Property—Not Just a Game

As successful business leaders, the proprietors understand that the sport needs promoting and protecting like a business. They talk about professional football being "America's game but NFL's property."

To promote the game, and to maximize profits, they established NFL Properties, which is responsible for licensing, merchandising, and publishing deals. In this, it is very effective. Of the $10 billion in revenues raised in 2013, just $2 billion came from ticket sales for the games. The rest came from several other sources. The biggest source is broadcasters. In 2013, the NFL received $5 billion—half of its revenues—from them. Overall, NBC, CBS, Fox, and ESPN have paid more than $40 billion for the broadcasting rights from 2014 through 2022. Then, there are the major sponsorship deals with big-name companies. Altogether, in 2013, the NFL received $2 billion from these deals.[34] Verizon has paid $1 billion for a four-year deal. Pepsi has paid the same for a 10-year deal. Finally, there is the merchandising and licensing of products, worth $1 billion in 2013. More than 70 licensees generate products with the names of around 2,000 players. In the 2013–2014 season, Russell Wilson, quarterback for the Seattle Seahawks, had the number-one-selling jersey.

To protect the brand, the NFL established a PR department and pioneered policies relating to player behavior on and off the field. These, of course, are now under great scrutiny. But there is no question that, over the years, the NFL has been at the fore-front of efforts to preserve the integrity of the game.

The NFL was the first American sport to introduce a league-wide drug-testing program. It also has a tough alcohol abuse policy. In their contract, players are required to recognize "the detriment to the League and professional football that would result from impairment of public confidence in the honest and orderly conduct of NFL games or the integrity and good char-acter of NFL players."[35] Failure to abide by this rule can lead to fines, suspension, and, in egregious cases, termination of contract.

Some observers have nicknamed the NFL the "No Fun League." But the reassurance that fans got from these rules helped the NFL build football's enormous popularity as a family sport.

Headline: Let's Make a Movie: Creating a Hollywood Image of the Brand

NFL sports stars are glamorous gladiators: almost every boy wants to be one, and many girls want to marry one. Much of the reason for this is NFL Films, the NFL's very own Hollywood studio that produces enough film every year to stretch from Madison Avenue to Pahokee.

It was back in 1965 that the NFL, looking to its future, acquired Blair Motion Pictures, a small studio founded by Steve Sabol. The following year, it released the film *They Call It Pro Football*, which documented the highs and lows of the season: slow-motion replays, magisterial musical scores, and a deep baritone narration that was quickly dubbed "the voice of God." The films that followed raised the status of an everyday football game to the level of a Shakespearean drama or Greek tragedy. On display were "ballet and brutality," beauty and the beast.[36]

And it worked. *Road to the Super Bowl*, first broadcast in 1974, is now the longest-running and most-honored sports special. In all, NFL Films has won more than 100 Emmys, the TV equivalent of the Oscars. It has redefined sports cinematography.

The archive of NFL Films, dating back 50 years, is the largest sports-film library in the world. It has allowed the NFL to reach the broadest possible audience and, at the same time, control the image of the sport with carefully edited clips of the games. The archive gives an insight into how the NFL thinks about its mission to create an emotional connection. It is cataloged in an extraordinarily detailed way. There are the product shots (for example, Adidas, Nike, Puma, and Reebok), and there are the personnel shots (for example, celebrities, coaches, "funky fans," and cheerleaders). But what is most interesting is that NFL Films catalogs the films according to defining emotions or vivid imagery: "angry," "blood," "dejection," "frustration," "patriotic," "praying," "sun," and "sweat."

It is not surprising that *Sports Illustrated* has described NFL Films as "perhaps the most effective propaganda organ in the history of corporate America."[37]

Headline: Target the Superfans: They Spread the Word

The NFL's fans are its customers, and they are segmented into very different groups so that the NFL can target them with appropriate products and services. At the top of the list are the 25 million superfans who make the NFL—and *their* team—their number one priority in life.

One such superfan is Anthony, a well-spoken 26-year-old financial analyst who supports the Chicago Bears. He can't remember a time when he didn't follow the Bears. His dad is a die-hard Chicago sports fan who refereed football games and has "a good eye" for the game. When he was a kid growing up, the house was strewn with team memorabilia. He recalls the thrill of going to Soldier Field and being part of the 50,000-plus crowd.[38]

Anthony is physically small: just 5 feet 8 inches. As a player, he was dwarfed by the linebackers on his school team. But, despite the bruises he got from playing, he always wanted to play because "it was an opportunity to prove my toughness."

His on-field experience has enhanced his understanding—and enjoyment—of the game that now dominates his adult life. He goes to almost every home game. "I plan my fall travel schedule around the Bears," he tells us. "I can't remember a Sunday in recent memory that the NFL didn't dominate my day." On one occasion, he left an engagement party early in order to get back for a Bears game. His girlfriend has learned that she rarely gets to see him during NFL season. The Bears take priority in his affections.

The home games are all-consuming. "It's always a full-day event," he said. Before the game, there is a "tailgate" party—fathers, sons, and friends celebrating in the parking lot, sometimes starting as early as 9 a.m. Then there's the game. Then there's the postmatch analysis and, it's hoped, more celebration. Anthony is a season ticket holder, so his tickets cost $152 per game. If he were to buy tickets on a one-off basis, he would have to pay as much as $1,000 for each one.

But he thinks the entertainment is worth every cent. And when there is an away game or he can't make the home game, he watches everything on TV. He pays a $10 monthly subscription to the NFL RedZone, a league-sponsored TV channel that allows fans to keep up to date on all the games across the league. "You can watch all the games at once," he says.

Overall, Anthony spends around 20 hours every week following the NFL: watching a home game; following matches on TV; playing Fantasy Football, where fans create teams of real-life players and score points based on their actual performance on the field of play; seeing the televised draft, where new players are recruited from U.S. colleges; and catching up on news and gossip about teams and players.

Talking to him is like talking to a football encyclopedia. He can reel off the names of 50 percent of the players in the league—about 1,000 people. He is already instilling the next generation with a love for the Bears. "Just the other day, I bought my godson a Bears 'onesie,'" he says. "And the second my nephew is old enough, I will take him to a game." But his proudest achievement is the influence he had on an ex-girlfriend. "After spending time with me, she turned from not knowing what a first down was to knowing the names of all the Bears' players."

Anthony shows all the emotions that we have identified as being central to the success of the NFL: anticipation, including the tailgate parties, the hopefulness, and the belief that the draft can help revive the Bears' fortunes; loyalty, with a commitment to the team even when his family moved to Texas for a few years; and connection, as shown in the camaraderie of the crowd and others who wear the Bears jersey.

He also likes the brutality. "I like the hitting aspect, the contact. I love that a 200-pound guy can take on a 300-pound guy." In this respect, he and other superfans are different from another important group of consumers, the moms and their kids.

Headline: Target the Moms and Their Kids: They Hold the Future in Their Hands

The NFL has long understood that kids and the moms who decide whether they participate in the sport while they are in high school are the future of the game. As long ago as 1961, the NFL introduced its Punt, Pass & Kick program, designed to entice youngsters into the game. Since then, it has introduced NFL FLAG Football for boys and girls. Today, more than 5 million kids, including 1 million girls, play this softer version of the game.

Women are also targeted as fans in their own right. The NFL calculates that 44 percent of its fan base is female. In particular, the NFL for Her apparel line is especially popular.[39]

But the NFL may need to do more to woo its female fans. Women are increasingly being seen as the demographic that will make or break the NFL. As the *New Yorker* noted: "The death of football, according to the declinist scenario, would have to originate with women—mothers who, having read the medical findings, would forbid their sons to play Pop Warner, which in turn would reduce the teen-age ranks aspiring to play under the lights on Friday night, and so on up the chain."[40]

Headline: Prevent the Downward Cycle of Schismogenesis: Striking the Right Balance Among Customers (the Fans), Employees (the Players), and Owners (the Billionaires)

The NFL has bold plans for growth. It wants to generate $25 billion in revenue every year by 2027, up from nearly $10 billion in 2013.[41]

But it faces a tough test.

For most brands, there is a fine line between success and irrelevance. Once you've crossed the line, it's hard to go back. The problem is this: How do you know when that's happened? Schismogenesis is the ever-present but hidden force that is ready to pull you across the line, to rip you apart.

Even the strongest brands are susceptible to its cataclysmic centrifugal power. This is because there is an essential fragility at the core of every brand: each is created with an invisible magnetism that emotionally connects owners, employees, and customers. These stakeholders are held together through a constantly managed dynamic equilibrium. But the moment you lose focus, you risk unsettling this equilibrium, and you risk breaking the bonds that define the brand. Things spiral out of control. The impact of this can be devastating, similar to that of the splitting of the atom.

Is this what is now happening to the NFL?

For a long time, the owners have gotten pretty much everything right. They have found a way to strike the proper balance among the contrasting—and, in some cases, competing—interests of the fans, the players, and themselves as custodians of treasured brands.

Now, however, they seem to have taken their eye off the ball. The NFL is being dubbed the *beleaguered league*. A glorious future is also being put in jeopardy by the way the NFL is responding to some features of the modern game.

One is the way it is trying to squeeze even more profit out of the game. The charge is that the NFL is becoming too greedy. Already, 45 of the 50 most-watched sports programs are NFL games.[42] Yet the NFL now wants to broadcast games every night of the week. According to Mark Cuban, the owner of the Dallas Mavericks, a basketball team, this spells danger for the NFL. "I think the NFL is 10 years away from an implosion," he said in an interview with journalists. "When you've got a good thing and you get greedy, it always, always, always, always, always turns on you. That's rule number one of business."[43]

His point is that if the NFL becomes ubiquitous, it will contravene one of the core emotional bonds that tie the stakeholders together: anticipation. For fans like Anthony, this is a core emotional need. What would happen if there were games every night of the week? Yes, there would be short-term profits for the NFL. Anthony would certainly watch. But what would happen in the long run?

A second issue—one that is far more serious than the frequency of NFL games on TV—is the growing incidence of domestic violence among players, their unforgivable mistreatment of their wives and girlfriends off the field. When a video was released showing Ray Rice, the Baltimore Ravens running back, knocking out Janay Palmer, his fiancée, in a casino elevator, he was handed only a two-match suspension. This shocked America.

In the past, the NFL has anticipated controversial issues. It has been one step ahead and has pioneered on many fronts, including alcohol and drug testing. On the issue of domestic violence, however, it has been too slow to react in an appropriate way. Even though domestic violence is a real and growing scourge across America, the NFL did not have a position on how it would respond in a crisis. Part of the problem is the NFL's failure to move with the times, to react quickly enough in the digital age. With NFL Films, it could control the images that fans saw. But it is powerless to stop the security camera video on YouTube showing Rice's assault on his fiancée.

The result has been that it has acted in the short-term interests of the owners and the players rather than in the long-term interests of the brand. It has exposed the NFL's values, and these values were not relevant to and aligned with moms and the rest of America.

The third issue, as we've seen, is the spate of serious head injuries that have left players paralyzed and suicidal. Here, the interests of the players seem to have been placed behind the interests of the superfans, who want to see a hard-fought contest.

So what will happen next? There are two scenarios.

One is that hubris reigns. There is no reform, no serious advocacy for player health, and no policing of players' behavior on and off the field. Everything is focused on exponential growth. If this happens, the NFL will become like the governing body of wrestling. And fans will turn to other sports.

The other scenario is that common sense reigns. There is reform. The game turns over a new leaf. Players are protected. There is proper policing of behavior. Players who maim or injure fellow players are thrown out of the game—forever. Also, players who are guilty of "ungentlemanly behavior" are thrown out of the game—forever. The NFL goes global, expanding beyond its American roots, and is no longer based on busted brains, broken backs, and beaten women.

There are already signs that the NFL is addressing the question of domestic violence. In the wake of the Ray Rice affair, Roger Goodell, the NFL commissioner, acknowledged that he had let down the game's fans when he gave Rice a two-game suspension. "I didn't get it right," he admitted. "My disciplinary decision led the public to question our sincerity, our commitment, and whether we understood the toll that domestic violence inflicts on so many families."[44] He issued a new memorandum to players, increasing the penalty for those who commit domestic violence or sexual assault. If they commit one offense, they get an automatic six-game ban, with no pay. Two offenses, and they get a lifetime ban.

The NFL has introduced some measures that seem to show that it is taking the concussion issue seriously. For instance, it has helped establish a series of so-called Moms Clinics, where worried mothers can get the latest information on the science of head injuries. It has also introduced new rules to ensure that players receive adequate treatment after a serious collision.

But these steps may not go far enough. Some fans are prepared to see more fundamental changes.

What will the moms in Pahokee think? They, and the millions like them in the Pahokees across America, are the people who the NFL needs to be most worried about.

As we found, many moms feel embittered and betrayed. The emotional connection that they once had with the NFL has been shattered. The memory of Junior Seau, the just-retired star of the San Diego Chargers who committed suicide in 2012 and was later discovered to have suffered from chronic traumatic encephalopathy, haunts the game.

There may be a way for the NFL to counter the relentless power of schismogenesis.

We shall have to wait and see what happens next.

Headline: Lessons from the NFL

No matter how strong your brand may be, it is always subject to the laws of schismogenesis: breaking up and dividing into pieces. No sporting brand is stronger than the NFL. Yet it is facing a crisis that threatens to overwhelm the guardians of the brand, the 32 owners.

There are three principles you need to observe if you are to counter the ravaging effects—the down cycle—of schismogenesis.

First, you need to restore the equilibrium among the various stakeholders—in the case of the NFL, among the owners themselves, the players (the employees), and the fans (the customers). If this equilibrium can be carefully managed, the NFL can enjoy success far into the future.

Second, you need to give priority to the long term if you want your brand to endure. Often, it is tempting to put the urgent ahead of the important. This is what the NFL has done because it failed to think ahead and failed to envisage a different future. It was forced to rush to judgment—and it miscalculated.

Third, you need to make sure that any changes you make are consistent with your brand—its history and its defining essence. This requires a deep understanding of the way consumers view the brand. In the NFL's case, the question is why people choose to follow the NFL. What are the core emotions that pull consumers toward it?

When we analyzed the emotions that really connected fans with the NFL, we found that violence wasn't one of them. This means that the NFL could adapt the game to make it less brutal without suffering a mass exodus of fans, a destruction of shareholder value, and a dynamic in which marginal teams slip below breakeven and into debt.

*****

One Conclusion

Brands are not stable. They rise and fall on the basis of what they did yesterday. Big brands generate sufficient resources to ensure that they can live in perpetuity. If you don't drain your cash, you will have the resources to create news, improvements, and expansion. If you take money from Peter to pay Paul (from the core brand for a new brand), then you can get into big trouble very fast. Premature abandonment can be a mortal sin. Pay attention to customer satisfaction and the willingness of your core customers to refer and repurchase. These are primary warning signals. Once a year, every company should call its leaders together and ask: How are we really doing? What are our core consumers saying about us? What have we done to drive loyalty, appreciation, and love? What do we know quantitatively? What do we know qualitatively? In our space, who is hot and why? In our space, how do we preempt and arrest?

Four Takeaways

1. **No brand stands still.** You're either moving up or falling down. From 1960 through 2010, the NFL was a story of conquest and emotional appeal. In contrast, the last five years have been a story of betrayal, danger, and nonresponsiveness. By any measure, notwithstanding the rapid rise in the size of Super Bowl audiences, the NFL is in trouble. In the next three years, we will know whether the NFL will go on to greater glory or become like boxing, a once-popular sport that is now in decline. You don't need to fall into the same trap. Respond before the curtain drops.

2. **Pay attention—don't fall asleep at the wheel.** The story Toyota tells is opposite to the NFL's. The story is about vigilance throughout the ranks of the organization. It's not about shirking danger. It's about facing up to the issues—confronting them and applying the trusted precepts of *kaizen* to the challenges.

3. **As the leader, you've got to stand up and be counted.** For every business, there will be a moment of truth when the leaders of the company are faced with challenges to the company's core values and principles. This is the time when real leaders rise to the challenge.

4. **Don't despair.** No matter how bad the news may be, you should never despair. You can be hit with headlines that accuse you of malfeasance. You can be hit with headlines about the state of the economy. But no matter how depressed the economy appears to be, there are always opportunities to recover. Toyota demonstrated an uncanny ability to return to the organization's value proposition: reliability, durability, and economy of use. It continues to draw strength from this value proposition.

SOME KEY ACTION POINTS

1. Learn to recognize a crisis, intervene early and proactively, accept responsibility, and adopt daily communication.
2. Track the data to see how you are really doing.
3. Create an alternative story line, get ahead of rumors, isolate the issue in consumers' minds, explain the cause, educate, and inform.
4. Repeat the message until you are blue in the face.
5. Hire the broadest range of experts possible to testify on your behalf.
6. Increase your total media spending. Develop a big voice on your story.
7. Respond to the issues with specificity and force; make consumers "whole" financially and emotionally.
8. Use the attention to drive toward long-term, higher share. Think big targets. Make them real and translate them into programs that energize.
9. Behind the scenes, create extensive "what-ifs" and respond preemptively; learn from the crisis.
10. Demonstrate tangible change—for example, improved plant processes, revised health and safety protocols, or better investment.

EPILOGUE

Tools, Techniques, Challenges, and Words of Advice

Every brand owner we have ever met has high aspirations. They all want their brand to be bigger and stronger, and to have more vitality. They want to have more power and establish themselves as fixtures in their consumers' minds. Few of them want to have anything less than 100 percent of their consumers' category requirements. However, very few achieve this, and even fewer hold on to it.

If you have read this book, you are one of the ambitious ones.

We will close this book with four steps that can help you get started. These are the four steps of the demand-centric growth approach.

This approach looks at how the dimensions of choice influence a customer's final purchase decision. We isolate who the consumers are by age, income, gender, life stage, marital status, and presence of children by age. We probe how they feel emotionally and what their purchase motivations are. We understand how they behave, how often they purchase and use the product, where they buy it, and how engaged they are with the category. The resulting model is drawn from three dimensions mathematically: who they are, how they feel, and what they do. It opens up new ways to think about the business, the market, adjacent categories, and growth vectors.

The goal is to deliver an astounding improvement in your customers' experience, to break down doors that create silos within companies, and to achieve a breakthrough in the technical, functional, and emotional aspects of your product or service. It is aimed at helping you answer some fundamental questions: Where do we fully bet? What resources will deliver victory? How do we anticipate a new and better world?

Before you begin the four-step process, you need to be ready and willing to engage. You need the humility to recognize that you may not have all the answers or the universal organizational desire to transform and elevate your brand and its performance. Not everyone has the courage of a Kevin Plank at Under Armour, the sports apparel company, or his audacity in turning football underclothing into a multibillion-dollar brand.

The telltale signs of trouble are declines in sales, losses in market share, squeezed gross margins, the fear of trying to pass along cost increases to customers, and, most important, an inability to crisply explain why and how you will grow and to resolutely pick a path to growth. Other signs you should watch out for include marketing double-talk when you ask questions, the absence of an institutional view of market segmentation, an innovation pipeline with no direction, and the inability of sales reps to succinctly explain what your brands stand for, how they are unique, and who your target audience is.

In our view, the first step is to do the right research to get the frame of reference right and to build a map of demand. The Boston Consulting Group begins here with something that we call *MindDiscovery*.[1] We meet consumers in their homes or accompany them on shopping trips in order to get a rich understanding of their behavior. This provides the foundation for our next step, a full-blown quantitative model.

We aim to understand what the consumers' true options are. We watch consumers buy, use, and repurchase products. We discover how they make decisions and hear their words describing those decisions. We use projective exercises that help consumers express and articulate things that are normally left unsaid. We look to understand what we call the *benefit attributes* that drive choice. These are 30 technical and 30 emotional attributes based on the language of the consumer. In the spirits business, for example, the most important technical attributes include "smooth," "smoky," and "light," whereas the most important emotional attributes include "helps me impress others," "makes me look cool," and "it's all about me."

Once you have this information, you can begin to develop, on the basis of customer segmentation, early hypotheses about what causes different people to buy different things. You can begin to understand how one individual can actually be buying for several different objectives and in several different circumstances. It is very rare, indeed, for individuals to buy one product for all their needs.

With the knowledge gained through our MindDiscovery sessions, we then launch the BCG demand spaces survey. This is a questionnaire with an expansive frame of reference. As we saw in Chapter 3, we defined Frito-Lay's market as "macro snacks" rather than the narrower "salty snack" market. To get clear findings, we ask consumers to rank and evaluate relevant brands and relevant emotional, functional, and technical attributes. We ask them to compare one brand against another brand—in what we call a *pairwise comparison*—so that we can understand the drivers of relative rank. We ask them about their last trip and their last purchase or consumption occasion.

In any survey, sample size is a critical element. For our survey, we target a minimum of 300 users for each segment and demand space. For a category "demand map," the total sample can quickly rise to more than 10,000 users.

A demand-space map is a mathematical representation of all the users' answers, providing the projected space, sizing, needs, and decision criteria. We generate heat maps so that we can match brands with particular demand spaces. We then take the time to digest the findings and ask many questions. Discussion, debate, and internalization are the critical next steps.

The purpose of the demand-space map is to define the specific set of emotional and functional benefits a brand requires in order to win a customer. It forces choices on companies. No longer does one size fit all. No longer can a brand be positioned as being equally valuable across segments. It pushes the company to come to conclusions: What spaces are we targeting? What are we saying and claiming? What is the substantive backup for what we believe? What will it take to win?

For many executives, a close understanding of the markets is a revolution of revelation. With a demand-space map, we can describe the consumer market and the relative position of different brands. We can explain patterns of winners and losers. This is not an academic exercise. It is about bringing clarity to a complex world, to a market where consumers make perplexing choices across categories to satisfy their needs and demands.

As Frito-Lay and Hilton Worldwide found, this is a broadening exercise that allows companies to compete outside their traditional channels, categories, and price points. It sets the foundation for strategy and the creation of a commercial development plan. We are able to demonstrate that the brands that outperform on the attributes that really matter in any given demand space are the ones with a disproportionate share. We have the data to prove this. It's not a conceptual consumer model. More than this, we can predict how big a share of a demand space you can win if you have the right mix of emotional and functional benefits that satisfy the attributes that matter. As such, we offer a road map for growth.

Once you have created a demand-space map—the singular focus of the first step—you need to set the strategic direction. This is the second step. We help you determine where your brand should play—in which demand space. We provide a supporting rationale that is based on the attractiveness of the demand space and your brand's economic "right to win."

For a company with a portfolio of brands, this step helps you identify independencies and forces you to make trade-offs. The goal is to maximize the position of each of your brands, minimize any overlap, and increase the probability of winning. This is a step that requires backbone and perseverance. Few companies make the hard choices. They say that they want to "distort" investment in their portfolio, so that every dollar goes toward the best brands with the best chance of winning in a particular demand space, but they often don't have the controls or the will to say no to hungry, ambitious brand managers. It is like choosing among your children to decide which of them will get extra nourishment and which will need to survive on the streets.

During this strategic review, we help you determine where you should place your investment bets, identifying which brands are best suited to win and which are most responsive to investment. We then turn this analysis into a business case; afterward, you know that you have to "spend this to get that."

For this to succeed, you need buy-in from your leaders. So an important part of the strategic review is building alignment, which is a foundational basis of the commercial strategy. Brand leaders are forced to address the realities of their business, their brands, the consumer landscape, and changes in consumer demand. They are forced to make the calls that are often avoided. This process creates friction—but friction that is ultimately healthy. It is a liberating battle, leading to investment decisions that are made with clear logic and a market foundation.

The third step is to create an integrated commercial plan. That means developing each of your offerings so that it can be the undisputed winner in a target demand space. This is a cross-functional process that embraces product development, packaging, shelving, pricing, and promotion, along with message development, store operations, delivery, and even employee engagement. We help you build and unify your plans for communication, innovation, and activation (pricing, in-store, store design, go-to-market) so that they are all focused on delivering the core benefits of a particular demand space. Each is to be in sync with the core drivers of choice. Communication is an art, and it requires the science of demand spaces to match the creativity of breakthrough message development.

The integration process calls for the various cross-functional experts to engage with one another. They need to share a common understanding of the demand spaces and the requisites for success. The process triggers a shift toward a common goal, away from a situation in which many well-intentioned people dispersed across the company do what they believe to be right for the business. It unleashes the power of mutual reinforcement—the true value of collaboration to win in the marketplace.

The final step is the encore. Do it again. Lay the foundation for a longitudinal understanding of the market. Use the second year to fine-tune your market understanding and to change the game. Stay vigilant; make sure that old bad habits do not creep back. Stick to what the facts are telling you. Track them and modify outdated data sources that are not aligned. Measure progress against goals. Focus on the parts of the change program that are falling behind schedule. Be quick to applaud your successes—they need to have adequate internal understanding and appreciation. Use the successes to convert more champions.

A culture change requires a broad organizational understanding of the process—how the map was generated, how opportunities were teased out, how priorities were ranked, what the biggest wins have been, why there have been calculated bets that did not pay off, and how the careers of the champions have accelerated. You need to communicate relentlessly, consistently, and broadly. People will give lip service to the changes and then attempt to carry on as before, shoehorning in their prior ideas and using the new strategy as their justification.

But remember, in the end, the consumer gets to decide, and there is no place to hide from the stark fact of progress or inertia.

A demand-centric growth approach is a story with many chapters of success. The objective is to have loyal consumers, apostles for your brand, and testimonial reviews explaining your fanatical attention to the details of your consumers' hopes and desires. Enduring success will often require adapting your business model to use new partners, new technology, new product designs, and new venues. We urge you to bring passion and humanity to the front line of your business. We urge you to use the demand-centric growth tool to break new ground, to reimagine a better future, and to map your growth strategy with confidence and a foundation of fact.

Headline: Brand Advocacy Index: A Tool to Help You Track Progress, Provide an Early Alert on Issues, and Predict Growth

Brands can move up and down in consumers' minds. They have momentum driven by emotional engagement, by recent innovation, and by reinvestment. Every successful brand prompts competition. Competitors enter your category with your wake as a marker. They will research your costs, your investment, and all the dimensions of your power. They will research your weaknesses, too. If you let them, they will exploit the cracks in your defenses.

To keep this from happening, you should continuously track the mood of the consumer. BCG's Brand Advocacy Index tracks the advocates and—this is important—the critics of a brand. For example, Apple is not only the world's favorite brand, but also one of the world's least favorite brands. In other words, it has large numbers of advocates and large numbers of critics. That fact raises red flags concerning Apple's future value.[2]

With the Brand Advocacy Index, you can uncover the real story behind a brand's strengths and weaknesses.

How does it do this? It asks about actual behavior rather than intention. This is because what people say they will do often differs from what they actually do. Also, it puts the questions to noncustomers as well as customers—that is, to everyone who could be talking about the brand.

In January 2015, as Apple prepared to announce world-record profits of $18 billion for the last quarter of 2014,[3] we surveyed U.S. consumers about the Apple iPhone. We asked them to pick one from the following list:

- ▶ I've recommended the iPhone spontaneously (without being asked).
- ▶ I've recommended the iPhone when asked about it.
- ▶ I haven't recommended the iPhone, nor criticized it.
- ▶ I've criticized the iPhone when asked about it.
- ▶ I've criticized the iPhone spontaneously (without being asked).

We found some powerful responses. Some 82 percent of customers recommended the iPhone; 46 percent were spontaneous advocates, and 36 percent were prompted advocates. But we also detected some dissatisfaction. Some 4 percent of customers were critics. This may not sound like much, but Samsung, Apple's great rival, had fewer critics. Also, it is important to remember that the voices of critics are twice as loud as the voices of advocates. We reflect this in the weighting we give to critics: a spontaneous advocate is given a score of +1; a spontaneous critic is given a score of –2.[4]

Once we knew how many advocates and critics Apple had, we probed further to find out why these people recommended or criticized the iPhone. We found out that the iPhone was regarded as above average in terms of its design, technical features, brand identification, brand innovation, compatibility with applications and software products, and user-friendliness. But it was regarded as below average in terms of its short battery life and value for money.

Drilling further down, we established what types of customers liked it and what types of customers still needed to be convinced of its merits. Apple's core strength is among women age 35 and older who earn more than $75,000. The iPhone is weaker among younger demographics and those with an income under $75,000. The iPhone is one of the strongest product brands in history. However, like all cell phones, it will ride a wave of success, and a time will probably come when a better, less expensive product with more features comes to market. At that point, price premiums will decline, phone company subsidies will erode, and the profits of its parent will come under pressure. Only powerful incremental improvements will sustain its market share, its price premiums, and the company's market value.[5]

The Brand Advocacy survey helps you identify not only the advocates and critics of your brand, but also your brand's areas of strength and weakness. You can understand whom you are connecting with and how you are connecting with them—or aren't, as the case may be. You can develop concrete actions for improving your advocacy score.

And if you can improve your advocacy score, you will certainly drive growth. Our research shows definitively that brands with high levels of advocacy significantly outperform heavily criticized companies. In the sample of brands we studied, we found that the average difference between the top-line growth of the highest- and lowest-scoring brands was 27 percentage points.

Positive advocacy is more common for "aspirational" categories, where consumers associate a purchase with a desire to improve their social standing. Also, it is much more common with very visible purchases and purchases that involve significant amounts of money or time. People are much more likely to have conversations with friends and colleagues about a car, a prominent purchase on which they spend a large percentage of their income and, in many cases, a lot of time researching.

By contrast, negative advocacy tends to be more common in service businesses, such as retail banking and mobile telecommunications. Service-oriented brands find it much more challenging to maintain a consistent customer experience than product-oriented brands. Every customer touchpoint has the potential to create a negative impression.

We have a database of more than 1,000 brands from 35 industries in 30 markets around the world. Our pool of consumers exceeds 1.5 million. In other words, we have compiled a Brand Advocacy score for the world's leading brands. This is available online at the BCG website.

Today's Apostles: A Snapshot of the Five Major Consumer Groups in the United States

Anyone can be an apostle. It's not about how affluent you are; it's about how influential you are. What's important is your network, not your net worth.

As part of our consumer work, we divide the population into different segments, each of which can contain apostles for your company. It is worth getting to know them and getting to understand them. These segments are defined by aspiration, appetite, and aperture.

At the top of the pyramid are the affluent, educated, and upwardly mobile. In the United States, they constitute 10 percent of households, have big dreams and fewer constraints, and control more than 20 percent of spending. But many consumers have been forced to live by the budget books. Even as the world pulls out of recession, they remain insecure about the future. They feel unprotected from global forces.

In the United States, we have identified five distinct, and distinctive, consumer segments:

1. **Rich, happy, and balanced.** These are couples or families who are mostly satisfied with their life today and who are focused on maintaining their lifestyle and enjoying themselves during

retirement. They aspire to see the world, spend time with their loved ones, and help their kids and grandkids with homes, college, and other expenses.

2. **So cheap, shoes squeak.** These are consumers who are pleased with their position in life, but who are concerned about the direction of the country and pessimistic about what the future holds. They want to be sure that they have the savings to retire without burdening others and to make their frugal dreams—updating their homes, going on a cruise, buying a car—come true.

3. **Rocket in the pocket.** These consumers are young and full of hope and expectations for the future. They are living comfortably now, and they believe that life will only get better. They have big dreams, from world travel to luxury cars, as well as more practical desires such as paying off student debts, finding love, and starting a family. They want it all.

4. **Families under siege.** These consumers are struggling to make ends meet. Their biggest worries are financial. But, despite this, these families have love in their lives and optimism that life will get better for them and for the next generation. They dream of a future in which they can enjoy time with their family without worrying about money, bills, and debt.

5. **Weight of the world.** These consumers are single parents who are having difficulty providing financial stability for their children, but who are determined to set them on the right path. They are very dissatisfied with their lives today, but they hope that they can find love, deliver opportunity to their children, and one day be able to enjoy a home of their own and financial success.

Let's now look at each of these consumer segments in greater detail.

Rich, Happy, and Balanced

These consumers are in the best financial position. Not surprisingly, they are more positive than the average American. They are more satisfied with their life, and their expectations for love, happiness, and money are exceeded at higher rates. Only

14 percent are financially insecure, and none of them—zero percent—face financial trouble.

They save at a higher rate than the average U.S. consumer: 15 percent versus 6 percent for all Americans. The 15 percent savings rate is the magic number. If this is maintained over the course of a career and invested prudently, it provides for a constant real retirement income. Since they have a financial cushion, fewer of these consumers are anxious about the future: 53 percent versus 60 percent for all Americans. Their biggest fears relate to financial stability, personal health, and the country's ability to overcome economic, diplomatic, and political challenges.

These consumers value time with their family and their spouse, the chance to travel, and the ability to relax and enjoy themselves. Their vision of a successful retirement includes a long, healthy life; the freedom to enjoy retirement without stress; and the opportunity to go on special trips with loved ones (for instance, to a Disney theme park, a great city such as Rome, or one country on each continent). Also, some of them are focused on the happiness or success of their children, maintaining relationships with their spouse, or the general betterment of society.

Most of the purchases on this segment's wish lists are connected with enjoying retirement or helping their loved ones. All the time, they are conscious of balancing their desire to buy luxury items with the need to secure funds for retirement. Vacations and cars are on their lists, and a minority would like to make more indulgent purchases such as vacation homes or boats. Some also want to spend their money on their kids' or grandkids' education or other practical expenses like mortgages.

These consumers believe that their lives will continue to be rosy, although some of them mention fear of social unrest and failing health. Given all their advantages, it is perhaps surprising that they are no more or less optimistic than the U.S. population overall—the proportion who believe that their life will get better in the next 10 years is the same as for the average American: 68 percent. Likewise, the proportion that says that the next generation will have a better life is the same, too: 24 percent.

So Cheap, Shoes Squeak

These consumers have more stability in their lives and more savings than most Americans, but they are no happier or more optimistic because of this. They are more satisfied with their financial situation (41 percent versus 14 percent), comfort (41 percent versus 26 percent), and success (37 percent versus 18 percent) than the average American, but when it comes to happiness (32 percent versus 31 percent) or love (40 percent versus 38 percent), they are no more satisfied.

Despite their stable financial situation, job security, and low anxiety about the future (41 percent versus 60 percent), these consumers don't believe that the next generation will have a better life (only 11 percent think it will versus 24 percent for the United States as a whole). Also, many of them don't think their own lives will be better in 10 years' time (52 percent versus 68 percent for the United States). In fact, many of them take an extremely pessimistic view of the social and political situation in the United States, with some 81 percent thinking that an economic or political global conflict will emerge in the near future.

Perhaps preparing for the worst, this group of consumers saves at a much higher rate than U.S. consumers on average: more than 20 percent versus 6 percent for all Americans. They want to have enough money to live on during retirement and enough for emergencies and for helping their kids and grand-kids. They are even thrifty when it comes to their wish lists. Most of the purchases they dream about are very practical—topping their lists are spending on vacations and travel, often to very attainable destinations; real estate; and home repairs or investments. Asked what they would do with extra income, they respond by saying that they wouldn't spend it on apparel, shoes, food and beverages, or electronics—in contrast to most American consumers. Instead, they dream of a long retirement with continued financial stability and the success and happi-ness of their children and their loved ones.

Rocket in the Pocket

These young consumers are living comfortably today, but they have big aspirations for tomorrow. They feel more comfortable than their fellow Americans (52 percent versus 26 percent) and happier, too (37 percent versus 31 percent). Very few of them feel insecure about their job (17 percent versus 22 percent) or their finances (33 percent versus 51 percent), although many long for a future without the burden of student loans to repay.

If they are content with today, they are even more content with their prospects for the future: they hope to find love, start families, and see the world. Their professional hopes are anchored in successful jobs with a good income, but meaning and fulfillment are important, too. They want to do more than just "make it." Their aspirations are to succeed in every aspect of life. They desire a meaningful career, the ability to have a positive impact on society at large, and the opportunity to start a family.

Rocket consumers save 5 percent of their income and spend 20 percent on paying back loans. The remainder is used to treat themselves to nice accommodations, dining out, and travel (34 percent, 7 percent, and 5 percent of current spending, respectively). International travel is more than a hope for these consumers—it is an expectation. When they are no longer paying back their loans, they want to spend their money on an experience or a luxury indulgence, with only a minority looking to purchase homes or cars. Also, these consumers mentioned upgrading their wardrobes, taking long trips with their loved ones, and sometimes treating themselves to something like season tickets for their favorite team.

With so much to look forward to, these consumers are very optimistic about the future, both for themselves and for society at large. Some 88 percent believe that they will be earning more in 10 years, and 38 percent believe that the generation to come will live better (versus 24 percent for the average American). Their hopes for the future center on continued success at work and building a fulfilling home life. They do not share the sense of helplessness that some consumers feel about climate change or the U.S. economy.

Families Under Siege

These consumers are striving for the American Dream—a house, a car, a happy family, and no debt. But it all feels out of reach. Their concern and stress over money permeate their thoughts, despite their having a good family life at home. Even with an average annual household income of $86,000, the vast majority of these families feel more financially insecure than the average American (70 percent versus 51 percent). Their average savings rate is below that for the average American (only 2 percent versus 6 percent). They struggle with debt, probably linked to the financial crisis, and having a large family to provide for (with an average of 2.5 children) may be at the root of these monetary struggles. Their top priority is achieving financial security by paying off their mortgages and credit card debt.

But despite their financial difficulties, they are relatively satisfied with their family relationships: 53 percent are satisfied with the love in their life (versus 38 percent for the average American). Only 23 percent say that they are unhappy. In the next 10 years, 70 percent believe they will earn more income (versus 60 percent), and nearly 80 percent believe that their lives will be better (versus 69 percent). But only 16 percent believe that the economy has bottomed out (versus 27 percent), and only 10 percent believe that the next generation will live a better life than their own (versus 24 percent). Although these families are hopeful about their own lives, their feelings about the direction of the country have been jaded by their struggles.

Weight of the World

These consumers are very dissatisfied with their current lives because of their financial struggles and their lack of a significant other. With an average household income of just $37,000 and an average of 2.1 children to take care of, these consumers struggle from day to day to make ends meet. This financial insecurity explains their perilously low average savings rate of just 1 percent (versus 6 percent). Across nearly all categories, they are more dissatisfied with their lot in life than the average American. They have high levels of dissatisfaction with love (56 percent versus 30 percent), stress (65 percent versus 46 percent), and happiness (44 percent versus 26 percent).

Along with their financial difficulties, their lack of a significant other to share their life with explains much of the unhappiness and dissatisfaction among this segment. These single parents hope that their children will learn from their mistakes, attend college, and live the stable life that they themselves haven't been able to achieve. Their purchase wish lists reflect their desire to achieve stability and provide for their children. Clearing debts and owning a home are their top goals. Providing their children with basic needs such as clothing and shoes, as well as money for education, is also important.

Although they don't have the money, many of the people in this group expressed a desire to get away from the stress and go on vacation. And, remarkably, despite the dire straits in which they find themselves, these consumers are optimistic about the future. They believe that in 10 years, their lives will be better and they will be earning more.

Meet the Millennials: The Next Generation of Apostle Consumers

Consumers between the ages of 24 and 35—the millennials—will make or break your brand. They are setting the tone for all of us. They are determining what language we use, what styles are "in," and what is cool and what is not. They are heavily influencing what, where, and why we're purchasing. Their aspirations and decisions are emulated by their friends and family members of all ages. This vital generation is beginning to hold sway over the fortunes of the world's most successful brands.

To become and remain apostle brands, companies need to understand how these consumers influence others, how they are activated, and how they think. The best companies have already learned to listen to millennial consumers. They teach their salespeople to collect information on "unstocked" items; to systematically record why an item is being considered, returned, or rejected; and to observe and report facts about fit, try-on rates, payment choice, the time spent from browsing to making a purchase, and the shopping bags of competitors.

Millennials go to college. They graduate with degrees in soft subjects, not the hard STEM (science, technology, engineering, and math) subjects. They take a first job, and then they try to grow up. They become consumers and brand connoisseurs. Their consumption is largely food and beverages away from home, clothing, rent, utilities, electronics, some furniture, and travel. In our quantitative research, they say that they eat out so often because they want to treat themselves, celebrate special occasions, and gather with friends and family, and—most important—they have neither the time to prepare and eat at home nor "the ability to prepare the same food" as what they eat when they're out.

Their readiness to shop frequently, experiment, and engage with brands makes them ideal customers and advocates for their favorite choices. They can quickly fill a new restaurant's seats and empty out an old-time favorite. This same behavior is true in other sectors, too—apparel, vehicles, entertainment, leisure time, vacations, and home.

If they represent an opportunity, they also represent a huge challenge. They buy and neglect products. They cycle through brands. They are highly influenced by peer recommendations. Also, they are hard to reach: they are always on the go; they are not home birds; and they do not consume much conventional media.

But you should go out of your way to meet them. They are too important for you to ignore. In the course of our work, we have met hundreds of millennials. In the final section of *Rocket*, we present our encounters with three of them: Mark, Andrea, and Erik.

Millennial Number 1: Mark

When we were looking for millennial consumers to talk with, we had some very specific requirements. They needed to be employed, less than 30 years of age, middle income, articulate, and willing to tell their whole life story (in exchange for a modest honorarium). Also, they needed to be willing to fill out an extensive questionnaire and to log their purchases for the previous month. Over the last 30 years, we have done thousands of interviews of this kind. Consumers love to talk. They enjoy sharing their tales. But although most of what they say is truthful, they have a tendency to exaggerate both the good and the bad.

A qualitative interview, balanced by related quantitative research, really gets to the heart of the matter.

We met Mark at the food court of a Paramus, New Jersey, mall less than an hour from Manhattan. We told him, "We're buying!" He was happy about that. The mall is midscale, with a JCPenney, a Lord & Taylor, a Macy's, a Neiman Marcus, and a Nordstrom. There are 281 other retail locations in the mall. You can purchase food and beverages there at 123 different outlets.

Mark chose McDonald's and, like a reflex, ordered a number one Big Mac meal. We ordered a grilled chicken salad. Lunch for two was just $12. Mark ate the meal according to his routine. He devoured the fries—which he thinks are "the best fries in the world." He then ate the sandwich slowly, taking eight bites to finish "two all-beef patties, special sauce, lettuce, cheese, pickles, onions—on a sesame seed bun." Mark says he's been eating the sandwich at McDonald's since he graduated from Happy Meals some 18 years ago.

Mark is a good-looking young man: 25 years old, just under six feet tall, with curly brown hair and a neat appearance. He has a stubble beard instead of being clean-shaven. He is part of the reason why blade salespeople at Gillette are in a state of panicked frenzy. Mark and his peers think that a clean shave is for their fathers.

Mark is moderately fit—his youth is his advantage. He exercises three times a week—two three-mile jogs and two hours of basketball every Sunday morning with a local twentysomething league. He played basketball in high school, but he was second string. He never tried out for the team at his state university. He wears a Jawbone fitness band that he tells us is "a conversation piece and a reminder." He graduated from college with $25,000 in student loans, and is paying them off at the rate of $225 a month. He does not resent the payments.

Mark is now in his first "real" job. "I've never had trouble getting a job," he tells us. "People like me are in demand. I'm industrious, curious, hardworking," he continues, somewhat immodestly.

As an entry-level salesman for a food company, Mark drives a company car. He is making about $45,000 a year and receives (and takes) three weeks of vacation per year: "I take every day I can." Recent trips include a "singles" cruise, a lazy Mexico beach vacation, and a week in Los Angeles. He has the potential for a $5,000 bonus (but he doesn't think he can count on it). Work is not quite what he expected. "Too much routine. Too much paperwork. Lots of hierarchy. I'm with customers 10 percent of the time. I am the bottom of the totem pole." He speaks with a touch of a New Jersey accent. His parents were blue collar.

Every week, Mark has to visit stores where his product is sold. He is aware of prices and values. He has an insider's view of the motivations of retailers and the role of merchandising in influencing consumer purchases. He knows how much his company pays for an end-of-aisle display, a temporary price reduction, and a space in the retailer's ads.

Mark lives in a suburb of New Jersey about 14 miles from Manhattan with three guys from college. His rent is $865 a month—his single biggest expense. "Too much!" he says. "But I want to live in a cool neighborhood in a cool building." He has his own bedroom and shares a bath with one of his friends. He spends every nickel he makes. He has only minimal savings; he keeps a $500 balance in his checking account and contributes the matching amount to his retirement account. He says that he can't really think 40 years out and he believes that his earnings will grow dramatically. He has heard that a district manager at his company makes $200,000 and that the higher-ups make a lot more than that.

Mark is a big discretionary spender, allocating about $1,250 per month—or $15,000 per year—to use any way he wants (making him a powerhouse compared to married couples with children who are scrimping to make ends meet or an older couple saving for retirement). "I'm living large," he tells us proudly. "When I'm older, I'll make more money, and then I'll save. When I am married, I'm sure my wife will have me on a budget."

Mark makes a clear separation between his buddies and his girlfriends. He is generally "sleep deprived," although he will sleep until noon on weekends. He goes out after work three nights a week, but he sets himself a curfew. "I have a 1 a.m.

rule on work nights," he reveals. But he needs a pick-me-up the following morning: "It means Red Bull and coffee the next day." Typically, he will see a movie or go to a bar or a club with his friends. He talks to a lot of women, but he rarely goes on a date. "Sex is easy. Relationships require a lot of time and money. I don't have either right now," he explains.

When it comes to buying for himself, Mark has a certain number of favorite brands. He chooses things that are visible to the world; clothing, athletic equipment, and electronics are top-priority categories. He has a strong preference for lifestyle brands: Nike, Under Armour, Apple, Sam Adams beer, Grey Goose vodka. He says that someday he'd love to drive a BMW or an Audi.

Mark grew up with an Apple computer—it was cool and sleek. When the iPod became available, he suddenly had an unlimited quantity and variety of music. He traded with his friends, broke the code to "free" music, and always had "buds" in his ears. To this day, he remains loyal to Apple, and he has an iPhone 5c and a full armament of apps.

Although he's constantly trying out new places, Mark's fast food "go to's" include Five Guys and Chipotle. Five Guys has a "great" burger made exactly the way he wants it—loaded with "everything." Chipotle is his fill-me-up meal.

The burrito he likes best is made with a flour tortilla, cilantro rice, adobo-marinated chicken with honey, garlic, black pepper, guacamole, salsa, cheese, and sour cream. He explains that Chipotle chicken has no added hormones and that the chickens are not "factory animals." By our calculation, when using the company's website, this meal without chips and salsa is a whopping 1,125 calories, with 57 grams of fat, 2,280 milligrams of salt, and 126 grams of carbohydrates.[6] It has more than 55 percent of the recommended daily calories, nearly three times the recommended fat, and a day's worth of salt. On different days, Mark will guide his group of friends and coworkers to one fast food place or the other, depending on his mood and taste at the moment.

Neither Chipotle nor Five Guys is in the mall. They have a "locational disadvantage"—our term for retailers that are in build-out mode and do not have a full network of locations. If they are to become apostle brands, they will need to increase their presence. That's because apostle brands operate under rules of ubiquity; this entails a race to prominence and visibility in the top 300 malls for apparel retailers; a 3,000-plus store network for a national restaurant chain; a near-100 percent distribution in the nation's grocery stores for a premium food product; and a richly capitalized, high-velocity network of at least 500 dealers to sell cars. Mark commented that McDonald's is a safe choice. "Everyone can get something," he said, pointing to my salad.

Mark almost never cooks. He tries to go to Whole Foods for lunch or dinner, but rationalizes that often he "doesn't have the time." Mark eats a lot of ethnic food, including cheap Indian, Vietnamese, Thai, and Americanized Mexican. He visits restaurants with a wide range of price points, from Subway and McDonald's to Starbucks and an occasional white-tablecloth restaurant. "It depends on who I am with and what they want."

His clothing preferences include Urban Outfitters, North Face, Banana Republic, and Nordstrom when Nordstrom is having its biannual men's sale. He wears a Tag Heuer stainless steel watch that he received as a graduation gift, but only on big dates. "Why do you need a watch," he asks us, "when you have a phone?" He broadly rejects his father's and mother's favorite brands. "They are conservative and older," he says.

Mark has a shaded view on the future: he believes that the world needs to fight pollution and global warming, protect U.S. security, and avoid global conflict.

Indeed, Mark has a deep-seated belief in social responsibility. He tells us that "we owe it to leave the world better, less polluted, with more opportunity." In college, he is proud that he led the campus effort to reduce cafeteria waste, driving total dining garbage down by nearly half by advocating recycling and composting. These days, he reads labels and studies menus carefully. We have a very active discussion about chickens. He has seen a television show about chickens that never see daylight, are genetically distorted to produce more white meat, and live sad 14-week lives. "If these chickens could talk," he says, "they would tell me, 'Find another way.'"

Mark also seems sensitive about how the companies behind his favorite brands treat their employees. He tells us that he "knows" which retailers are paying a fair wage and treating their employees decently—and which ones aren't. He is willing to pay somewhat more for products from what we call *good companies*—the ones that manage their supply chains and the ones that pay above minimum wage. He likes the attention his generation is getting. "We are concerned; we are caring; we want more than just money," he says. "If you want to sell me something, it's gonna happen because my friends tell me or someone I trust tells me on Facebook." He thinks that if companies pay enough attention to him and his fellow millennials, they will be rewarded. But he does not consider himself to be either a trendsetter or a creator or destroyer of brands.

Mark has "at least" 500 friends on Facebook, and he is on Facebook every day. He changes his cover photo every other week. He tries to spread his "philosophy of life," which is, "Do good, work hard, play hard, don't sweat the small stuff, and treat people well." He received 300 birthday wishes. He is a big user of Wikipedia—"a college term-paper habit"—and he believes that almost everything on it is true. He reads a newspaper once a month when it is left around and free. He devours *Rolling Stone*, the music magazine, from cover to cover.

After lunch, we walk the mall with Mark. Mark struts through it as though he is walking the perimeter of a basketball court that he has run 1,000 times. He tells us that he doesn't actually go to mall department stores very often because they usually have "nothing for me—and no one to help me." Mark will use the malls for specialty establishments—athletic shoes, a haircutter, movies, and a dine-in restaurant like the Cheesecake Factory at the nearby Short Hills mall.

It is clear that Mark knows the different retailers well, even if he doesn't go into them. There are stores that he just won't enter, and there are stores that he "adores." He calls Abercrombie & Fitch overpriced and "so '90s." He carefully stops at the Victoria's Secret window "just so I know what to look for." When it finally comes to purchasing his "free" item courtesy of the authors, we walk into Banana Republic. He is modest in his desires. He picks three T-shirts, medium stretch cotton in gray. They are on sale for 40 percent off, and the price is under the magic $50 gift. "I like them tight," he says.

Mark says that he probably has put "thousands" of hours into purchases and that he is an expert on the "design" and quality that work for him. He says that he tells his friends about all of his major (and many of his minor) purchases and that most of his male friends have the same level of conviction on retail brands. He goes out of his way to tell them the horror stories and to offer a quick endorsement of the good experiences. He says his good-to-bad ratio is two to one. He is a savvy shopper, and he says that he learned his skills from his mom. "Cheap is good for most things. But not for vacations, cars, computers, TVs, and music."

Our questions to Mark are like short commas in our conversation. He answers them indirectly and stays on his line. He laughs a lot when he talks about his behavior and motivations. He is energetic and happy to share.

You need to get to know consumers like Mark.

Millennial Number 2: Andrea

Andrea is another classic millennial consumer. We met her through our BCG Consumer Sentiment Survey. She responded as an advocate of Nordstrom, the department store. She is also a big fan of 7 For All Mankind, the jeans maker; Lululemon, the sports apparel outfitter; and Kenneth Cole, the fashion retailer—an interesting menagerie of brands.

She grew up in an affluent suburb of Chicago, the daughter of a lawyer and a French immigrant. She lived in a two-story, brick, 100-year-old home in a neat, manicured suburb. Her parents have been married for nearly 40 years, but they now sleep in separate bedrooms and have grown apart. She was a top 1 percent student at her high school. She went to a neighboring "Big Ten" college, where she majored in French because it was "easy."

Her first job out of college was as a rental leasing agent. She found that she had natural selling skills and went from "agent-at-large" to top agent at a major new 500-unit apartment complex. In five years, her annual income jumped from $40,000 to $90,000. The rental apartment building charges $2,000 for a studio and up to $12,000 a month for a penthouse.

Andrea is fit and beautiful—she has sparkling white teeth, neatly styled short hair, and an easy smile. She stands 5 feet 5 inches and weighs 127 pounds. She weighs herself every day. She works out five days a week and spends at least 20 percent of her income on apparel and personal care products. She's been through a string of men, but no one has tempted her with marriage.

Her big budget items are rent, clothing, food, alcohol, and travel. She eats out almost every lunch and dinner and goes out drinking with friends five nights a week. Budgeting is hard for her. She has one credit card, but she uses only her debit card so that she doesn't go into debt. "I spend most of my money on rent, food, dining, cabs, and shopping," she says. She proudly carries a Céline purse. "It is my first expensive purse—$2,500. I'm 27; I think it's appropriate."

She has a new favorite shoe brand—Saint Laurent, where pairs range from $600 to $1,200. She buys them at the semiannual sale at Nordstrom. She also has a preference for Victoria's Secret. In her lingerie drawer, there are 10 bras and 40 pairs of underwear—"classic, simple, solid colors." In her closet, there are 40 pairs of jeans, but her active jeans wardrobe is 10 favorite pairs. The remaining pairs are "old or too small," but she is not prepared to part with them just yet.

She has limited savings. "I have a savings account with maybe $1,000 in it," Andrea confesses. "If I had an emergency come up, I could get help from my parents." She says that if she had more money, she would spend it on travel—New York, Miami, Los Angeles, or perhaps a return to Paris, where she completed her junior year. When she travels, she likes to go to bars and clubs.

Her one-bedroom apartment is clean and uncluttered. "It's not always like this," she says. "Most of the time it looks like a big closet, but my cleaning lady comes once a week and straightens things out. I don't ever cook, so there are no food messes."

On the walls are pictures of her family and her dog. Her small bedroom has a queen-size bed with purchased

Ritz-Carlton sheets, a dresser, and gift boxes from Gucci. The closet is packed with dresses, blouses, pants, jeans, and shoes. She keeps the Saint Laurent shoe boxes. Her reading material includes *Shape* and Chicago's social magazine *Modern Luxury.* There is a 40-inch flat-screen TV in her living area. The furniture was a gift from her parents. Her refrigerator is virtually empty. It contains a case of Miller Lite, two opened bottles of white wine, a bottle of soy sauce, aerosol whipped cream, a jar of Grey Poupon mustard, a bag of Trader Joe's frozen brown rice, and a frozen Stouffer spinach soufflé.

As we sit and talk, it is clear that Andrea wants advice and direction. We are strangers, but she thinks nothing of asking, "What would you be doing if you were me?" Her parents want her to get married, but she is resisting. "I have not met 'the one.' I don't know if I ever will. Everyone requires compromises. Looks, job, love—they're hard to find in one person."

She has fond memories of her original boyfriend from high school, Kevin, but has no intention of going back to him. "He has not aged well," she says. "He gained weight, lost his hair, and is stuck in a go-nowhere job." Last night, her ex-boyfriend came over. "We broke up a year and a half ago, and he wants to hang out all the time. He's a good person, and he loves me unconditionally. But there is no hot passion."

Millennial Number 3: Erik

Erik grew up in Raleigh, North Carolina. He is the son of two lawyers and attended a private school with 875 students and a full-time faculty of 100. He grew up rich, loved, catered to, and protected. At the very last minute, just before he graduated from high school, he switched his college choice to the University of Michigan, where he knew "no one." He had been set to go to the University of North Carolina, which his high school sweetheart was attending and where he knew "many" people. He just felt that he had to get out of the Deep South.

In school, he dressed "preppy"—polo shirts and khaki pants—and drove the family Range Rover. He is now 25 years old, but his mother still buys many of his clothes.

At the University of Michigan, he joined a fraternity for the parties, the friendship, and a sense of belonging. He was a business major, but he had a very active social life. "Drinking bourbon, whiskey, and beer" three or four nights a week was routine. It was a time of hookups, cram studying, and fun. He describes life in the fraternity as similar to the movie *Animal House*. He was a mediocre student as a freshman, but he got serious by his junior and senior years. His family helped with good jobs for the summers.

He comes across as a polite, refined southern gentleman with an edge. "Do you remember the character Eddie Haskell from *Leave It to Beaver*?" he asks over breakfast in Manhattan. "They say I'm like him: charming to the parents on meeting, a hell-raiser when out of sight."

Today, he works for a media start-up. He wants to work in the venture capital industry. He used to work at a major New York bank, where he was part of a team that helped private investors with wealth management. "My boss believed you needed to look the part," he says as he describes his clothing preferences. "So I upgraded my wardrobe. Ferragamo loafers, Hermès ties, and I traded in my Brooks Brothers suits for Suitsupply—a $900 suit that they make to look custom." Erik explains that investment counselors like suit coats with buttonholes that open and coat linings that make the suit look custom. "In the financial world, people comment on your dress. I've heard the bosses say, 'We would never take Jim (a coworker and coassociate) to a client.' It's not what you know. It's what you look like that counts."

Erik admits that working in a big financial institution was a source of anxiety. "There were so many people on top of me. There was nowhere to go." He took a major pay cut to work in the social media company that now employs him. "I am learning how start-ups work." His life goal is to be a successful investor. But for Erik, money has never been an issue. He has $25,000 in the bank—enough for a rainy day. His current income covers all his expenses. He still gets help from his parents.

Erik spends virtually all his income. He has the proverbial summer share in the Hamptons for $1,800 a season (with 30 other participants), one room in a three-bedroom apartment for $2,000 a month, and an "entertainment" budget of close to $2,000 a month. He provided us with a week of receipts for his purchases.

His budget is divided into thirds: one-third for taxes, one-third for rent, and one-third for entertainment and personal consumption. He was lucky enough to graduate without any debt, so his entertainment budget is for food, clothing, transportation, and "girls." He claims to be a master of the "pickup." His routine is to meet his date at his favorite speakeasy, Little Branch on Seventh Avenue in the West Village. He is known at this dark underground bar where live jazz is played a few nights a week. Little Branch makes custom cocktails and takes only cash. "We go for three drinks each, and then I call it a night. If I like her a lot, I send her home in a cab and send a text message 20 minutes later inviting her for a second date," he says. "Otherwise we go to her house or mine."

Little Branch is very different from the bar he used to go to when he lived in Ann Arbor. That was Scorekeepers, or simply Skeepers if you were a local. It was "big, loud, dirty," according to Erik. But pitchers of beer are $2.50, and some weekends he is tempted to go back. "I'd pay for the airfare by just saving on the drinks I buy in Manhattan."

Erik's postgraduation lifestyle is work, drink, and women. He does not work out, even though he has an Equinox fitness club membership and even though he was a three-letter sportsman in high school. "No time, no energy," he says about staying fit. Age is working to his benefit for now. He is 6 feet tall, weighs 180 pounds, and looks clean-cut—short hair, close shave, neat dress.

Erik says that he is starting to mature and to see a path to his future. His friends in North Carolina are getting married, but he says that people living in New York don't even think about marriage until age 30 or later. He wants to have a relationship. Three weeks ago, he saw his first girlfriend, Lizzie, on her first trip to New York. He describes her as a "blond, blue-eyed, 5 foot 8, 115 pounds, southern beauty." Then he confides: "I'd marry her if I could, but she's involved with another guy and wouldn't think about taking me back." He later e-mails us, suggesting that our discussion has gotten him thinking, and he is going to make a run at her. "If she will take me back, I'm hers," he writes.

Erik cares about only a handful of brands. Hermès, Ferragamo shoes, and McDonald's are at the top of his list. He thinks the ties are distinctive, the shoes carry prestige, and McDonald's offers better quality than anyone would think at the price point. His home furnishings are from IKEA and Pottery Barn.

Like the other millennials who we met, Erik pays little attention to advertising and watches only sports on TV. "I listen to friends about brands. They vote thumbs up or down," he says.

On any given day, he will be on Facebook, Google+, Yelp, or other social media sites. He can be found in bars, at sports events, and at concerts. But it's not easy. Millennials "hear" about hot new brands, but they may only sluggishly adopt them.

FINAL WORDS OF ADVICE

So What Does It Take
to Build a Great Brand?

*You can create "bedazzled": consumers who love you
and tell your story.*

This requires brand vision from conception to legacy.

Consumer brands are not created by genius alone.

*There are no accidents when it comes to creating "cravers,"
"apostles," or "brand ambassadors."*

*You get into a consumer's head through a comprehensive
understanding of users, usage, repurchase, and "raving."*

Your level of knowledge is comprehensive and anticipatory.

*Demand spaces are the quantitative tool that allows you
to dissect and respond to dissatisfactions.*

*Consumer complaints that are met with humility, apology,
enthusiasm, engagement, and curiosity are a gift.*

Say it loudly from across the berm.

*Your frontline sales partner to your consumer needs to be
vibrant, primed with knowledge, engaged in the moment, and
compensated for the riches that he creates.*

*She shops with her eyes and her emotions. Help it all come
to life for her; tell the story with images and with words that
bite.*

Apply the Golden Rule up, down, and around.

Digital raises the stakes.

Innovation remains the game changer; leadership is inherently unstable.

Success breeds competition and destruction.

See around the corner; be ready for whatever is "next."

We've told quite a few success stories in this book. We've described how, in his late twenties, Howard Schultz discovered and remade Starbucks. We've described how the 23-year-old Les Wexner bought sportswear and became the king of specialty retail. We've told the story of Tony Hsieh and his accidental investment in Zappos and ultimate appointment as CEO.

You can now recount the story of John Mackey as a "hippie" opening a healthy grocery store. Or the tale of Kip Tindell, who slaved away for two years to open his "container store"—where his friends joked that he was selling expensive boxes. Or the one about the wad of cashmere that Brunello Cucinelli knitted into sweaters that he sold to wealthy German consumers at a three-times markup.

None of these entrepreneurs had a master plan. They had the germ of an idea—what became their secret sauce. But the truth is, they won big-time because of their passion. That's what you need if you are going to succeed, if you are going to create a brand that has an emotional connection with the consumer.

These entrepreneurs were:

- ▶ Present in the moment and at the front of the battle line.
- ▶ Learning every day.
- ▶ Invested in continuous innovation ("small R, big D").
- ▶ Always worrying; always preparing; always ready for what was "next."
- ▶ Caring deeply about their followers—most considered them their "partners."
- ▶ Both fearless and fearful. They would jump to what was "next" without worrying about the business. They may have cowered in bed at night at the risks that they could enumerate—but they were willing to ignore them.

In their minds, there was a common thread: the consumer was the "boss." She needed to be happy—and if she was happy, she would tell her friends. She could be influenced and persuaded, but the evidence had to be compelling. What she was buying had to give her pleasure. It had to take her to a new place. Brands were her touchpoint as an explanation and to save time.

By now, you know the Eight Brand Rules. It's now your job to bring passion to your category. Invent something bigger, something bolder. Change the consumer frame. Whether you are a multibillion-dollar enterprise or a start-up, the rules are the same. You need to know more about your consumers and their consumption than anyone else. There really is a knowledge advantage. It starts with the data. It requires intuition and expertise. You need to get deep into the details of product creation to understand the true possibilities. You need to create a red thread that links all the logic points together.

The road map to getting started is a version of demand spaces (either the big macro study that we have described or a slimmed-down version based on your budget and your skill). You then need to call your team members together for a cross-functional response: design the great leaps forward together. Reinvention is not optional. To paraphrase Shakespeare writing about Henry V before the battle of Agincourt, "We few, we happy few, we band of brothers [and sisters]" will be remembered from this day forward for our invention, the joy we created in our consumers, the words of reverence that we generated, and the legacy of our inspiration.

NOTES

Introduction

1. The Boston Consulting Group (hereafter cited as BCG) Value Science Database; S&P Capital IQ.
2. BCG 2012; "Howard Schultz on Global Reach and Local Relevance at Starbucks," *BCG Perspectives*, October 17, 2012, https://www.bcgperspectives.com/content/videos/leadership_management_two_speed_economy_howard_schultz_global_reach_and_local_relevance/.
3. BCG Value Science Database; Starbucks Corporation public filings.
4. Matt Ryan (global chief strategy officer), Starbucks 2014 Biennial Investor Day, http://news.starbucks.com/news/live-blog-starbucks-path-for-growth-outlined-at-2014-biennial-investor-day/.
5. BCG Value Science Database; Starbucks Corporation public filings.
6. Jessica Wohl, "Starbucks Rolling out Upscale Teavana Tea Cafes," *Chicago Tribune*, April 29, 2014, http://articles.chicagotribune.com/2014-04-29/business/ct-starbucks-teavana-0429-biz-20140429_1_tazo-ceo-howard-schultz-seattle-based-coffee-chain.
7. BCG proprietary consumer research; BCG analysis.
8. BCG conducted a consumer survey in September 2014 (hereafter cited as BCG 2014 consumer survey) of more than 15,000 people in the United States and Europe, including representation from all income levels.
9. Ibid.
10. Ibid.
11. Jay Yarow, "Apple Crushes Earnings," *Business Insider*, January 27, 2015, http://www.businessinsider.com/apple-q1-earnings-2015-1.

12. BCG proprietary company data; demand spaces have been introduced to companies worldwide.
13. Source data compiled from BCG 2014 consumer survey; image developed at http://www.wordle.net/.

Chapter 1

1. BCG Value Science Database; L Brands public filings and analyst reports.
2. Michael J. Silverstein and Neil Fiske, *Trading Up: Why Consumers Want New Luxury Goods—and How Companies Create Them* (New York: Penguin, 2003).
3. E. Jerome McCarthy, in *Basic Marketing: A Managerial Approach* (Homewood, IL: Irwin, 1964), developed the Four Ps of marketing; BCG analysis.
4. BCG proprietary company research.
5. BCG proprietary consumer interview.
6. Samuel Ullman, "Youth," in Jane Manner, *The Silver Treasury: Prose and Verse for Every Mood* (New York: S. French, 1934), pp. 323–324.

Chapter 2

1. BCG proprietary company research.
2. BCG Value Science Database; Whole Foods public filings and analyst reports.
3. Whole Foods Market History, company website, http://www.wholefoodsmarket.com/company-info/whole-foods-market-history.
4. Whole Foods Core Values, company website, http://www.wholefoodsmarket.com/mission-values/core-values.
5. Twitter, http://www.twitter.com/wholefoods/; Elizabeth Holmes, "Tweeting Without Fear—How Three Companies Have Built Their Twitter Strategies," *Wall Street Journal*, December 9, 2011, http://online.wsj.com/article/SB10001424052970204319004577086140865075800.html#ixzz1g46GK5SA.
6. Whole Foods Market careers page, company website, http://www.wholefoodsmarket.com/careers.
7. BCG 2014 consumer survey.
8. Ibid.
9. Ibid.

10. BCG Value Science Database; Whole Foods public filings and analyst reports; BCG analysis.

11. Container Store company website, http://standfor. containerstore.com/our-foundation-principles/.

12. Dan Schawbel, "Kip Tindell: How He Created an Employee-First Culture at The Container Store," *Forbes*, October 7, 2014, http:// www.forbes.com/sites/danschawbel/2014/10/07/kip-tindell-how-he-created-an-employee-first-culture-at-the-container-store/.

13. Contained Home consultations can be scheduled in-store or online at http://www.containerstore.com/containedhome/index.htm.

Chapter 3

1. Jim Motavalli, "Frito-Lay Adds Electric Trucks to Its Fleet," *New York Times*, September 8, 2010, http://wheels.blogs.nytimes. com/2010/09/08/frito-lay-adds-electric-trucks-to-its-fleet/.

2. BCG proprietary company research and analytics; IRI Worldwide market research.

3. BCG proprietary demand-space research delivered to Frito-Lay; Kacey Culliney, "Frito-Lay CEO: We Went Very, Very Deep on Snack Occasions," *Bakeryandsnacks.com*, February 21, 2014, http://www.bakeryandsnacks.com/Manufacturers/ Frito-Lay-CEO-We-went-very-very-deep-on-snack-occasions.

4. Frito-Lay North America, "Do Us a Flavor," https://www. dousaflavor.com/#!/; Samantha Bonar, "Cappuccino One of Four Finalists in Lay's Potato Chip Flavor Contest," *LA Weekly*, September 10, 2014.

5. BCG proprietary company data, supported by John Ellett, "5 Marketing Takeaways from the ANA Digital Conference," *Forbes*, July 14, 2014.

6. William D. Cohan, "Blackstone's $26 Billion Hilton Deal: The Best Leveraged Buyout Ever," *Bloomberg Businessweek*, September 11, 2014, http://www.bloomberg.com/bw/articles/2014-09-11/ blackstones-hilton-deal-best-leveraged-buyout-ever.

7. Hilton History & Heritage, company website, http://www. hiltonworldwide.com/about/history.

8. Hilton News, "Caribe Hilton, Birthplace of the Piña Colada, Celebrates the 60th Anniversary of Puerto Rico's Official Drink," August 4, 2014, http://news.hilton.com/index.cfm/newsroom/ detail/27240/.

9. Multiple facts in this section are attributable to Thomas Heath, "Christopher Nassetta: The Man Who Turned Around Hilton," *Washington Post*, July 6, 2014, http://www.washingtonpost.com/ business/capitalbusiness/christopher-nassetta-the-man-who-turned-around-hilton/2014/07/03/43071478-fd5a-11e3-932c-0a55b81f48ce_story.html.

10. *Entrepreneur* 2015 Franchise 500, http://www.entrepreneur. com/franchise500/index.html; Embassy Suites Media Center, Brand Milestones, http://embassysuitesmediacenter.com/index. cfm/page/4005/.

11. BCG proprietary consumer interview.

12. BCG 2014 consumer survey; BCG analysis.

13. Customer review on Trip Advisor, December 22, 2014, http:// www.tripadvisor.co.uk/Hotel_Review-g58258-d84021-Reviews-or60-Hilton_McLean_Tysons_Corner-Tysons_Corner_Fairfax_ County_Virginia.html#REVIEWS.

14. Hilton/DoubleTree marketing literature, "The DoubleTree by Hilton Cookie," http://doubletree3.hilton.com/en/about/cookie. html.

15. Multiple facts in this section are attributable to Hilton HHonors Global Media Center, http://news.hiltonhhonors.com/index. cfm/page/9001/.

16. Hilton/DoubleTree Brand Portfolio; Hilton Worldwide public filings.

17. Hui-yong Yu, Leslie Picker, and Stephanie Ruhle, "Blackstone's Hilton Raises $2.35 Billion in Record Hotel IPO," *Bloomberg Business*, December 12, 2013, http://www.bloomberg.com/ news/articles/2013-12-11/blackstone-s-hilton-raises-2-34-billion-in-largest-hotel-ipo.

18. Hilton/DoubleTree Brand Portfolio; Hilton Worldwide public filings.

19. Hilton Worldwide Annual Report 2013, http://ir.hiltonworldwide. com/files/doc_financials/Hilton_2013_AR.pdf.

20. Ibid.

Chapter 4

1. See Theodore Levitt, "Marketing Myopia," *Harvard Business Review* 38 (July–August 1960), 24–47.

2. BCG Value Science Database.

3. BCG proprietary consumer interview.
4. BCG Value Science Database; Walt Disney Company public filings.
5. Information regarding Disneyland Park, https://disneyland. disney.go.com/ca/disneyland/.
6. Attendance data available at *Theme Park Insider*, http://www. themeparkinsider.com/flume/201406/4049/.
7. Gus Lubin, "Disney Now Has EIGHT Billion-Dollar Merchandise Brands," *Business Insider*, August 6, 2014, http://www.businessinsider.com/ disneys-billion-dollar-merchandise-brands-2014-8.
8. Bob Iger, Fiscal Year 2013 Annual Financial Report and Shareholder Letter, http://thewaltdisneycompany.com/sites/ default/files/reports/10k-wrap-2013.pdf.
9. BCG 2014 consumer survey.
10. BCG proprietary consumer interview.
11. BCG Value Science Database; Walt Disney Company public filings.

Chapter 5

1. About Zappos, company website, "Tony Hsieh—Author of 'Delivering Happiness' and CEO of Zappos.com, Inc.," http:// about.zappos.com/meet-our-monkeys/tony-hsieh-ceo.
2. Keith McFarland, "Why Zappos Offers New Hires $2,000 to Quit," *Bloomberg Businessweek*, September 16, 2008, http://www.bloomberg.com/bw/stories/2008-09-16/ why-zappos-offers-new-hires-2-000-to-quitbusinessweek-business-news-stock-market-and-financial-advice. Additional sources were used to compile information on Zappos's training and culture, including live interviews with management and employees.
3. Robin Wauters, "Amazon Closes Zappos Deal, Ends Up Paying $1.2 Billion," *TechCrunch*, November 2, 2009, http://techcrunch.com/2009/11/02/ amazon-closes-zappos-deal-ends-up-paying-1-2-billion/.
4. Zappos Insights, internal brand literature, "Culture Book," 2012–2013.
5. "100 Best Companies to Work For: Zappos.com," *Forbes*, 2014. Zappos has made the list for six years in a row.

6. Zappos recruiting literature, "The Good Jobs—Zappos Family," https://www.thegoodjobs.com/company/zappos.

7. About Zappos, company website, "Tony Hsieh."

8. About Zappos, company website, "Zappos Family Core Values," http://about.zappos.com/our-unique-culture/zappos-core-values.

9. BCG proprietary customer interview, Chicago 2014.

10. About Us, Four Seasons company website, "Founder and Chairman Isadore Sharp," http://www.fourseasons.com/about_four_seasons/isadore-sharp/.

11. Multiple facts in this section are attributed to Isadore Sharp's autobiography, *Four Seasons: The Story of a Business Philosophy* (New York: Portfolio, 2012).

12. Tsunami survivor stories, Four Seasons press releases. Full accounts are at http://phukettsunami.blogspot.com/2005/12/survivor-dave-lowe.html.

13. Ibid.

14. Ibid. Also "Rebuilding Maldives After the Asian Tsunami Tragedy," *Sport Diver*, http://www.sportdiver.com/article/news/rebuilding-maldives-after-asian-tsunami-tragedy.

15. Ibid. Also full Jet Li account at "ONE Foundation Jet Li," *SG Forums*, April 19, 2010, http://sgforums.com/forums/1728/topics/397013?page=1.

16. About Us, Four Seasons company website, "Founder and Chairman Isadore Sharp."

17. Roger Martin, "Isadore Sharp: Creating the Four Seasons Difference," *Toronto Globe and Mail*, November 20, 2007, http://www.theglobeandmail.com/report-on-business/isadore-sharp-creating-the-four-seasons-difference/article20405869/.

18. Helen Arnold, "World's 15 Most Expensive Hotel Suites," *CNN Travel*, March 25, 2012, http://travel.cnn.com/explorations/escape/worlds-15-most-expensive-hotel-suites-747256.

19. Peter Bregman, "The Real Secret of Thoroughly Excellent Companies," *Harvard Business Review*, March 18, 2009, https://hbr.org/2009/03/the-real-secret-of-thoroughly.html.

20. BCG proprietary customer interview, Chicago 2014.

21. David Segal, "Pillow Fights at the Four Seasons," *New York Times*, June 27, 2009.

Chapter 6

1. David Dean, Sebastian DiGrande, Dominic Field, Andreas Lundmark, James O'Day, John Pineda, and Paul Zwillenberg, "The Internet Economy in the G-20: The $4.2 Trillion Growth Opportunity," *BCG Perspectives*, March 19, 2012, https://www.bcgperspectives.com/content/articles/ media_entertainment_strategic_planning_4_2_trillion_ opportunity_internet_economy_g20/.

2. Ibid. For pdf: https://www.bcgperspectives.com/Images/ Internet_Economy_G20_Appendix.pdf. Also: Chendra Ngak, "Would You Give Up Sex for the Internet? Report Reveals Surprising Data," CBS News, March 22, 2012, http://www. cbsnews.com/news/would-you-give-up-sex-for-the-internet- report-reveals-surprising-data/.

3. Multiple quotes and facts in this section are attributable to Brad Stone, *The Everything Store: Jeff Bezos and the Age of Amazon* (New York: Little, Brown, 2013), and Brad Stone, "The Secrets of Bezos: How Amazon Became the Everything Store," *Bloomberg Businessweek*, October 10, 2013, http://www.bloomberg.com/ bw/articles/2013-10-10/jeff-bezos-and-the-age-of-amazon- excerpt-from-the-everything-store-by-brad-stone.

4. Douglas MacMillan, Mike Spector, and Evelyn M. Rusli, "Airbnb Weighs Employee Stock Sale at $13 Billion Valuation," *Wall Street Journal*, October 23, 2014, http://www.wsj.com/ articles/airbnb-mulls-employee-stock-sale-at-13-billion- valuation-1414100930.

5. BCG conducted a 2014 survey asking consumers to identify the "up-and-coming" brands of tomorrow (hereafter cited as BCG Consumer Sentiment Index).

6. Multiple quotes and facts in this chapter are attributable to Richard L. Brandt, "Birth of a Salesman," *Wall Street Journal*, October 15, 2011, http://www.wsj.com/articles/SB100014240529 7020391430457662710299683200.

7. BCG 2014 consumer survey; BCG analysis.

8. Multiple quotes and facts in this section are attributable to George Packer, "Cheap Words," *New Yorker*, February 17, 2014, http://www.newyorker.com/magazine/2014/02/17/cheap-words.

9. Cited in Packer, "Cheap Words."

10. Frank Konkel, "The Details About the CIA's Deal with Amazon," *Atlantic*, July 17, 2014, http://www. theatlantic.com/technology/archive/2014/07/ the-details-about-the-cias-deal-with-amazon/374632/.

11. Matthew Garrahan, "Amazon Arrives on Golden Globes Stage," *Financial Times*, January 12, 2015, http://www. ft.com/cms/s/0/17dfe66c-9a17-11e4-8426-00144feabdc0. html#axzz3Xr0mAzYD.

12. Matthew Garrahan and Shannon Bond, "Amazon: A Very Modern Media Mogul," *Financial Times*, January 21, 2015, http://www.ft.com/intl/cms/s/0/ad0811e4-a14f-11e4-8d19-00144feab7de.html#axzz3WXSiY3ym.

13. See comments in Stone, *The Everything Store*.

14. Amazon's Leadership Principles, company website, http://www. amazon.jobs/principles.

15. Ibid.

16. Stone, *The Everything Store*.

17. Cited in Brandt, "Birth of a Salesman."

18. Jeff Bezos, Amazon Annual Letter to Shareholders, April 2014, http://phx.corporate-ir.net/phoenix. zhtml?c=97664&p=irol-reportsAnnual.

19. Ibid.

20. Packer, "Cheap Words."

21. Bezos, Amazon Annual Letter to Shareholders, April 2014.

22. Garrahan and Bond, "Amazon."

23. Bezos, Amazon Annual Letter to Shareholders, April 2014.

24. Stone, *The Everything Store*.

25. Bezos, Amazon Annual Letter to Shareholders, April 2014.

26. BCG 2014 consumer survey; BCG analysis.

27. BCG proprietary consumer interview, Chicago 2014.

28. Brandt, "Birth of a Salesman."

29. Amazon's Leadership Principles. Also Julie Bort, "Here's a Peek Inside Amazon's Culture of 'Frugality,'" *Business Insider*, April 15, 2014, http://www.businessinsider. com/a-peek-at-amazons-culture-of-frugality-2014-4.

30. See Interactive Map, Airbnb website, https://www.airbnb.co.uk/ map. Also Jessica Plautz, "550,000 Travelers Used Airbnb on New Year's Eve," *Mashable*, January 12, 2015, http://mashable. com/2015/01/12/airbnb-new-year/.

31. BCG Consumer Sentiment Index. Also Tim Bradshaw and Robert Wright, "SpaceX Claims $10bn Value on New Funding," *Financial Times*, January 21, 2015, http://www. ft.com/cms/s/0/8e4659c0-a0f3-11e4-b8b9-00144feab7de. html#axzz3Xr0mAzYD.

32. Multiple facts in this chapter are attributable to Sara Rosenthal and Andrew Rachlett, "Airbnb," Stanford Graduate School of Business Case Study E470, April 4, 2013, http://www.gsb. stanford.edu/faculty-research/case-studies/airbnb.

33. Danielle Sacks, "The Sharing Economy," *Fast Company*, April 18, 2011, http://www.fastcompany.com/1747551/sharing-economy.

34. Tomio Geron, "How Sharing and Renting Is Creating a New Economy in the West," *Forbes India*, February 16, 2013, http:// forbesindia.com/article/cross-border/how-sharing-and-renting-is-creating-a-new-economy-in-the-west/34711/0.

35. Sequoia Capital website, http://www.sequoiacap.com/us/airbnb/ info.

36. Tim Bradshaw, "Airbnb Valued at $13bn Ahead of Staff Stock Sale," *Financial Times*, October 24, 2014, http://www. ft.com/intl/cms/s/0/99312b96-5b05-11e4-8625-00144feab7de. html#axzz3caCc7isq.

37. Tim Bradshaw, "Lunch with the FT: Brian Chesky," *Financial Times*, December 26, 2014, www.ft.com/intl/cms/s/0/fd685212-8768-11e4-bc7c-00144feabdc0.html#axzz3WXSiY3ym.

38. Thomas L. Friedman, "And Now for a Bit of Good News . . . ," *New York Times Sunday Review*, July 19, 2014, http://www. nytimes.com/2014/07/20/opinion/sunday/thomas-l-friedman-and-now-for-a-bit-of-good-news.html.

39. BCG proprietary consumer interview, Nashville, 2014.

40. Tomio Geron, "Airbnb and the Unstoppable Rise of the Share Economy," *Forbes*, February 10, 2013, http:// www.forbes.com/sites/tomiogeron/2013/01/23/ airbnb-and-the-unstoppable-rise-of-the-share-economy/.

41. Michael Arrington, "The Moment of Truth for Airbnb as User's Home is Utterly Trashed," *TechCrunch*, July 27, 2011, http:// techcrunch.com/2011/07/27/the-moment-of-truth-for-airbnb-as-users-home-is-utterly-trashed/. Also Brian Chesky, "Our Commitment to Trust and Safety," *Airbnb blog*, August 1, 2011, http://blog.airbnb.com/our-commitment-to-trust-and-safety/.

42. Airbnb website, user listing for a *Central Paris Apt—Le Marais,* https://www.airbnb.com/rooms/726267.

43. Ibid.

44. Jason Tanz, "How Airbnb and Lyft Finally Got Americans to Trust Each Other," *Wired,* April 23, 2014, http://www.wired. com/2014/04/trust-in-the-share-economy/.

45. BCG proprietary consumer interview, Washington, DC, 2014.

46. Airbnb's website, https://www.airbnb.co.uk/about/about-us.

47. BCG 2012 Travel and Tourism Digital Marketing Survey.

48. BCG-conducted customer focus groups, 2014.

49. Austin Carr, "Inside AirBNB's Grand Hotel Plans," *Fast Company,* May 15, 2014, http://www.fastcompany.com/3027107/ punk-meet-rock-airbnb-brian-chesky-chip-conley.

50. Friedman, "And Now for a Bit of Good News . . . ."

Chapter 7

1. Throughout Mercadona marketing literature, as well as its public filings, customers are referred to as the "boss" or "bosses."

2. WWF Global (World Wild Fund for Nature) company website, "The Amazon Rainforest," http://wwf.panda.org/about_our_ earth/teacher_resources/best_place_species/current_top_10/ amazon_rainforest.cfm.

3. Rhett Butler, "Rainforests of Brazil—An Environmental Status Report," *Mongabay.com,* http://rainforests.mongabay. com/20brazil.htm, last updated July 13, 2014.

4. Leslie Taylor, *The Healing Power of Rainforest Herbs* (New York: Square One Publishers, 2005).

5. Geoffrey Jones, "The Growth Opportunity That Lies Next Door," *Harvard Business Review: Emerging Markets,* July 2012, https:// hbr.org/2012/07/the-growth-opportunity-that-lies-next-door.

6. Luciana Hashiba (manager for partnerships and technological innovation at Natura Cosmeticos), "Innovation in Well-Being—The Creation of Sustainable Value at Natura," *Management Innovation Exchange,* May 18, 2012, http://www. managementexchange.com/story/innovation-in-well-being.

7. PBS Home Videos, *Conquistadors,* June 6, 2006, http://www. pbs.org/conquistadors/.

8. Natura marketing literature, company website, https://www. naturabrasil.fr/en/our-values/brasilian-beauty-rituals.

9. Ibid.

10. BCG proprietary company interview, 2014.

11. Vivian Broge (Natura) and Suba Sivakumaran (UN Development Programme), "Natura Cosmeticos Empowers Women in Mexico: Brazil-Based Firm Aims to Scale-up Training for Consultants," *Business Call to Action*, March 8, 2013, http://www.businesscalltoaction.org/news-highlights/2013/03/natura-cosmeticos-empowers-women-in-mexico/.

12. Alexandre Spatuzza, "Natura Cosmeticos Gets a Sustainability Makeover," *Green Biz*, February 4, 2014, http://www.greenbiz.com/blog/2014/02/04/natura-cosmetics-sustainability-amazon.

13. Natura Annual Report 2013; company public filings.

14. João Paulo Ferreira (VP operations and logistics, Natura Cosmetics Brazil), "Natura: The Challenges in Building a Sustainable Supply Chain," Stanford Graduate School of Business, *Slideshare*, June 15, 2012.

15. Ian Fraser, "Natura's Back-to-Nature Success," *Management Today*, July 10, 2006, http://www.managementtoday.co.uk/news/566630/Naturas-back-to-nature-success/; Robert Ford (Merrill Lynch), Merrill Lynch analyst reports.

16. Hashiba, "Innovation in Well-Being."

17. BCG proprietary consumer interview, Chicago 2014.

18. "Looks Good: Brazilian Cosmetics Firms and Other Consumer Brands Are Powering Ahead," *Economist*, September 28, 2013, http://www.economist.com/news/special-report/21586681-brazilian-cosmetics-and-other-consumer-brands-are-powering-ahead-looks-good.

19. BCG Brand Advocacy Index, 2014.

20. "The World's Billionaires," *Forbes*, 2015, http://www.forbes.com/billionaires/list/#version:static_country:Spain.

21. Multiple facts in this chapter are attributable to Zeynep Ton and Simon Harrow, "Mercadona," Harvard Business School Case Study, April 20, 2010, http://www.hbs.edu/faculty/Pages/item.aspx?num=38682.

22. Mercadona Annual Report 2014; company public filings.

23. Ibid.

24. "Spanish Aisles: Why a Low-Cost Retailer Is Thriving," *Economist*, June 2, 2011, http://www.economist.com/ node/18775460.

25. Cited in Ton and Harrow, "Mercadona."

26. Message from the President, Mercadona Annual Report 2013, https://www.mercadona.es/corp/ing-html/memoria2013. html#menuB.

27. BCG analysis.

28. BCG proprietary consumer interview.

29. Zeynep Ton, *The Good Jobs Strategy: How the Smartest Companies Invest in Employees to Lower Costs and Boost Profits* (Boston: Houghton Mifflin Harcourt, 2014).

30. Cited in Ton and Harrow, "Mercadona."

31. Ibid.

32. Cited in Tom Metcalf, "Spanish Billionaires Hire 4,000 Amid Country's Job Slump," *Bloomberg Business*, May 14, 2013, http://www.bloomberg.com/news/articles/2013-05-13/ spanish-billionaires-hire-4-000-amid-country-s-job-slump.

33. "Spanish Aisles."

34. Mercadona Annual Report 2014; company public filings.

35. Message from the President, Mercadona Annual Report 2013.

36. BCG Brand Advocacy Index, 2014.

37. BCG proprietary consumer interview, 2014.

38. BCG 2014 Consumer Survey.

39. Coop Italia company history, company website, http://www. e-coop.it/.

40. Dana Biasetti, "2013 Italian Food Retail and Distribution Sector Report," USDA Foreign Agricultural Service, December 27, 2013.

Chapter 8

1. Toyota company history, marketing literature, http://corporatenews. pressroom.toyota.com/corporate/company+history/.

2. Toyota press releases, "Toyota Boosting Manufacturing Investment in Alabama, Missouri and Tennessee," June 20, 2013.

3. "Toyoda Precepts: The Base of the Global Vision," Toyota Traditions, http://www.toyota-global.com/company/toyota_ traditions/company/apr_2012.html, April 2012.

4. *Toyota: A History of the First 50 Years* (Toyota City, Japan: Toyota Motor Corporation, 1988); BCG Value Science Database.

5. Jeffrey K. Liker, *The Toyota Way: 14 Management Principles from the World's Greatest Manufacturer* (New York: McGraw-Hill, 2004).

6. John A. Quelch, Carin-Isabel Knoop, and Ryan Johnson, "Toyota Recalls (A): Hitting the Skids," *Harvard Business Review*, October 19, 2010.

7. BCG proprietary consumer interview, Chicago 2014.

8. Scott Evans and Angus MacKenzie, "The Toyota Recall Crisis: A Chronology of How the World's Largest and Most Profitable Automaker Drove into a PR Disaster," *Motor Trend*, January 2010.

9. James B. Meigs, "Target Toyota: Why the Recall Backlash Is Overblown," *Popular Mechanics*, February 9, 2010.

10. BCG proprietary consumer interview, Chicago 2014.

11. Akio Toyoda Executive Profile, *Bloomberg Business*, http://www.bloomberg.com/research/stocks/people/person.asp?personId=1828739&ticker=TM.

12. "Akio Toyoda's Statement to Congress," February 2010, http://blog.toyota.co.uk/akio-toyodas-statement-to-congress.

13. Akio Toyoda, "Toyota's Plan to Repair Its Public Image," *Washington Post*, February 9, 2010, http://www.washingtonpost.com/wp-dyn/content/article/2010/02/08/AR2010020803078.html.

14. BCG proprietary company interview, 2014.

15. BCG Value Science Database; GM, Toyota public filings and analyst reports.

16. BCG proprietary company interview, 2014.

17. Toyota 2014 Annual Report and public filings; Toyota analyst reports; BCG Value Science Database.

18. Ben McGrath, "Beleaguered League," *New Yorker*, September 29, 2014, http://www.newyorker.com/magazine/2014/09/29/beleaguered-league.

19. Beau Riffenburgh, *Official NFL Encyclopedia* (New York: New American Library, 1986).

20. NFL press releases, "NFL, Ex-players Agree to $765M Settlement in Concussions Suit," Associated Press, August 2013.

21. Michael Powell, "A League Grins as a Star Grimaces: Given the NFL's Culture of Manliness, an Injured Tony Romo Likely Will Play in London," *New York Times*, November 6, 2014, http://www.nytimes.com/2014/11/07/sports/football/given-the-nfls-culture-of-manliness-an-injured-tony-romo-likely-will-play-in-london.html.

22. David Remnick, "Going the Distance: On and Off the Road with Barack Obama," *New Yorker*, January 27, 2014, http://www.newyorker.com/magazine/2014/01/27/going-the-distance-2.

23. John Burn-Murdoch and Gavin Jackson, "Football Sees Deeper Drop-Off than Other Youth Sports in the US," *Financial Times*, December 1, 2014, http://www.ft.com/intl/cms/s/0/3f4fcbf8-7718-11e4-8273-00144feabdc0.html#axzz3WXSiY3ym.

24. Ibid.

25. Laura Sinberg, "Women in the FanHouse," *Forbes*, February 2, 2010, http://www.forbes.com/2010/02/02/super-bowl-women-fans-forbes-woman-time-commercials.html.

26. BCG proprietary consumer interview, Chicago 2014.

27. J. R. Moehringer, "Football Is Dead. Long Live Football," ESPN, April 14, 2013, http://espn.go.com/nfl/story/_/page/Mag15footballisdead/jr-moehringer-120-reasons-why-football-last-forever-espn-magazine.

28. Mike Ozanian, "The NFL's Most Valuable Teams," *Forbes*, August 20, 2014, http://www.forbes.com/sites/mikeozanian/2014/08/20/the-nfls-most-valuable-teams/.

29. "NFL & Legend of the Rabbits," ESPN, on YouTube, https://www.youtube.com/watch?v=aan4Kagq_7Y; Scott Purks, "Florida Stars Go from Muck Bowl to Super Bowl," *ESPN Rise/Football*, January 30, 2009, http://sports.espn.go.com/highschool/rise/football/news/story?id=3869165.

30. Ibid.

31. Ibid.

32. Stefan Deeran, "NFL Owners: '32 Republicans That Vote Socialist,'" *CBS News*, September 2009.

33. Ozanian, "NFL's Most Valuable Teams."

34. BCG research. Also Shalini Ramachandran and Kevin Clark, "In Television Deals, NFL Plays by Its Own Rules: League Has Huge Leverage as TV Networks Look to Live Games for an Edge Over Online Services," *Wall Street Journal*, September 3, 2014.

35. NFL Players Association, Collective Bargaining Agreement, August 4, 2011, https://nflpaweb.blob.core.windows.net/media/Default/PDFs/General/2011_Final_CBA_Searchable_Bookmarked.pdf.

36. Steve Sabol, *They Call It Pro Football*, NFL Films, 1967.

37. Douglas Martin, "Steve Sabol, Cinematic Force for NFL, Dies at 69," *New York Times*, September 18, 2012, http://www.nytimes.com/2012/09/19/sports/football/steve-sabol-creative-force-behind-nfl-films-dies-at-69.html.

38. BCG proprietary consumer interview, Chicago 2014.

39. Vanessa Golembewski, "How the NFL Is Growing Its Female Fan Base," *Refinery29*, February 1, 2014, http://www.refinery29.com/2014/02/61545/nfl-women#slide.

40. McGrath, "Beleaguered League."

41. Brent Schrotenboer, "NFL Takes Aim at $25 Billion, but at What Price?" *USA Today*, February 5, 2014, http://www.usatoday.com/story/sports/nfl/super/2014/01/30/super-bowl-nfl-revenue-denver-broncos-seattle-seahawks/5061197/; Ben Liedenberg (AP), "NFL v EPL: A League of Their Own," *Economia*, September 2, 2014, http://economia.icaew.com/business/september-2014/nfl-v-epl-a-league-of-their-own.

42. NFL press release, "NFL 2014 TV Recap: 202 Million Viewers, Game Viewership Nearly Triples Broadcast Primetime," January 12, 2015, http://sportsmedianews.com/nfl-2014-tv-recap-202-million-fans-tuned-in-nfl-game-viewership-nearly-triples-broadcast-primetime-45-of-50-most-watched-shows-this-fall/.

43. Chris Chase, "Mark Cuban Thinks the 'Greedy' NFL Is 10 Years Away from Implosion," *USA Today*, March 24, 2014, http://ftw.usatoday.com/2014/03/mark-cuban-nfl-implosion-10-years.

44. Letter to Owners, August 28, 2014, http://www.nfl.com/static/content/public/photo/2014/08/28/0ap3000000384873.pdf; Tom Pelissero, "NFL Toughens Its Stance on Domestic Violence," *USA Today*, August 28, 2014, http://www.usatoday.com/story/sports/nfl/2014/08/28/nfl-toughens-its-stance-on-domestic-violence/14746187/.

Epilogue

1. Dylan Bolden, Antonella Mei-Pochtler, Rohan Sajdeh, Gaby Barrios, Erin George, Deran Taskiran, and Keith Melker,

"Data-Driven Insight: BCG's MindDiscovery and More," *BCG Perspectives*, https://www.bcgperspectives.com/content/articles/branding_communication_consumer_insight_data_driven_insight/, July 28, 2011.

2. "BCG Inaugurates the Brand Advocacy Index," press release, December 2, 2013, http://www.bcg.com/media/pressreleasedetails.aspx?id=tcm:12-150778.

3. BCG Value Science Database; Apple 2014 Annual Report; public filings.

4. BCG 2014 consumer survey.

5. Ibid.

6. Chipotle company website, http://www.chipotle.com/en-US/menu/nutrition_calculator/nutrition_calculator.aspx; BCG analysis.

SELECTED BIBLIOGRAPHY

Brandt, Richard L. *One Click: Jeff Bezos and the Rise of Amazon.com.* New York: Portfolio, 2012.

Capodagli, Bill, and Lynn Jackson. *The Disney Way: Harnessing the Management Secrets of Disney in Your Company,* rev. ed. New York: McGraw-Hill, 2006.

Hsieh, Tony. *Delivering Happiness: A Path to Profits, Passion, and Purpose.* New York: Business Plus, 2010.

MacCambridge, Michael. *America's Game.* New York: Anchor, 2005.

Mackey, John. *Conscious Capitalism: Liberating the Heroic Spirit of Business.* Boston: Harvard Business Review Press, 2013.

Oriard, Michael. *Brand NFL.* Chapel Hill: University of North Carolina Press, 2007.

Schultz, Howard, and Dori Jones Yang. *Pour Your Heart into It: How Starbucks Built a Company One Cup at a Time.* New York: Hyperion, 1997.

Schultz, Howard, and Joanne Gordon. *Onward: How Starbucks Fought for Its Life Without Losing Its Soul.* New York: Rodale, 2011.

Schultz, Howard, and Rajiv Chandrasekaran. *For Love of Country.* New York: Knopf, 2014.

Sharp, Isadore. *Four Seasons: The Story of a Business Philosophy.* Toronto: Penguin, 2009.

Stone, Brad. *The Everything Store: Jeff Bezos and the Age of Amazon.* New York: Little, Brown, 2013.

Tindell, Kip. *Uncontainable: How Passion, Commitment, and Conscious Capitalism Built a Business Where Everyone Thrives.* New York: Grand Central Publishing, 2014.

Zimmerman, Paul. *The New Thinking Man's Guide to Professional Football.* New York: HarperCollins, 1987.

ACKNOWLEDGMENTS

Creating *Rocket* involved many contributors—case team members, partners around the world at BCG, and many friends from outside the firm. Special thanks go to Simon Targett, a former associate editor of the *Financial Times*, who provided discipline and original thought to the construction of the book. Thank you, Simon, for your special sense of humor and intelligence. Todd Shuster of Zachary Shuster Harmsworth has been our agent, friend, and counselor. From the beginning, he was our strongest proponent and advisor. Thank you, Todd, for helping us find a very special publisher in the form of Mary Glenn at McGraw-Hill, and for your many suggestions. Carrie Vaccaro Nelkin delivered fast and precise copy editing of the final manuscript.

Our project team was led by Aaron Mass and Chris Prochak. They supplied us with direction, synthesis, and insights. Dave Blowers, a young consultant, provided us with energy, enthusiasm, and connections for interviews, and was deep in research for many of the stories. Shruti Jindal furnished excellent one-on-one interviews with consumers. Special thanks to Ioana Calcev for insightful, original research on many of the companies discussed in the book. Thanks are also due to Nick Ling. Special thanks to Tom Robinson for all his help and insights into making the book come alive in the market. Our gratitude also goes to Eric Gregoire for postproduction support and to Gary Callahan for cover design. Much appreciation to Bennett Siegel for exploring the world of social media on our behalf. We also thank the many people who participated in our interviews and quantitative surveys.

BCG has a strong writing tradition. Our first book was sponsored under the direction of then-CEO John Clarkeson. His successor, Carl Stern, provided sponsorship and encouragement for our second book. BCG chairman Hans Paul Buerkner was the principal sponsor for books three and four. He contributed feedback, insight, and direction. CEO Rich Lesser, who was supportive of *Rocket* from our first discussion of it, offered substantive suggestions and direction. We thank these four leaders for their help. Former senior partner George Stalk got us writing. He gave us the original suggestion to "write this up," and we've followed his lead ever since. Two practice area leaders stepped up to provide visible support for the project: Tom Lutz from the Consumer practice and Rich Hutchinson from our Marketing & Sales practice.

In addition, a number of partners around the world supplied suggestions, input, and help in securing interviews. They include Mark Abraham, Antonio Achille, Ivan Bascle, Lamberto Biscarini, Lucy Brady, Nicolas Catoggio, Peter Dawe, Jeff Gell, Marin Gjaja, Cliff Grevler, Jeff Hill, Jim Jewell, Mark Kistulinec, Lara Koslow, Jeff Kotzen, Matt Krentz, Megan Lyon, Sharon Marcil, Ivan Marten, Bjorn Matre, Brian Myerholtz, Hans Pichler, Martin Reeves, Sam Ridesic, Abheek Singhi, Janme Sinha, Hal Sirkin, Miki Tsusaka, Karin von Funck, Dan Wald, and Sarah Willersdorf.

Michael's long-tenure executive assistant, Kristin Claire, rose once again to the challenge of another book on top of the usual client work and global travel. Kristin, thank you for your spirit and your help.

A comprehensive editorial review by Professor Silvia Hodges Silverstein is gratefully acknowledged. Thank you, Silvia, for reading the many drafts and for your insights, clarifications, and wonderful suggestions.

INDEX

ABOUT THE AUTHORS

Michael J. Silverstein is one of BCG's most prolific and published authors. He has written five consumer books since 2003, each published in a three-year sequence. He wrote *Trading Up: The New American Luxury*, the story of middle-class consumers trading up to luxury goods. Michael predicted dramatic growth in the top of the market in all consumer categories. He created the rule of 20-40-60: 20 percent of almost all consumer categories became premium, delivering 40 percent of volume and as much as 60 percent of category profitability. The companies identified in *Trading Up* and premium players have delivered total shareholder return dramatically higher than the market. In 2006, he launched *Treasure Hunt: Inside the Mind of the New Consumer*, a book about the consumer search for higher-value goods at lower prices. In this book, he showed how consumers were going to cut back on their spending and begin the road to savings. He predicted a global recession as a result. In 2009, he led BCG's largest consumer-research effort with women. This culminated in *Women Want More: How to Capture Your Share of the World's Largest, Fastest-Growing Market*. He predicted dramatic growth in the value of purchases controlled by women. He also found that women want more time, more money, and more love. His fourth book was *The $10 Trillion Prize: Captivating the Newly Affluent in China and India*. The book forecast the size of the consumer market in China and India in the year 2020. The forecast is on track.

Michael joined BCG in 1980, after completing his MBA with honors at Harvard University and an AB degree in economics and history at Brown University. Based in Chicago, he has been a worldwide leader of BCG's consumer practice and a member of the firm's executive committee. He actively serves global clients in retail and consumer packaged goods. He is considered one of the firm's experts in branding and innovation.

Dylan Bolden is the head of BCG's loyalty practice. Based in Dallas, he joined BCG in 2002, and he is an expert on global branding, customer experience, multichannel retailing, and turnaround strategy. Dylan earned an MBA with highest honors from Columbia Business School, graduating Beta Gamma Sigma, and a BS in chemical engineering with honors from Florida State University.

Rune Jacobsen is the worldwide head of the firm's global consumer retail sector practice. Based in Oslo, and a graduate of the Norwegian School of Business, he joined BCG in 1999. He has led more than 80 retail projects around the world. Rune is an expert in market turnaround, growth strategy, private-label development, retail transformation, and change management. He has worked in food, nonfood, DIY, apparel, sports, and home retailing.

Rohan Sajdeh is a senior partner who joined BCG in 1995. Based in Chicago, he has extensive consumer goods experience, advising companies around the world. Rohan has a master of management degree from Northwestern University's Kellogg School of Management, an MPhil in international relations from Cambridge University, and a bachelor of business degree with the university medal from the University of Technology, Sydney.